组织与人力资源管理系列精品教材

国际商务沟通

余晓泓　赵洱崟　主　编
王红夏　戚　淳　董　梅　副主编

电子工业出版社
Publishing House of Electronics Industry
北京·BEIJING

内 容 简 介

本书是一部融合国际商务沟通理论和实践的商务类应用型专业教材，共有 21 个单元。本书立足中国文化背景，同时保持全球视野和未来眼光；从理论到实际操作，详细阐述国际商务沟通的基本原理，分析商务沟通的过程和要素，揭示解决具体问题的策略和技巧；内容涵盖国际商务的主要活动和环节，为学习者提供国际商务沟通实践指南。

本书可作为高等院校国际经济与贸易、国际金融、国际物流、商务英语等专业学生的教材，也适合作为从事外贸工作的专业人士的自学参考资料。

未经许可，不得以任何方式复制或抄袭本书之部分或全部内容。
版权所有，侵权必究。

图书在版编目（CIP）数据

国际商务沟通 / 余晓泓，赵洱崟主编. -- 北京：电子工业出版社，2024.10. -- ISBN 978-7-121-48969-3

Ⅰ．F740

中国国家版本馆 CIP 数据核字第 2024DC6766 号

责任编辑：张天运
印　　刷：河北鑫兆源印刷有限公司
装　　订：河北鑫兆源印刷有限公司
出版发行：电子工业出版社
　　　　　北京市海淀区万寿路 173 信箱　　邮编：100036
开　　本：787×1092　1/16　印张：13.25　字数：440.96 千字
版　　次：2024 年 10 月第 1 版
印　　次：2024 年 10 月第 1 次印刷
定　　价：49.00 元

凡所购买电子工业出版社图书有缺损问题，请向购买书店调换。若书店售缺，请与本社发行部联系，联系及邮购电话：(010) 88254888，88258888。
质量投诉请发邮件至 zlts@phei.com.cn，盗版侵权举报请发邮件至 dbqq@phei.com.cn。
本书咨询联系方式：zhangty@phei.com.cn。

前　　言

一、教材编写的时代背景

随着我国经济的快速发展，信息技术取得了长足进步，移动互联网、大数据、社交网络、人工智能、VR/AR 等技术正在改变着社会的运行方式和我们的生活方式、学习方式。在数字化时代，高校教师如何以教书育人的初心，培养面向未来的人才？

党的二十大报告指出："必须坚持科技是第一生产力、人才是第一资源、创新是第一动力，深入实施科教兴国战略、人才强国战略、创新驱动发展战略，开辟发展新领域新赛道，不断塑造发展新动能新优势"。教育部部长怀进鹏也在 2023 年全国教育工作会议上强调，坚持守正创新，在教材中充分反映马克思主义立场、观点、方法，充分反映中华民族灿烂文化、民族精神、时代精神和党的百年奋斗重大成就、历史经验，打好中国底色、厚植红色基因，紧密对接国家战略需求，善用现代信息技术，真正把"培根铸魂、启智增慧"融入好、落实好。如何用新时代中国特色社会主义"培根铸魂、启智增慧"？教材无疑是核心载体。新时代的高校教育，需要以信息技术为工具、以课程思政为引领，培养国家所需要的既有扎实的理论基础，又有较强的问题解决能力，更有家国情怀的新时代大学生。

二、教材的定位与特色

教材的定位：用世界语言讲中国文化，学科学沟通说中国故事，以商务合作促多方共赢，建构适应课程国际化改革的新形态一体化教材。

教材的主要特色如下。

第一，数字体系新形态。本教材以纸质教材为核心，联结在线课程和课堂教学，构建"在线课程、纸质教材、课堂教学"三位一体的新形态课程体系，纸质教材更精要，数字资源更丰富，线上线下学习相联通。

第二，资源载体新形态。利用网络化、智能化传播介质，以纸质教材为核心，依托信息技术等手段立体呈现多模态资源，为学生创设立体化学习环境。

第三，知识获取新形态。以课堂教学为中心，利用在线课程平台和移动学习终端，引导发现式、建构式、自主式、开放式的知识获取。

第四，教学方式新形态。采取线上线下混合式教学方式，以学习者为中心，使教学双方深度参与教与学全过程。

第五，学习方式新形态。实现随时、随地、随意学习，包括以纸质教材为核心的线上学习、线下学习、移动学习、协作学习、互动式学习、探究式学习等。

三、教材的编写原则

本教材秉持一体化原则，做好教材的规划建设。其主要体现在四个方面：教材研发与课程建设一体化、教材内容与线上线下资源一体化、教学内容设计与教学过程设计一体化、学习过程与应用过程一体化。

第一，教材研发与课程建设一体化，围绕"培养大学生跨文化商务沟通能力"的教学目标，明确跨文化沟通的策略，掌握沟通技巧，拆分技能知识点，整体设计课程及教材主要内容。

第二，教材内容与线上线下资源一体化，发挥纸质教材完整呈现技能知识体系的优势，线上资源呈现形态丰富、检索便捷等特点，实现纸质教材重点呈现课程内容，并与线上学习内容相互依存、互补融合。线上资源对接首批国家精品在线开放课程"管理沟通"、首批上线"学习强国"的慕课"管理沟通"、edX全球MOOC平台"Management Communication"课程。

第三，教学内容设计与教学过程设计一体化，建构多元融合的课前、课中、课后的教学模式，强化教材内容支持实践教学过程的能力。

第四，学习过程与应用过程一体化，通过任务设计掌握国际商务沟通的基本原理、科学规律的学习过程与跨文化沟通实践能力应用过程，实现学习技能知识的过程与实际应用技能知识的过程高度相关，提高教材的实用性和服务学生学习知识、应用知识的能力。

本教材基于国际商务沟通领域的最新教学研究成果，以培养学生的跨文化沟通实践能力为核心，以任务型教学为主导，建构了40余篇特色案例和21个场景学习模块。

四、教材的主要教学目标

1. 知识传授：学习国际商务沟通的基本原理，理解科学沟通的过程与要素，掌握解决国际商务具体环节沟通卡点和问题的策略，学会跨文化沟通技能，培养适应模糊、复杂沟通情境下的理性思维和科学思考能力。

2. 能力培养：掌握清晰表达、情绪管理、积极倾听、即时反馈、磋商与谈判等知识和技巧，能够将国际商务沟通的基础知识和跨文化交际的实践能力相结合，娴熟运用沟通技能，运用有效和适当的方法解决国际商务谈判和贸易实务环节中的沟通问题。

3. 价值塑造：在国际商务沟通中嵌入中国优秀传统文化、中华历史智慧等中国元素，讲好中国故事。为学生树立理想信念提供价值引领，在内容体系中体现思政观，引导学生养成遵循责任担当、德行并举和经世济民的职业操守与伦理规范的习惯，引导学生从我国特定的人文环境中体会国际商务沟通的特色。

本教材是集体智慧的结晶，由北京理工大学余晓泓副教授、赵洱崟教授担任主编，负责全书的各项工作，教材建设团队其他成员包括北京理工大学戚淳老师（单元1、16、

18、19、20)、王红夏老师(单元2、3、4、6、17)、董梅老师(单元5、11、12、13、14)。本教材是未来管理学习研究中心(Research Center of Future Management Learning)的系列成果之一。

  由于作者的知识和水平有限，教材编写中难免存在缺陷和不足，需要不断地打磨和完善，在此恳请应用本教材的同行和业内人士不吝赐教，以便更好地服务于学习者。

国际商务沟通教材建设团队
2024 年 3 月

目 录

Unit 1　The Nature of Negotiation ··1
   1.1　Learning Objectives ···2
   1.2　The Nature of Negotiation ···2
   1.3　Interdependence ··2
   1.4　Mutual Adjustment ···2
   1.5　Examples for Your Check List ··3
   1.6　Value Claiming and Value Creation ··4
   1.7　Effective Conflict Management ···5
   1.8　Case Study ···6
   1.9　Business Ethics ··8
   1.10　Exercises ··9

Unit 2　Strategy and Tactics of Negotiation ··11
   2.1　Learning Objectives ···12
   2.2　Tactical Tasks ···12
   2.3　Position Taken During Negotiation ··13
   2.4　Key Steps in the Negotiation ··16
   2.5　Factors That Facilitate Successful Negotiation ··17
   2.6　Case Study ···18
   2.7　Business Ethics ··19
   2.8　Exercises ··19

Unit 3　Relationships in Negotiation ··20
   3.1　Learning Objectives ···21
   3.2　Negotiation in Communal Sharing Relationship ······································21
   3.3　Key Elements in Managing Negotiations within Relationship ···············22
   3.4　Case Study ···27
   3.5　Business Ethics ··28
   3.6　Exercises ··28

Unit 4　Strategy and Planning of Negotiation ···29
   4.1　Learning Objectives ···30
   4.2　Goals and Effects of Negotiation Strategy ··30
   4.3　Strategy and Tactics ···31

4.4	The Planning Process of Implementing Strategy	32
4.5	Case Study	35
4.6	Business Ethics	35
4.7	Exercises	36

Unit 5 Cross-Cultural Negotiation ··········· 37

5.1	Learning Objectives	38
5.2	The Nature of Culture	38
5.3	Dimensions of Culture	38
5.4	Why Culture Influences Negotiations	40
5.5	How Culture Influences Negotiations	41
5.6	Cross-Cultural Negotiation Strategies	43
5.7	Case Study	45
5.8	Business Ethics	46
5.9	Exercises	47

Unit 6 Essential of Business Letter Writing ··········· 48

6.1	Learn Objectives	49
6.2	Brief Introduction	49
6.3	Requirements for Business Letter and Email Writers	49
6.4	Seven Guidelines in Business Letter Writing	49
6.5	Letter Format and Placement of Major Parts	51
6.6	The Layout of Emails	53
6.7	The Layout of Business Letters	54
6.8	Addressing Envelopes	55
6.9	Writing Procedure	56
6.10	The Outline of Business Letters	57
6.11	Case Study	58
6.12	Business Ethics	60
6.13	Exercises	60

Unit 7 Establishing Business Relations ··········· 61

7.1	Learning Objectives	62
7.2	The Significance of Establishing Business Relations	62
7.3	The Channels of Establishing Business Relations	62
7.4	Writing Skills	63
7.5	Typical Expressions for Letters Requesting for Establishment of Business Relations (See Table 7.1) and Replies (See Table 7.2)	63
7.6	Specimen Letters	64
7.7	Situational Conversation	65
7.8	Useful Patterns & Examples	66
7.9	Case Study	67

7.10	Business Ethics	68
7.11	Exercises	68

Unit 8 Enquiry and Reply ··· 70

8.1	Learning Objectives	71
8.2	The Importance and Nature of Enquiry	71
8.3	Categories of Enquiry	71
8.4	Writing Skills	71
8.5	Typical Expressions for Letters Making Enquiry (See Table 8.1) and Reply (See Table 8.2)	72
8.6	Specimen Letters	73
8.7	Situational Conversation	74
8.8	Useful Patterns & Examples	75
8.9	Case Study	76
8.10	Business Ethics	76
8.11	Exercises	77

Unit 9 Quotation and Offer ··· 79

9.1	Learning Objectives	81
9.2	The Importance and Nature of Offer	81
9.3	Categories of Offer	81
9.4	Differences between Offer & Quotation	82
9.5	Writing Skills	82
9.6	Typical Expressions for Letters Making Offer (See Table 9.1)	82
9.7	Specimen Letters	83
9.8	Situational Conversation	84
9.9	Useful Patterns & Examples	85
9.10	Case Study	86
9.11	Business Ethics	86
9.12	Exercises	87

Unit 10 Order and Acknowledgement ··· 89

10.1	Learning Objectives	90
10.2	Orders and Their Effects	90
10.3	About Acknowledgement	90
10.4	Writing Skills and Typical Expressions of Placing Orders (See Table 10.1)	91
10.5	Specimen Letters	93
10.6	Situational Conversation	95
10.7	Useful Patterns & Examples	96
10.8	Case Study	97
10.9	Business Ethics	97
10.10	Exercises	98

Unit 11　Conclusion of Business ·········· 100
  11.1　Learning Objectives ·········· 101
  11.2　Function of Contract ·········· 101
  11.3　The Contents of a Contract ·········· 101
  11.4　Writing Skills ·········· 102
  11.5　Typical Writing Steps of Conclusion of Business (See Table 11.1) ·········· 103
  11.6　Specimen Letters ·········· 103
  11.7　Situational Conversation ·········· 105
  11.8　Useful Patterns & Examples ·········· 105
  11.9　Case Study ·········· 107
  11.10　Business Ethics ·········· 107
  11.11　Exercises ·········· 107

Unit 12　Payment Methods ·········· 109
  12.1　Learning Objectives ·········· 110
  12.2　Modes of Payment ·········· 110
  12.3　Writing Skills and Typical Expressions (See Table 12.1—12.4) ·········· 111
  12.4　Specimen Letters ·········· 112
  12.5　Useful Patterns & Examples ·········· 113
  12.6　Case Study ·········· 114
  12.7　Business Ethics ·········· 114
  12.8　Exercises ·········· 115

Unit 13　Packing ·········· 117
  13.1　Learning Objectives ·········· 118
  13.2　Types of Packing ·········· 118
  13.3　Function of Packing ·········· 118
  13.4　Writing Skills ·········· 118
  13.5　Typical Expressions for Letters of Packing (See Table 13.1) and Replies (See Table 13.2) ·········· 119
  13.6　Specimen Letters ·········· 119
  13.7　Useful Patterns & Examples ·········· 121
  13.8　Case Study ·········· 122
  13.9　Business Ethics ·········· 122
  13.10　Exercises ·········· 122

Unit 14　Shipment ·········· 124
  14.1　Learning Objectives ·········· 125
  14.2　About Shipment ·········· 125
  14.3　Method of Shipment ·········· 125
  14.4　Writing Skills and Typical Expressions ·········· 125
  14.5　Specimen Letters ·········· 127

14.6	Useful Patterns and Examples	128
14.7	Case Study	129
14.8	Business Ethics	129
14.9	Exercises	129

Unit 15 Insurance · 131
15.1	Learning Objectives	132
15.2	About International Cargo Transportation Insurance	132
15.3	The Field of International Cargo Insurance	132
15.4	Writing Skills and Typical Expressions	133
15.5	Specimen Letters	134
15.6	Useful Patterns & Examples	135
15.7	Case Study	136
15.8	Business Ethics	137
15.9	Exercises	137

Unit 16 Claim and Settlement · 139
16.1	Learning Objectives	140
16.2	Brief Introduction of Complaints and Claims	140
16.3	The Different Types of Claims	140
16.4	Writing Skills	141
16.5	Typical Expressions for Letters Requesting for Claim and Settlements	141
16.6	Specimen Letters	142
16.7	Useful Patterns & Examples	143
16.8	Case Study	145
16.9	Business Ethics	145
16.10	Exercises	145

Unit 17 Telephone Etiquette · 146
17.1	Learning Objectives	147
17.2	The Significance of Telephone Etiquette	147
17.3	The Guidelines for Handling Outgoing Calls	147
17.4	The Guidelines for Receiving Incoming Calls	148
17.5	Typical Expressions for Handling Outgoing and Incoming Calls	148
17.6	The Guidelines for Teleconferencing	149
17.7	Case Study	150
17.8	Situational Conversation	152
17.9	Business Ethics	153

Unit 18 Job Application and Interview · 154
| 18.1 | Learning Objectives | 155 |
| 18.2 | Brief Introduction | 155 |

18.3	Resumes and Application Letters	155
18.4	The Job Interview	158
18.5	Case Study	160
18.6	Business Ethics	163
18.7	Exercises	163

Unit 19　Business Travel Etiquette 164

19.1	Learning Objectives	165
19.2	The Significance of Business Travel Etiquette	165
19.3	Basic Etiquette of Business Travel	165
19.4	Foreign Custom and Holiday Etiquette	167
19.5	Typical Greeting Behaviors	171
19.6	Basic Etiquette of Conference, Seminar or Training Program	171
19.7	Basic Etiquette of Trade Fair	172
19.8	Case Study	172
19.9	Business Ethics	173
19.10	Exercises	173

Unit 20　Business Negotiation Etiquette 175

20.1	Learning Objectives	176
20.2	Brief Introduction	176
20.3	Negotiators as Hosts	176
20.4	Negotiators as Guests	178
20.5	Verbal and Nonverbal Communication	178
20.6	Taboos of Business Negotiation of Different Cultures	179
20.7	Case Study	180
20.8	Situational Etiquette	181
20.9	Business Ethics	182
20.10	Exercises	183

Unit 21　Business Dinner Etiquette 187

21.1	Learning Objectives	188
21.2	The Significance of Dining Etiquette	188
21.3	Forms of Business Entertaining	188
21.4	Preparations for Business Meals	188
21.5	Etiquette for Business Dinner	190
21.6	Toasts	192
21.7	Useful Tips	193
21.8	Case Study	194
21.9	Business Ethics	195
21.10	Exercises	195

参考文献 198

Unit 1

The Nature of Negotiation

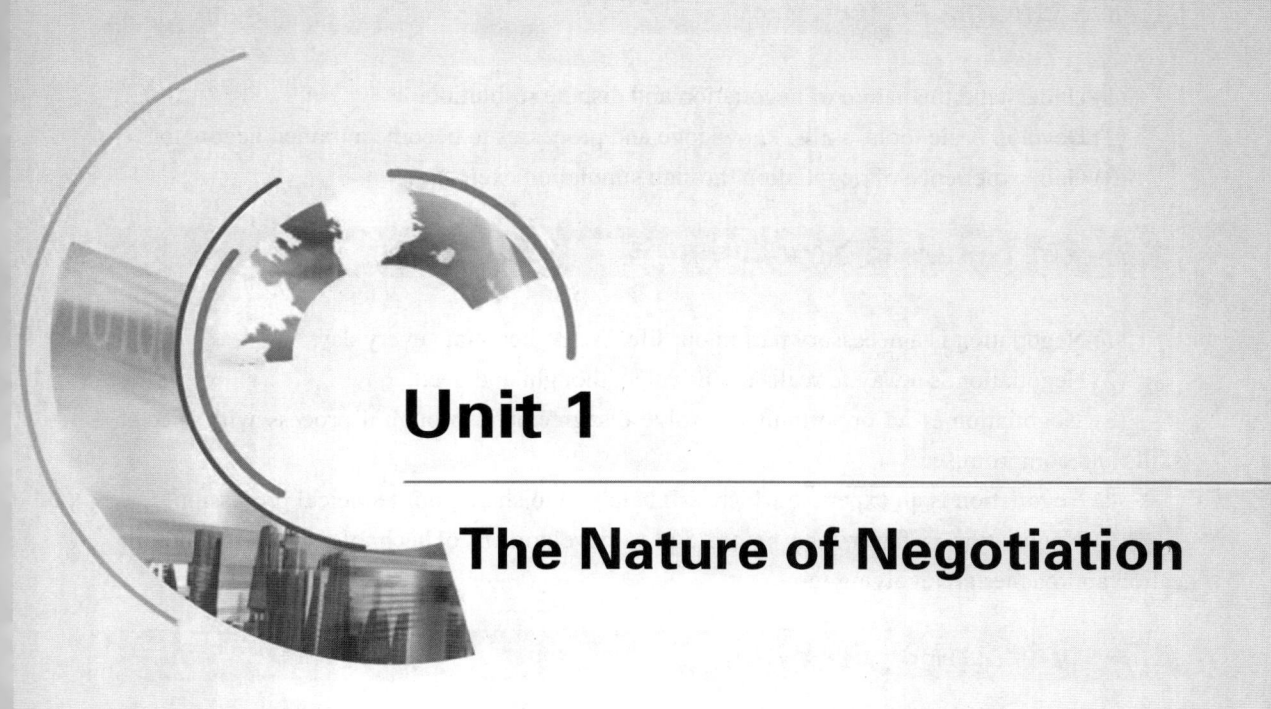

✧ **Case-Lead-in**

Say you were assigned as leading negotiator of your company in a key project: to purchase major raw materials for your company's produts. This project has a very tied schedule and till now, nothing was settled down. Your task is to work all issues out which are including: price, quality, quantity, payment, and delivery. How did you do it?

1.1　Learning Objectives

(1) Understand the nature of negotiation and dispute resolution.
(2) Develop basic tools, skills, knowledge and processes to become a trained negotiator.
(3) Gain experience of negotiation through simulation exercises.

1.2　The Nature of Negotiation

(1) Negotiation is a necessary part in our life. We do negotiate every day.
(2) Negotiation is a way to realize your value, thought and need.
(3) Negotiation is an opportunity to solve disagreement through a process with special skills and compromise.
(4) Negotiation is an expertise which will help you to sharp your technical profession.
(5) Negotiation is faster than before due to development of technology, and communication approaches are evolving too.

1.3　Interdependence

Negotiation is a process to reach collaboration with a partner regarding both parties' interests, feelings, and concerns. As we have demonstrated in lead-in case, we negotiate for something important for us or something we want, and we might have something other parts want too. How can we trade with each other? How much will be a proper price and who is going to decide it? If you step into a negotiation with an opinion that you are going to push your counterpart to the corner. Then you do not understand the true beauty of negotiation.

A negotiation is about communication, understanding the other party's position, encoding and decoding information, interpreting oral and body language, asking the right question, and win wisely. An effective negotiation provides both sides opportunity to achieve their goals, but how can we define a negotiation which is effective or success? Here we classify negotiations into following four categories: (1)win-win; (2)lose-lose; (3)win-lose; (4)partial win-partial lose. Among these, a win-win negotiation is the best outcome, because both parties get what they want. But in real life, it is very hard to reach a win-win solution. People always need to deal with many contentious issues and if you can reach satisfaction through collaboration, when you leave negotiation table, you may have a win-win end in your mind. Then you can call it an effective negotiation.

1.4　Mutual Adjustment

Before you start to prepare a negotiation, you need to draw a map for what you really want from it. The map can be drawn by solution-driven approach, you need to imagine what will be the final solution you want. That picture may not be the real one you finally have, but you need to build a blueprint before you start everything. In the map, you could draw some key points which will help you walk in the right path.

(1) What is my ultimate goal? Is this goal the best solution for me?

(2) If so, to achieve this final goal, how can I break it down into several objectives?

(3) How can I distinguish between: what I must achieve, and what I can achieve?

(4) What are my strength and weakness?

(5) What is my plan B?

Like any competition, knowing yourself is not enough, in management field, you will not make any decision without knowing external environment which includes your competitors' position. So, the similar questions should be asked for your counterpart.

(1) What is their ultimate goal? Is this goal the best solution for them?

(2) If so, to achieve this final goal, how can they break it down into several objectives?

(3) Which objectives they must achieve, and what they can achieve?

(4) What are their strength and weakness?

(5) What is their plan B?

These questions may help you understand your general ground in this negotiation as well as your counterpart's. With this information, you might understand both positions in the negotiation and could be better to predict what will be the best strategy for you to reach a collaboration.

1.5 Examples for Your Check List

Here we use the lead-in case as background information to outline questions negotiator should consider before walking into a negotiation (see Table 1.1 and Table 1.2).

Table 1.1 Questions for Before Negotiation

Elements	My Company	Seller
Who are the other party?		
Do we have a long-term relationship?		
Are there potential sellers as well?		
If my time constraint is severe, how much time-related cost my company might pay?		
Where does the negotiation take place?		
Is the negotiation on-line or off-line?		
Is there any language issue?		
Is there any legal issue?		

Table 1.2 Questions for During Negotiation

Elements	My Company	Seller
Does the contract need to be concluded in or evidenced by writing?		
Should the goods be handed over to the first carrier for transmission to the buyer or placed to a specific place?		
If there is no industrial standard, how can we determine the quality match required by the contract?		
If the seller has delivered goods late than the date for delivery, what my company should do?		
If the goods do not conform with the contract, can my company reduce the price?		
Where should my company pay to the seller?		
If my company fails to perform payment, what the seller should do?		
When the risk passes from the seller to my company?		

1.6 Value Claiming and Value Creation

In management analysis, there is one term always used to analyze company's competitiveness: bargaining power. An effective negotiation needs the power too. In a negotiation, you need to claim your interests and concern about interests of the counterpart as well. How can you end up with a win-win result instead of a win-lose end? There are several things you must/must not do.

Must do:

(1) to control yourself;

(2) to have an open mind;

(3) to listen to the counterpart's needs;

(4) to build mutual trust;

(5) to access the counterpart's strengths and weaknesses;

(6) to focus on the counterpart's concern not negotiators themselves;

(7) to identify the key difference;

(8) to aim to creative result;

(9) to help the counterpart at their interests;

(10) to adopt compromise if it is necessary.

Must not do:

(1) not to lead negotiation all the time;

(2) not to let your emotion or pressure to influence language/behavior;

(3) not to be subjective, negotiation is a game;
(4) not to label the counterpart negatively;
(5) not to point fingers;
(6) not to concern your interests only;
(7) not to be rude.

1.7 Effective Conflict Management

Negotiation is a game, and conflict is inevitable. Negotiation itself is a process of finding differences, resolving differences and finally reaching agreement. Each party has their fundamental interests, and it is their nature to focus on their interests firstly. In the process, conflict is necessary and cannot be avoid.

Conflict is not bad, in the phase, both parts should use their information, collected before and during negotiation, to identify the primary goal that they both need to achieve, and secondary, or even third goals. They both should perceive alternatives for the counterpart based on cost, time schedule, risk, capacity, and long-term relationship, etc. To do so, both need to have some knowledge about conflict, and if conflict management techniques are available will be better. It requires that both should probe their boundary to conflict and recognize their own path in dealing with conflict. This is the key to resolving conflicts.

As shown in Figure 1.1, when there is a conflict in the negotiation, both parties should investigate source of the conflict, diagnose real reasons behind the conflict, and actively seek alternative solutions to solve it. The difficulty here is both might insist on their own interests and refuse to take any step forward. The other side should determine whether the insistence is driven by subjective or objective factors. Then based on the factor, two parts can work on objective criteria to solve the conflict.

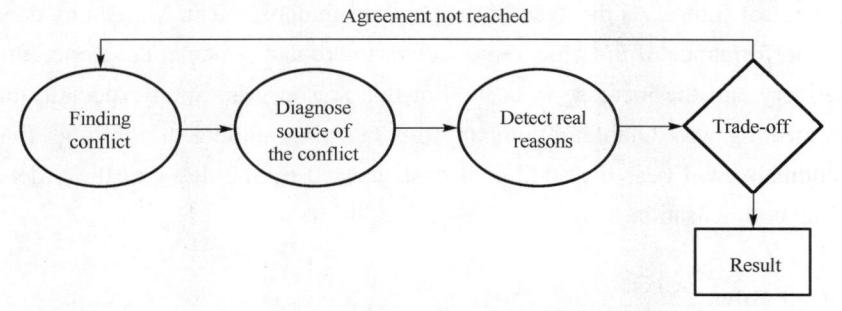

Figure 1.1 Process of Resolving Conflicts

When you want to conduct this process, you need to be aware that some phrases might increase tensions between your two, please put red flag for them.

(1) You are not reasonable.
(2) You don't know what you are talking about.

(3) You are going to ruin your business.

(4) It is unfair.

(5) The result is obvious.

1.8　Case Study

Side A: Meifu

At the beginning of 2022, the purchasing department of Meifu company outsourced a large number of prepared dishes orders planned for first quarter sales to Qianfeng company for production, but there were a lot of delays in order delivery. The two companies have cooperated for many years, and Qianfeng company has undertaken many batches of prepared dishes orders from Meifu company, and there has never been any delay in delivery. However, due to the impact of the epidemic, the delivery of orders was delayed. Ms. Sunny, a representative of Meifu company, claimed that in order to meet the demand of offline stores and online sales for prefabricated dishes of core products, Meifu company had to arrange its own production line to expedite production orders and use expedited transportation to transport products to retail stores across the country, resulting in a large number of additional costs and high opportunity cost losses.

In May, the two sides had a negotiation on the delay of delivery of 130000 boxes of orders. At that time, Qianfeng company compensated 850000 yuan to Meifu for the long-term cooperation between the two sides and the idea of jointly bearing the losses. The total losses caused by the order delay now is as high as 2.79 million yuan. Both companies must take this negotiation seriously and try to clarify the responsibilities and obligations of both parties to minimize the losses of the company.

2022 is the critical year for the IPO of Meifu company and to do so, the company may lay off staff in the near future. As the head of the purchasing department, Ms. Sunny does not want to affect the performance of the procurement department and personal development due to the delay in delivery and the increase in costs. For this reason, Ms. Sunny specially organized a negotiation meeting with Qianfeng company this morning, hoping that through this meeting, Qianfeng company will bear the additional costs caused by the delay of the order and make corresponding compensation.

Side B: Qianfeng

The compensation incident also had a great impact on Qianfeng company and disrupted the company's future development plan. Qianfeng company was also conducting internal negotiations before negotiating with Meifu company.

Mr. Wall (CEO): at the beginning of the year, when we found that due to the epidemic, the order of Meifu company might be delayed, we have decided to compensate Meifu company accordingly. This is also because our two companies have a long-term cooperative relationship, and we don't want to lose this important customer. But now, the losses calculated by Meifu company far exceed our expectations. Now they ask us to compensate, which will be a great blow to the financial performance of our company.

Ms. Clare, purchasing department: at the beginning of the year, Meifu company's forecast for the prepared dishes market was not very optimistic, so it gave us a small order, according to which we arranged production. However, three weeks later, Meifu adjusted their market expectations and increased the number of orders. The number of new orders greatly exceeded our capacity, which caused subsequent problems. In fact, this was caused by their own judgment, and the responsibility should be borne by them.

Mr. Tony, production department: our department has been responsible for the production of prepared dishes from the beginning. We have a better understanding of the situation. First of all, because of the additional orders, the production volume has greatly exceeded our expectations. In order to complete the orders of Mobil, the workers in our department have been working overtime. Secondly, the seasoning of this prepared dish is a unique material, and we need to order from a third-party manufacturer. Due to their additional orders, the third-party manufacturers also need to reproduce due to insufficient inventory, which is also the reason for the production delay. Due to the insufficient supply of raw materials, we can't complete the production, which is due to the third-party manufacturers to a certain extent, but it is fundamentally due to the United States service company.

Ms. Clare: from the event of Meifu company, I deeply realize that there are problems in our company's development strategy in recent years. At the beginning of the establishment of our company, we mainly used OEM, but the profit of OEM is very thin and low, and the risk is also high. With the development of these years, our company has certain strength, and we should vigorously develop our own brands, which can not only improve our profit margin, but also enhance our popularity.

Mr. Tony: our company has not developed its own brand. A few years ago, we also launched a self-developed product. However, due to insufficient popularity, the market response was not good. The product not only did not make profits, but also brought a lot of losses to the company. If we launch new products rashly, we may repeat the mistakes.

Mr. Wall: independent brands must develop in the future, but at present, what we need to solve is the cooperation with Meifu company. In the short term, OEM for Meifu company is still a major part of our profits. Therefore, this time, we should have a good discussion with Meifu company. After all, we should maintain a long-term cooperative relationship. However, they should not make too much compensation. The amount of compensation should be discussed with them. They should not dominate the direction of negotiation in the negotiation. After all, the overall operation and profits of the company this year are not good. In my psychological expectation, the total compensation cannot exceed 1.5 million. If it exceeds this value, it will also have an impact on our company.

Based on the above information, please prepare to participate in this negotiation as Ms. Sunny. Please clarify the relevant background information in the case and the relationship between the two companies in Table 1.3. On this basis, set your primary and secondary goals and predict the primary and secondary goals of the Qianfeng company, as well as the conflicts that may occur in the negotiation. In view of these conflicts, please diagnose the sources of them and offer possible trade-offs.

Table 1.3 Background Information

Goals	Conflicts	Meifu	Qianfeng
Primary goal	Interest		
	Possible conflict		
	Source of conflict		
	Driven force		
	Bargaining power		
	Alternative solution		
Secondary goal	Interest		
	Possible conflict		
	Source of conflict		
	Driven force		
	Bargaining power		
	Alternative solution		
Third goal (if available)	Interest		
	Possible conflict		
	Source of conflict		
	Driven force		
	Bargaining power		
	Alternative solution		

1.9 Business Ethics

《战国策》：苏秦从燕之赵，始合从，说赵王曰："天下之卿相人臣，乃至布衣之士，莫不高贤大王之行义，皆愿奉教陈忠于前之日久矣。虽然，奉阳君妒，大王不得任事，是以外宾客游谈之士，无敢尽忠于前者。今奉阳君捐馆舍，大王乃今然后得与士民相亲，臣故敢献其愚，效愚忠。为大王计，莫若安民无事，请无庸有为也。安民之本，在于择交，择交而得则民安，择交不得则民终身不得安。请言外患：齐、秦为两敌，而民不得安；倚秦攻齐，而民不得安；倚齐攻秦，而民不得安。故夫谋人之主，伐人之国，常苦出辞断绝人之交，愿大王慎无出与口也。"

"请屏左右，曰言所以异，阴阳而已矣。大王诚能听臣，燕必致毡裘狗马之地，齐必致海隅鱼盐之地，楚必致桔柚云梦之地，韩、魏皆可使致封地汤沐之邑，贵戚父兄皆可以受封侯。夫割地效实，五伯之所以复军禽将而求也；封侯贵戚，汤、武之所以放杀而争也。今大王垂拱而两有之，是臣之所以为大王愿也。大王与秦，则秦必弱韩、魏；与齐，则齐必弱楚、魏。魏弱则割河外，韩弱则效宜阳。宜阳效则上郡绝，河外割则道不通。楚弱则无援。此三策者，不可不熟计也。夫秦下轵道则南阳动，劫韩包周则赵自销铄，据卫取淇则齐必入朝。秦欲已得行于山东，则必举甲而向赵。秦甲涉河逾漳，据番吾，则兵必战于邯郸之下矣。此臣之所以为大王患也。"

"当今之时，山东之建国，莫如赵强。赵地方二千里，带甲数十万，车千乘，骑万匹，粟支十年；西有常山，南有河、漳，东有清河，北有燕国。燕固弱国，不足畏也。且秦之所畏害于天下者，莫如赵。然而秦不敢举兵甲而伐赵者，何也？畏韩、魏之议其后也。然则韩、魏，赵之南蔽也。秦之攻韩、魏也，则不然。无有名山大川之限，稍稍蚕食之，傅之国都而止矣。韩、魏不能支秦，必入臣。韩、魏臣于秦，秦无韩、魏之隔，祸中于赵矣。此臣之所以为大王患也。"

讨论

《战国策》中的这一篇是我国历史上关于游说（谈判）的知名的文章，文中苏秦在说服赵肃侯的时候，充分利用谈判的诸多技巧，在对对方国内情况了如指掌的情况下，巧妙地分析了双方的首要目标，并通过创造一个安全的谈话环境，拉近了与对方的距离，取得了对方的信任。

在谈话的过程中，苏秦一直关注对方的利益，通过分析内外环境和赵国的优势，层层递进地阐述自己的观点。苏秦还主动提出双方有冲突的观点，分析该冲突产生的原因和可能造成的结果。在谈判的过程中，苏秦并没有一直输出自己的观点，而是不时地站在对方的角度思考问题，使得对方更容易接受自己的观点，为最终的胜利奠定了基础。同时，在交谈中注意语言的运用，包括提醒对方在与别国交往和谈判的过程中，不要使用负面语言。

在整个过程中，苏秦注重事前信息的收集，寻找双方利益的共同点，基于对方的利益分析问题，主动提出冲突观点，并针对冲突点进行分析，让对方明晰利弊。这是一篇值得我们深入学习和思考的文章。

1.10　Exercises

1. Case Practice

Please read extra information and conduct a further preparation for the second-round negotiation between Meifu & Qianfeng, this time, you can pick your side.

Results of the first-round negotiation.

The negotiation between Ms. Sunny and Qianfeng company was not smooth, showing a stalemate. Both parties were unwilling to make concessions, and no agreement was reached at the final meeting. Meifu company hopes Qianfeng company can compensate at least 2 million losses, so as not to affect the performance of Sunny's purchasing department; Considering the cost, Qianfeng company is willing to pay 1.5 million yuan at most to ensure that it will not affect the company's profits. Although the contract signed between Meifu company and Qianfeng company mentioned that if Qianfeng company's products have quality problems or product delivery delays, they should be fully responsible for the delay in delivery date, it did not specify what responsibilities should be borne by both parties if there is a large deviation between the number of Meifu orders and the actual number of orders.

2. Case Practice

Please read the case and answer the following questions.

You are the CEO of a startup company. Your company has developed a new product and wants to settle on an online sales platform. The sales platform has never heard of your company's products and brands, and rejected your proposal.

Requirement:

(1) How should you persuade the other party to accept your proposal in the negotiation?

(2) Please analyze the difference between negotiation and sales in this case.

3. Case Practice

Please read the case and answer the following questions.

You are the creative director of an art company. An internationally renowned singer asked your company to design the cover of his new album. You gave this job to the most famous project team in your company. There are two main employees in this project team. A is outgoing and keeps close communication with colleagues in different departments of the company. B is calm and introverted and does not associate with colleagues in other departments. After receiving the task of designing the cover for famous singers, the project team finally established two plans after many discussions. These two plans were proposed by A and B respectively, and the project team was also divided into two factions, with no dispute. Now the project team asks you to mediate. How do you preside over this internal negotiation? Please think about and use your own understanding to distinguish between mediation and negotiation.

Unit 2

Strategy and Tactics of Negotiation

✧ **Case-Lead-in**

Two years ago, an African country began a large set of equipment for a government department of its country selective bidding procurement, amounting to tens of millions of dollars, the bidders involved the United Kingdom, Germany, South Africa and China's more than a dozen large companies. The major companies have their own advantages, some of which have certain origins with the country. Germany is known for its excellent technology, strict attitude and high product quality; the African country used to be a British colony, with deeper historical roots; the South African company has a better relationship with the local Indians and Pakistanis, who have some power in the government. In this situation, Chinese company A was ready to participate in the competition and actively made preparations.

2.1 Learning Objectives

(1) To master the negotiation tactical tasks.
(2) To understand position taken during negotiation.
(3) To master steps in the negotiation.
(4) To understand the factors that facilitate successful negotiation.

2.2 Tactical Tasks

Some negotiators seem to believe that hard-bargaining tactics are the key to success. They resort to threats, extreme demands, and even unethical behavior to try to get the upper hand in a negotiation.

In fact, negotiators who fall back on hard-bargaining strategies in negotiation are typically betraying a lack of understanding about the gains that can be achieved in most business negotiations. When negotiators resort to hard-bargaining tactics, they convey that they view negotiation as a win-lose enterprise. A small percentage of business negotiations that concern only one issue, such as price, can indeed be viewed as win-lose negotiations, or distributive negotiations.

Here is a list of the 10 tactics in negotiation.

(1) Extreme demands followed up by small, slow concessions. Perhaps the most common of all hard-bargaining tactics, this one protects deal makers from making concessions too quickly. However, it can keep parties from making a deal and unnecessarily drag out business negotiations. To head off this tactic, have a clear sense of your own goals, best alternative to a negotiated agreement (BATNA), and bottom line—and don't be rattled by an aggressive opponent.

(2) Commitment tactics. Your opponent may say that his hands are tied or that he has only limited discretion to negotiate with you. Do what you can to find out if these commitment tactics are genuine. You may find that you need to negotiate with someone who has greater authority to do business with you.

(3) Take-it-or-leave-it negotiation strategy. Offers should rarely be nonnegotiable. To defuse this hard-bargaining tactic, try ignoring it and focus on the content of the offer instead, then make a counter-offer that meets both parties' needs.

(4) Inviting unreciprocated offers. When you make an offer, you may find that your counterpart asks you to make a concession before making a counteroffer herself. Don't bid against yourself by reducing your demands; instead, indicate that you are waiting for a counteroffer.

(5) Trying to make you flinch. Sometimes you may find that your opponent keeps making greater and greater demands, waiting for you to reach your breaking point and concede.

Name the hard-bargaining tactic and clarify that you will only engage in a reciprocal exchange of offers.

(6) Personal insults and feather ruffling. Personal attacks can feed on your insecurities and make you vulnerable. Take a break if you feel yourself getting flustered, and let the other party know that you won't tolerate insults and other cheap ploys.

(7) Bluffing, puffing, and lying. Exaggerating and misrepresenting facts can throw you off guard. Be skeptical about claims that seem too good to be true and investigate them closely.

(8) Threats and warnings. Want to know how to deal with threats? The first step is recognizing threats and oblique warnings as the hard-bargaining tactics they are. Ignoring a threat and naming a threat can be two effective strategies for defusing them.

(9) Belittling your alternatives. The other party might try to make you cave in by belittling your best alternative to an egotiated agreement. Don't let her shake your resolve.

(10) Good cop, bad cop. When facing off with a two-negotiator team, you may find that one person is reasonable and the other is tough. Realize that they are working together and don't be taken in by such hard-bargaining tactics.

2.3 Position Taken During Negotiation

Bargaining position is the position of a person, group, or organization in a negotiation, with respect to their ability to achieve a deal which is favorable to themselves. Negotiators' positions are the things they demand you give them and also the things that they refuse to provide you with. Negotiation positions are typically communicated in meetings, emails, and proposals. Inexperienced negotiators too often take the positions of the other side at face value and don't probe with questions or challenge sufficiently.

Competitive negotiators are infamous for employing positions—they're clear on what they want and communicate this early, strongly, and repeatedly. It's usually unwise to give in to someone's first position or demand. Wiser is to ask them questions, with "Why?" being the most useful question. There are many ways of asking "why" questions, such as:
- What will this enable you to do?
- What will happen if you don't get this?
- How will having this help you?

1. Opening Offers

While knowledge about the other party helps negotiators set their opening offers, it does not tell them exactly what to do. Making the first offer is advantageous as it can anchor a negotiation. Higher initial offers have a strong effect on negotiation outcomes. Negotiators can dampen the "first-offer effect" by concentrating on their own target and focusing on the other negotiator's resistance point.

The fundamental question is whether the opening offer should be exaggerated or modest.

Exaggerating an opening offer is advantageous because it gives the negotiator room for movement thereby giving his or her time to learn about the other party's priorities; it may create an impression in the other party's mind that: there is a long way to go before a reasonable settlement will be achieved; a greater number of concessions will have to be made to find a common zone of potential agreement (ZOPA); the other may have incorrectly estimated his or her own resistance point.

Two disadvantages to exaggerae an offer include: potential rejection by the other party, halting negotiations prematurely, and the perception of a "tough" attitude can harm a long-term relationship.

2. Opening Stance

A second decision negotiators should make at the outset of distributive bargaining concerns the stance, or attitude, to adopt during the negotiation. Is it competitive or moderate? Belligerence may be met with belligerence from the other party. Negotiators tend to match distributive tactics from the other party with their own distributive tactics, especially appropriate tactics.

To communicate effectively, a negotiator should try to send a consistent message through both the opening offer and opening stance. When the messages are in conflict, the other party will find them confusing to interpret and answer.

3. Initial Concessions

An opening offer is usually met with a counteroffer, and these two offers define the initial bargaining range.

After the first round of offers, what movement or concessions are to be made? It is not an option to escalate one's opening offer—that is, to set an offer further away from the other party's target point than one's first offer. If concessions are to be made, how large should they be? The first concession conveys a message, frequently a symbolic one, to the other party about how you will proceed.

Opening offers, opening stances, and initial concessions are elements at the beginning of a negotiation that parties can use to communicate how they intend to negotiate. Negotiators who take a hard line during negotiations achieve better economic outcomes, but at a cost of being perceived negatively by the other party.

There are several good reasons for adopting a flexible position.

First, when taking different stances throughout the negotiation, you can learn about the other party's targets and perceived possibilities by observing how they respond to different proposals.

Second, flexibility keeps the negotiations proceeding—the more flexible you seem, the more the other party will believe a settlement is possible.

4. Role of Concessions

Concessions are central to negotiation—without them, negotiation would not exist. People enter negotiations expecting concessions. Immediate concessions are perceived less valuable than gradual, delayed concessions. Research suggests that more straightforward negotiators and those with greater concern for the other party make more concessions during negotiation. Negotiators generally resent a take-it-or-leave-it approach.

There is ample data to show that parties feel better about a settlement when the negotiation involved a progression of concessions than when it didn't. Concessions imply recognition of the other's position and its legitimacy. Intangible factors of status and recognition may be as important as the tangible issues. Not reciprocating a concession may send a powerful message about firmness and leaves the concession maker open to feeling their esteem has been damaged.

A reciprocal concession cannot be haphazard. It must be on the same item or one of similar weight and comparable magnitude. Making additional concessions when none are received implies weakness. Negotiators may not accept inadequate reciprocal concessions.

To encourage further concessions, negotiators may link their concessions to a prior concession made by the other. Packaging concessions can lead to better outcomes than making concessions singly on individual issues.

5. Pattern of Concession Making

The pattern of concessions a negotiator makes contains valuable information, but it is not always easy to interpret. When successive concessions get smaller, the message is that the concession maker's position is getting firmer and the resistance point is being approached. Note that a concession late in negotiations may also indicate that there is little room left to move.

6. Final Offers

Eventually, a negotiator wants to convey the message that there is no further room for movement – that the present offer is the final one. But sometimes a simple statement of "This all I can do" does not suffice and a negotiator may use concessions to convey the point.

A simple absence of further concessions conveys the message, but the other party may feel the pattern of concessions is being violated. One way to accomplish this is to make the last concession more substantial. Large enough to be dramatic yet not so large it creates suspicion that the negotiator has been holding back. A concession may also be personalized to the other party signaling, this is the last concession the negotiator will make—"I went to my boss and got a special deal just for you."

2.4　Key Steps in the Negotiation

In today's business world, more negotiators are striving for win-win outcomes. It's easy to understand why: as more and more companies enter into long-term business relationships and partnerships, win-win agreements are becoming indispensable. Companies that depend on each other need to maintain positive relationships and conduct transactions that are mutually beneficial. As a result of this shift, traditionally trained win-lose negotiators are left wondering how to achieve win-win results.

Before you even walk into a negotiation, you should have outlined your own interests and made some educated guesses about those of the other party. Set your priorities beforehand and determine what is negotiable and what is not.

Depending on what you know or guess about the other party's interests, you may be able to identify in advance some areas where you can make concessions that are of more value to them than they are to you, and vice versa. This is an ideal opportunity to create value by finding ways for each party to give up a little in order to gain a lot, which is a valuable strategy for reaching a win-win agreement.

Concessions are the terms, conditions and dollars that may be traded in order to reach a win-win. The exchange of concessions is what moves a negotiation to a satisfactory conclusion. Here are some general guidelines for trading concessions.

(1) Since negotiation is a give-and-take process, remember that you must have something to give if you expect to receive anything?

(2) Never give a concession unless you expect to get one in return.

(3) Remember that what you perceive as having low value, the other party may perceive as having high value, and vice versa.

(4) Whoever gives a large first concession without getting one in return generally gives up the most in the entire negotiation.

(5) Plan a supporting statement for each concession to demonstrate its value. The other party must feel that each concession has been earned; something given for free has little perceived value.

(6) Don't accept, but always explore, the first offer. Chances are you can do better, and the other party will probably become concerned if they don't have to work a bit to get your agreement.

(7) Anticipate what concessions you think the other party will trade freely, and how the other party will react to each of your concessions.

(8) Remember that how you give out concessions is just as important as what concessions you give. Different concession patterns will send different messages.

Through effectively using concessions you can eliminate the zero-sum game, win-lose mentality, by increasing the size of the pie. By focusing on interests instead of positions, creative concessions become a key tool for reaching mutual satisfaction and achieving win-win outcomes in negotiations.

While there are many approaches to negotiation tactics, there are five common steps that most effective negotiations follow to achieve a successful outcome.

(1) Prepare: Negotiation preparation is easy to ignore, but it's a vital first stage of the negotiating process. To prepare, research both sides of the discussion, identify any possible trade-offs, determine your most-desired and least-desired possible outcomes. Then, make a list of what concessions you're willing to put on the bargaining table, understand who in your organization has the decision-making power, know the relationship that you want to build or maintain with the other party, and prepare your BATNA. Preparation can also include the definition of the ground rules: determining where, when, with whom, and under what time constraints the negotiations will take place.

(2) Exchange information: This is the part of the negotiation when both parties exchange their initial positions. Each side should be allowed to share their underlying interests and concerns uninterrupted, including what they aim to receive at the end of the negotiation and why they feel the way they do.

(3) Clarify: During the clarification step, both sides continue the discussion that they began when exchanging information by justifying and bolstering their claims. If one side disagrees with something the other side is saying, they should discuss that disagreement in calm terms to reach a point of understanding.

(4) Bargain and problem-solve: This step is the meat of the process of negotiation, during which both sides begin a give-and-take. After the initial first offer, each negotiating party should propose different counter-offers for the problem, all the while making and managing their concessions. During the bargaining process, keep your emotions in check; the best negotiators use strong verbal communication skills (active listening and calm feedback; in face-to-face negotiation, this also includes body language). The goal of this step is to emerge with a win-win outcome—a positive course of action.

(5) Conclude and implement: Once an acceptable solution has been agreed upon, both sides should thank each other for the discussion, no matter the outcome of the negotiation; successful negotiations are all about creating and maintaining good long-term relationships. Then they should outline the expectations of each party and ensure that the compromise will be implemented effectively. This step often includes a written contract and a follow-up to confirm the implementation is going smoothly.

2.5 Factors That Facilitate Successful Negotiation

Successful negotiation is not always easy. But if you want to learn how to negotiate like a professional, take a look at this effective process with key factors that can increase your leverage.

First, preparation.

(1) Focus on the benefits of the product you're offering.

(2) Learn what your competitors offer and stress the advantages your product has over theirs.

(3) Set your walk-away price.

(4) Develop your sales presentation—practice until you cover all the points.

(5) Key factor: resources.

Second, research your buyer.

(1) Learn what motivates him by looking at his social profiles on networks you can find him.

(2) Ask questions to learn more about his needs and motivations.

(3) Look at your customer and his surroundings and use anything that can help your negotiation.

(4) Key factor: power, leverage.

Third, during negotiation.

(1) Set your best price 10%—15% higher so you can be able to give up a few percentage points. This will make the other party feel as though they won some concessions.

(2) Add value for your price and price for your value.

(3) Key factor: concession, attitude.

Here are 7 steps to a successful negotiation.

(1) Be confident.

(2) Be aware of why the customer is looking at your product.

(3) Know what the customer values/doesn't value.

(4) Know the timeline for making a decision.

(5) Make sure you're dealing with a decision-maker.

(6) Give the customer value that doesn't cost you much.

(7) Know your walk-away point.

2.6　Case Study

Donald Hendon, Matthew Roy, and Zafar Ahmed (2003) provide the following 12 guidelines for making concessions in negotiation.

(1) Give yourself enough room to make concessions.

(2) Try to get the other party to start revealing their needs and objectives first.

(3) Be the first to concede on a minor issue but not the first to concede on a major issue.

(4) Make unimportant concessions and portray them as more valuable than they are.

(5) Make the other party work hard for every concession you make.

(6) Use trade-offs to obtain something for every concession you make.

(7) Generally, concede slowly and give a little with each concession.

(8) Do not reveal your deadline to the other party.
(9) Occasionally say "no" to the other negotiator.
(10) Be careful trying to take back concessions even in "tentative" negotiations.
(11) Keep a record of concessions made in the negotiation to try to identify a pattern.
(12) Do not concede "too often, too soon, or too much".
You can exercise with your partner according to the above instructions.

2.7 Business Ethics

汉王复使侯公往说项王。项王乃与汉约，中分天下，割鸿沟以西者为汉，鸿沟而东者为楚。项王许之，即归汉王父母妻子。军皆呼万岁。

——摘自《史记·项羽本纪》

"鸿沟"现在表示"分隔线"，也引申为"严重分歧后的界限"，但它本是一个河流名称。鸿沟是一条中国古代最早贯通黄河和淮河的人工运河，今位于河南郑州荥阳，黄河南岸，由战国时的魏国兴建。秦统一中国后利用鸿沟和济水等运粮，当时还在荥阳兴建规模庞大的敖仓作为转运站。一直到南北朝时期都是中原主要水运交通线，今天仅剩遗存。鸿沟之所以有名，主要还是因为"楚汉谈判、鸿沟为界"——中国象棋盘上的"楚河汉界"的"河"就是鸿沟。这也很好地展现了古人谈判的技巧。

公元前 204—203 年，楚汉两军在广武相持数月。项羽屡次挑战，汉王并不应战。刘邦眼看撑不住（所谓粮草充足和韩信马上回兵，那只是谈判说辞），看似死局。侯公在谈判中，灵活采用虚实两手，先直指"痛点"，然后"角色互换"，同时"看人上菜""见神说神话"，以刘邦为衬托给项羽戴高帽，搞"道德绑架"。在分析形势时，又"辩证看利弊"进行具体分析，让对方很难反驳。而项羽的缺点就是以贵族为傲，其痛点就是明明占优势却又一时不好得手，怎样以最小代价获得最大利益？侯公指出，放了人质，收获"仁义礼智信"，既可控制地盘还能拉拢人心，利于长远。万一失去难得机遇，就不能"互利共赢"。谈判中候公还多次"东扯西拉""转换话题"，大讲楚怀王、晋文公、伍子胥、魏惠王、王陵……来进行案例分析，最后"冠冕堂皇"地保证说刘邦老了，愿意从此不争霸……

该案例是死局做活的经典案例，虚实结合的谈判，让项羽情绪转变、目瞪口呆，然后沉思不语，最后心花怒放，实在精彩。当然，这只是谈判而已。事实上刘邦很快撕毁盟约，反攻项羽一直打到垓下，项羽被逼自刎乌江。

讨论

刘邦如何利用谈判技巧挽回败局。

2.8 Exercises

(1) How to take position during negotiation?
(2) How many key steps in the negotiation, and how to do them?
(3) What's the main factor effecting the successful negotiation?

Unit 3

Relationships in Negotiation

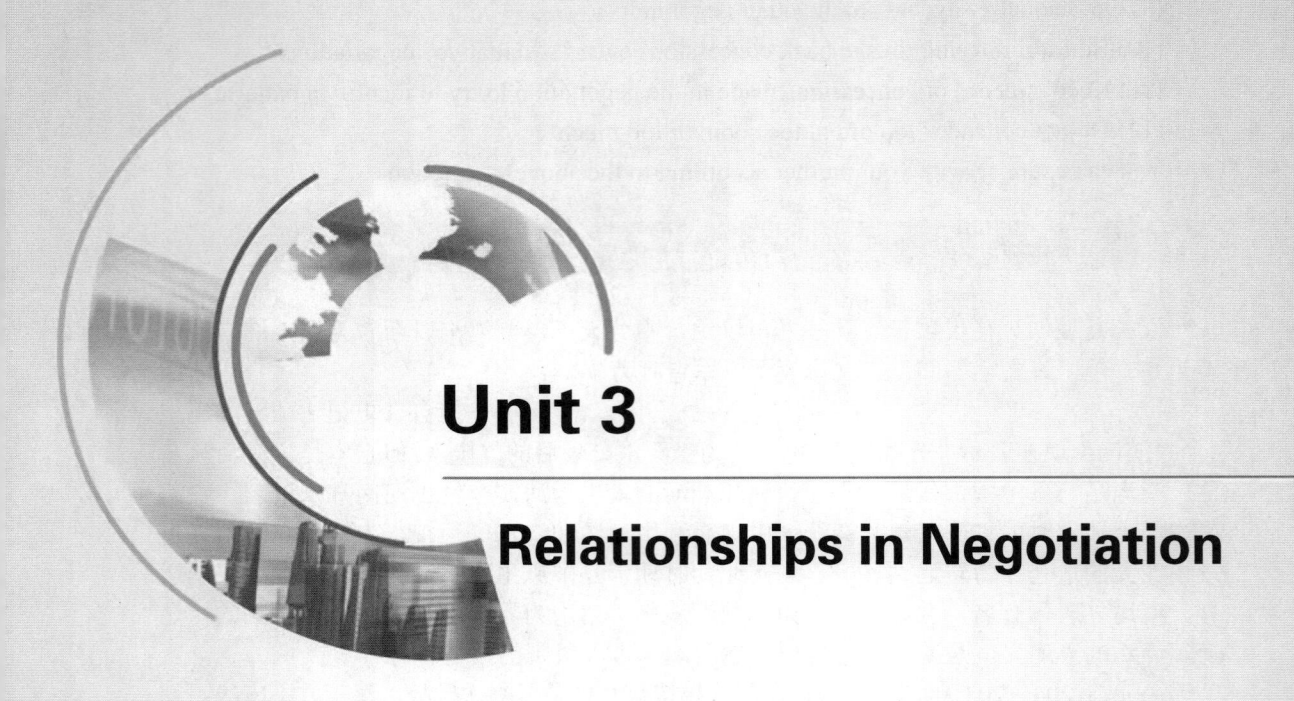

✧ **Case-Lead-in**

A semiconductor factory in Tianjin wanted to update its production line, and needed to purchase equipment and technology. Several suppliers suitable for this plant can be found in the United States and Japan. At that time, a salesman from a semiconductor company in Hong Kong went to Tianjin to visit, and found the factory's purchasing personnel and said that they could assist the factory in purchasing the required equipment and technology. Since the Hong Kong businessman speaks Chinese and easy to communicate with them, the relationship soon became familiar, and the factory agreed to buy it on his behalf. Since the factory has no foreign trade rights, it must entrust a company with foreign trade rights to act as an agent. After receiving the entrustment, Company A will inquire with the manufacturers in the United States and Japan. As a result, some manufacturers in the United States and Japan do not offer quotations, but ask: What is the relationship between the Company A and Hong Kong Company B? Some bids are very high. The inquiry results obtained by Company A did not meet the expected goals.

Unit 3　Relationships in Negotiation

3.1　Learning Objectives

(1) Understand how negotiation within an exiting relationship changes the nature of negotiation dynamics.

(2) Grasp the different forms of relationships in which negotiation can occur.

(3) Gain insight into how to rebuild trust and repair damaged relationship.

3.2　Negotiation in Communal Sharing Relationship

At the negotiation table, what's the best way to uncover your negotiation counterpart's hidden interests? Build a relationship in negotiation by asking questions, then listening carefully. Even if you have decided to make the first offer and are ready with a number of alternatives, you should always open by asking and listening to assess your counterpart's interests. Note that if your style of listening isn't sufficiently empathetic, it won't elicit honest responses.

There has been somewhat more research on negotiation in communal-sharing relationships and compared to those in other kinds of negotiations, researchers have found that parties who are in a communal-sharing relationships are more cooperative and empathetic. They focus their attention on other party's outcomes as well as their own and are more likely to share information with the other. They are more likely to use compromise or problem solving as strategies for resolving their conflicts, and hence, by some standards, perform better on both decision-making and performance-coordination tasks. More recent research emphasizes the uniqueness of communal negotiations.

- Perform better on both decision-making and performance-coordination tasks.
- Focus their attention on the other party's outcomes as well as their own.
- Are more likely to share information with the other and less likely to use coercive tactics.
- May be more likely to use compromise or problem solving as strategies for resolving conflicts.

Relational identity theory holds that groups defined by common ethnic, economic, or political interests often function as a "tribe", drawn together by a strong common identity that creates such rigid boundaries around it that most efforts at using traditional negotiation techniques to resolve the disputes are almost predestined to fail. Moreover, the strong emotionality that is also characteristic of the conflict between these groups often blind them to tools that help them identify their interests and manage the emotionality so as to effectively move toward conflict resolution.

It is unclear whether parties in close relationships produce better solutions than other negotiators do. Some studies found that parties who did not have a close relationship are more likely to arrive at integrative solutions. It may be that parties in a relationship may not push hard for a preferred solution in order to minimize the conflict level in the relationship or alternatively may sacrifice their own preferences in order to preserve the relationship.

3.3　Key Elements in Managing Negotiations within Relationship

Given the complexity of most close personal relationships, it is difficult to know which dimensions might be most relevant to negotiation. Reputation, trust, and justice are the three key elements that become more critical and pronounced when they occur within a relationship negotiation.

1. Reputation

Your reputation is how other people remember their past experiences with you. Reputation is the legacy that negotiators leave behind after a negotiation encounter with another party. Reputation is a "perceptual identity, reflective of the combination of salient personal characteristics and accomplishments, demonstrated behavior and intended images preserved over time, as observed directly and/or as reported from secondary sources." Based on this definition, we can say several things about the importance of reputations.

- Reputations are perceived and highly subjective in nature. It is not how we would like to be known by others, or how we think we are known—it is what they actually think of us, and their judgment, that count. Once a reputation is formed, it acts as a lens or "schema" by which people form their expectations for future behavior.

- An individual can have a number of different, even conflicting reputations because she may act quite differently in different situations. She may distributively bargain with the person who regularly services her computer. While individuals can elicit different reputations in different contexts, most commonly a reputation is a single and consistent image from many different persons across many contexts—in most cases, there I generally shared agreement on who we are and how we are seen.

- Reputations are shaped by past behavior. On the one hand, we may know someone's reputation based on our own past experience with him. On the other hand, our expectations may be shaped by the way the other behaves with other people. Thus, "direct" reputations may be different from "hearsay" reputations. Individuals tend to trust more those with better experiential reputations, and rely more on experiential reputations than hearsay reputations in deciding whether to trust another.

- Reputations are also influenced by an individual's personal characteristics and accomplishments. These may include qualities such as age, race and gender; education and past experience; personality traits, skills and behaviors. All of these work together over time to create a broad reputation—how other people remember us in general—as well as a specific reputation that comes from how we, or others, have experiences this particular other person in the past.

- Reputations develop over time; once developed, they are hard to change. Our early experiences with another—or what we have heard about them from other people—shape our views of them, which we bring to new situations in the form of expectations about the other. These expectations are then form of expectations about the other. These expectations are then confirmed or disconfirmed by the next set of experiences. Thus, first impressions and early experiences with others are powerful in shaping others' expectations; once these expectations are shaped, they become hard to change. A negotiator who develops a reputation as a distributive "shark" early on will have a difficult time convincing the current other negotiator that he is honest and trustworthy and wants to work toward a mutually acceptable agreement. In contrast, individuals with favorable personal reputations tend to be seen as more competent and trustworthy and are often accorded higher status.

- Others' reputations can shape emotional state as well as their expectations. Good hearsay reputations create positive emotional responses from others, and bad hearsay reputations elicit negative emotional responses from others.

- Finally, negative reputations are difficult to "repair". The more long-standing the negative reputation, the harder it is to change that reputation to a more positive one. Reputations need to be actively defended and renewed in others' eyes. Particularly when an event is likely to be seen by others in a negative light, we must work hard to defend and protect our reputation and to make sure that others do not remember the experience in a negative way. How we account for past behavior, how we apologize and ask another person to overlook or discount the past, or how we use excuses or justifications to explain why we did something the other views as unfavorable will have a major impact on how others remember us and their experiences with us. We say more about the role of apologies, excuses, and other "accounts" in the next section, on trust.

2. Trust

Many of the scholars who have written about relationships have identified trust as central to any relationship. Daniel McAllister defined trust as "an individual's belief in and willingness to act on the words, actions and decisions of another". There are three things that contribute to the level of trust one negotiator may have for another: the individual's chronic disposition toward trust (i.e., individual differences in personality that make some people more trusting than others), situation factors (e.g., the opportunity for the parties to communicate with each other adequately), and the history of the relationship between the parties.

The third major issue in relationships is the question of what is fair or just. Again, justice has been a major issue in the organizational sciences; individuals in organizations often debate whether their pay is fair, whether they are being fairly treated, or whether the organization might be treating some group of people (e.g., women, minorities, people from other cultures) in an unfair manner. As research has shown, justice can take several forms.

- Distributive justice is about the distribution of outcomes. Parties may be concerned that one party is receiving more than he or she deserves, that outcomes should be distributed equally, or that outcomes should be distributed based on needs. For example, one study showed that outcome fairness is often determined in a distributive negotiation as the point midway between the opening positions of the two parties. The presence of such an obvious settlement point appears to increase both concession making and the likelihood of settlement.

- Procedural justice is about the process of determining outcomes. Parties may be concerned that they were not treated fairly during the negotiation, that they were not given a chance to offer their point of view or side of the story, or that they were not treated with respect. Because negotiation is an environment in which parties are offered an opportunity to shape the outcome they receive, procedural fairness is generally high in most negotiations. Concerns about procedural fairness are more likely to arise when negotiators are judging the behavior of third parties: viewing the third party as neutral; seeing that party as trustworthy; accepting the third party's decisions; and in the case of formal authorities such as police, voluntarily accepting the party's decisions and directives.

- Interactional justice is about how parties treat each other in one-to-one relationships. Research has shown that people have strong expectations about the ways another party should treat them; when those standards are violated, parties feel unfairly treated. When the other party practices deception, is not candid and forthcoming, acts rudely, asks improper questions, makes prejudicial and discriminatory statements, makes decisions or takes precipitous actions without justification, negotiators feel that fairness standards have been violated.

- Finally, systemic justice is about how organizations appear to treat groups of individuals and the norms that develop for how they should be treated. When some groups are discriminated against, disfranchised, or systematically given poorer salaries or working conditions, the parties may be less concerned about specific procedural elements and more concerned that the overall system may be biased or discriminatory in its treatment of certain groups and their concerns.

The issue of fairness has received some systematic investigation in research on negotiation dynamics. The following conclusions can be drawn from key studies.

- Involvement in the process of helping to shape a negotiation strategy increases commitment to that strategy and willingness to pursue it. This is the familiar "procedural justice effect" in that parties involved in the process of shaping a decision are more committed to that decision. Negotiators who helped develop a group negotiation strategy were more committed to it and to the group's negotiation goals.

- Procedural justice also appears to have an impact on the way that negotiators approach the negotiation process. In a complex analysis of 11 historical cases of intergovernmental negotiations, one study showed that procedural justice was strongly related to using problem-solving processes and achieving integrative outcomes. On the other hand, the durability of the negotiated agreement was strongly related to distributive justice—that is, the parties assured that the agreement itself was perceived by the all parties as "fair" in the way that each party gave/received something in the outcome.

● Negotiators (buyers in a market transaction) who are encouraged ("primed") to think about fairness are more cooperative in distributive negotiations. They make greater concessions, act more fairly, reach agreement faster, and have stronger positive attitudes toward the other party. They also demand fair treatment from the other party in return. However, when the other party did not reciprocate the negotiator's cooperative behavior, the negotiator actively retaliated and punished the other's competitive behavior. Thus, stating your own intention to be fair and encouraging the other party to be fair may be an excellent way to support fair exchanges; but watch out for the negotiator whose fairness gestures are double-crossed!

● Similarly, parties who receive offers they perceive as unfair may reject them out of hand, even though the amount offered may be better than the alternative settlement, which is to receive nothing at all. Here, we see the role of intangibles entering into a negotiation. Economists would predict that any deal better than zero should be accepted (if the only alternative is zero), but research has shown that negotiators will often reject these small offers. Clearly, a less-than-fair small offer creates feelings of anger and wounded pride, and negotiators will often act spitefully to sink the entire deal rather than accept a token settlement.

● Negotiations and satisfaction with the outcome. We discussed the role of setting an "objective standard" for fairness. Among students who participated in a simulation of a corporate takeover, buyers who knew what a fair selling price would be for the company were more satisfied with those offered selling prices, more willing to buy the company, and more willing to do business with the other party in the future. Also, knowledge of an opponent's BATNA, as well as information about estimated market prices for the negotiated object, most strongly determine negotiator's judgments of fairness.

● Judgments about fairness are subject to the type of cognitive biases described earlier. For example, most negotiators have an egocentric bias, which is the tendency to regard a larger share for oneself as fair, even if the obvious fairness rule is an equal split. Research has shown that this egocentric bias can be diminished by strong interactional justice. That is, recognizing the need to treat the other person fairly, and actually treating the other fairly, lead to a smaller egocentric bias, a more even split of the resources, quicker settlements, and fewer stalemates.

● Not unsurprisingly, these egocentric biases vary across cultures. At least one study has shown that egocentric biases are stronger in cultures that are individualistic (e.g., the United States), where the self is served by focusing on one's positive attributes in order to stand out and be better than others, compared with more collectivist cultures (e.g., Japan) where the self is served by focusing on one's negative characteristics, so as to blend in with others.

Given the pervasiveness of concerns about fairness—how parties view the distribution of outcomes, how they view the process of arriving at that decision, or how they treat each other—it is remarkable that more research has not explicitly addressed justice issues in negotiation contexts. For example, justice issues are raised when individuals negotiate inside their organizations, such as to create a unique or specialized set of job duties and responsibilities. These "idiosyncratic deals" have to be managed effectively in order to make sure that they can continue to exist without disrupting others' sense of fairness about equal treatment. And they may not always be as fair as they seemed at the outset. Negotiated exchanges might be seen as procedurally fair because the parties collectively make the decision, know the terms in advance, give mutual assent to the process, and make binding decisions. Yet at least one study has shown that after such agreements are struck, negotiators perceive their partners as less fair and are unwilling to engage in future exchanges with them. Thus, rather than making things more fair, negotiated exchanges may serve to emphasize the conflict between actors who are blind to their own biases and inclined to see the other party's motives and characteristics in an unfavorable light.

3. Relationships among Reputation, Trust, and Justice

Not only are various forms of justice interrelated, but reputation, trust and justice all interact in shaping expectations of the other's behavior. For example, when one party feels the other has acted fairly in the past or will act fairly in the future, he or she is more likely to trust the other. We would also predict that acting fairly leads to being trusted and also enhances a positive reputation. Conversely, several theoretical and empirical works have shown that when parties are unfairly treated, they often become angry and retaliate against either the injustice itself or those who are seen as having caused it. Unfair treatment is likely to lead to distrust and a bad reputation. Trust, justice, and reputation are all central to relationship negotiations and feed each other; we cannot understand negotiation within complex relationships without prominently considering how we judge the other (and ourselves) on these dimensions.

4. Repairing a Relationship

There are many steps to repair a relationship. Trying to overcome a bad reputation, rebuilding trust, or restoring fairness to a relationship are much easier to talk about than to actually do. Roger Fisher and Dennis Ertel suggest the following diagnostic steps one can take when seeking to improve a relationship.

- What might be causing any present misunderstanding, and what can I do to understand it better? If the relationship is in difficulty, what might have caused it, and how can I gather information or perspective to improve the situation?

- What might be causing a lack of trust, and what can I do to begin to repair trust that might have been broken? Trust repair is a long and slow process. It requires adequate explanations for past behavior, apologies, and perhaps even reparations.

- What might be causing one or both of us to feel coerced, and what can I do to put the focus on persuasion rather than coercion? How can we take the pressure off each other so that we can give each other the freedom of choice to talk about what has happened and what is necessary to fix it?

- What might be causing one or both of us to feel disrespected, and what can I do to demonstrate acceptance and respect? How can we begin to appreciate each other's contributions and the positive things that we have done together in the past? How can we restore that respect and value each other's contributions?

- What might be causing one or both of us to get upset, and what can I do to balance emotion and reason? How can we surface the deeply felt emotions that have produced anger, frustration, rejection and disappointment? How can we effectively vent these emotions, or understand their causes, so that we can move beyond them?

3.4 Case Study

JetBlue Apologizes

On February 14th, 2007(Valentine's Day in the United States), airline JetBlue suffered a major crisis.

Two inches of snow and ice at New York's JFK airport led to 1,000 flight cancellations, massive delays, and passengers stranded on planes for up to nine hours. The event received massive media visibility, and it took almost a week for JetBlue to resume normal operations. While other airlines also suffered service disruptions because of the storm, JetBlue received most of the visibility for the breakdown—largely because, in its seven-year history, it had inspired much higher expectations of good treatment from its loyal customers.

JetBlue founder and CEO David Neeleman was faced with the challenge of how to repair the public's trust in a way that would strengthen the strong brand identity that the company had created.

In the week following the crisis, he appeared in every local and national news media. He accepted responsibility for bad decisions and organizational problems. He apologized repeatedly, promised refunds for stranded passengers, and promised to fix the problems that created the disaster. He also introduced a customer "bill of rights." Two weeks after the meltdown, 43 percent of a sample of people visiting JetBlue's website said the airline was still their number-one favorite. In a time when most airlines enjoy very little customer confidence, Neeleman's successful handling of the crisis has been highlighted as an example of creating a trustworthy brand identity—and being able to sustain it in a time of crisis. Bruce Blythe, CEO of Crisis Management International, sums it up well: "The single most important thing that a company needs to show in a crisis is that it cares. That's not a feeling. It's a behavior."

Here is an abbreviated text of JetBlue's apology, which is considered by many to be a "gold standard" for a good apology:

Words cannot express how truly sorry we are for the anxiety, frustration and inconvenience that you, your family, friends, and colleagues experienced … JetBlue was founded on the promise of bringing humanity back to (our industry), and making the experience happier. We know we failed to deliver on this promise last week. You deserve better—a lot better—and we let you down.

❓ Why JetBlue solving crisis problem is faster than other companies?

3.5 Business Ethics

"澶渊之盟"——宋辽百年再无战事

公元 1004 年 8 月，辽国准备大举南伐，宋朝震惊。宋朝宰相寇准力主出兵抗击，皇帝宋真宗决定御驾亲征。

宋时，黄河从今濮阳县城南穿过，河南北两岸分别筑城，时称南澶、北澶，中有浮桥相连。

同年闰九月初八，辽军开始大举南伐，一路上势如破竹，连续攻陷多座城池。十一月二十日，拖延 3 个多月的宋真宗御驾亲征才算付诸行动，从东京（今河南开封）出发，进驻韦城县（今河南滑县东南）后，督促民夫凿开黄河的封冰，以防辽骑渡河。

同日，辽圣宗与萧太后率主力进抵澶州北城外，立即从东北西三面将北城团团围住。在宋澶州守将的严防死守下，辽军痛失大将萧挞凛，但仍以主力围困澶州，并分兵继续南进，又攻下通利军（今河南浚县东北），大有越过澶州，进逼宋都东京（今河南开封）之势。

宋真宗驻韦城，见辽有渡河之势，群臣中有的重提迁都之事，有的说应该避辽锋芒，再做它计。宋真宗迟疑不决，在寇准等主战派的力陈下，宋真宗才下了进驻澶州的决心，从南面进入澶州。

由于一时谁也不能取得胜利，于是辽宋在澶州城下边打边谈。辽写信给宋真宗表达愿与宋重修"旧好"，宋真宗也派殿直曹利用为宋和义使臣。因为辽坚持索取关南之地，而宋坚持地不可归，只许金帛的意见，所以未能谈成。经过反复磋商，曹利用指出："若北朝（指辽朝）不恤后悔，恣其邀求（归关南之地），地固不可得，兵亦未易息也！"辽圣宗和萧太后权衡利弊之后，同意了宋的条件，在十二月初达成了宋朝每年给辽绢 20 万匹，银 10 万两；辽国主"愿兄事南朝（指北宋）"的停战协议，史称"澶渊之盟"。历经近 4 个月的澶渊之战至此宣告结束。

自从订立了澶渊之盟，辽宋之间的和好关系延续了近 120 年，这样长久的和好关系，在我国古代边疆王朝与中原王朝、边疆民族与中原民族相互关系的历史上，是罕有其匹的。

📔 讨论

澶渊之盟是如何达成的？

3.6 Exercises

Give some examples to explain the key elements in managing negotiations within relationship.

Unit 4

Strategy and Planning of Negotiation

✧ **Case-Lead-in**

A Brazilian company traveled to the United States to purchase complete equipment. The members of the Brazilian negotiating team were delayed by a shopping trip to the street. When they arrived at the negotiation site, they were 45 minutes behind the scheduled time. The US representative was extremely dissatisfied with this and spent a long time to accuse the Brazilian representative of not keeping time and having no credit, and that if things continued like this, it would be difficult to cooperate in the future. And wasting time was a waste of resources and money. In this regard, the Brazilian representative felt deficient and had to keep apologizing to the US representative.

After start, the negotiations also seems to be the Brazilian representative to come late to the matter of nagging, a time to make Brazilian representative at passive position. He did not care to bargain with the US representative, and did not quietly consider many of the requests made by the US, and hastily signed the contract. After the contract was signed, the Brazilian representative calmed down and realized that he had suffered a big loss and had fallen for the US side's trick when his mind was no longer feverish, but it was already too late.

4.1　Learning Objectives

(1) Understand the goals and effects of negotiation strategy.
(2) Gain a comprehensive implementing strategy.

4.2　Goals and Effects of Negotiation Strategy

Effective strategy and planning are the most critical precursors for achieving negotiation objectives. Remember, strategy is made up of Orientation, Objectives and Tactics. These strategic elements are primarily objectives to be achieved through specific tactics.

Strategy is the orientation or holistic approach of an individual toward achieving an outcome or objective. Strategy is often used to identify the plan for achieving that objective. Collectively, we will use the term strategy to refer to:

Strategic Orientation—this is the orientation toward a conflict of interest or dispute.

Strategic Objective—this is a method for achieving a desired outcome or objective.

Strategic Plan—a plan for achieving that outcome or objective that implements specific tactics.

Generally, a party develops a plan, objectives, and orientation together. Tactics, which are often confused with strategies, are short-term, adaptive moves designed to enact or pursue broad strategies. Strategy is carried out through tactics. Tactics are subordinate to strategy in that they are structured, directed, and driven by strategic considerations.

Aiming high can lead to dramatic payoffs if you succeed, but the difficulty of orchestrating complicated negotiations can increase the risk of impasse. By contrast, starting with more modest negotiation goals may suggest a lack of ambition or resolve, but might increase negotiators' odds of slowly building momentum and trust.

In the same vein, inexperienced negotiators and even many experienced negotiators tend to assume they have a choice between two main strategies: negotiate in a tough, demanding manner or in a friendly, accommodating manner. In fact, there's a better, third way of negotiating—one that doesn't rely on toughness or accommodation, but that will improve your likelihood of meeting your negotiation goals. Principled negotiation can produce wise outcomes efficiently and amicably.

How can you set and reach your negotiation goals while bearing this somewhat conflicting information in mind?

Set modest negotiation goals. Rather than announcing ambitious plans right from the start, considering setting more conservative goals.

Empower other parties to find solutions. By stepping back and prompting others to lead, you can invest them in problem solving.

But don't underestimate your odds. Play it too safe, and you may find yourself with no significant goals at all.

Finally, ensure that goals incorporate all the factors that will help you and your organization succeed. Clarify acceptable levels of risk, and promote cooperation by setting team negotiation goals.

There are four ways that goals affect negotiation.

(1) Wishes are not goals, especially in negotiation. Wishes may be related to interests or needs that motivate goals, but they are not goals themselves. A wish is fantasy, a hope that something might happen; a goal is specific, focused target that one can realistically develop a plan to achieve.

(2) One's goals may be, but are not necessarily, linked to the other party's goals. Linkage between two parties' goal defines an issue to be settled and is often the source of conflict. At the beginning, my goal is to get a car cheaply, and the seller's goal is to sell it at the highest possible price; thus, the "issue" is the price I will pay for the car. If I could achieve my goal by myself, without the other party, I probably wouldn't need to negotiate.

(3) There are boundaries or limits to what "realistic" goals can be. If what we want exceeds these limits (i.e., what the other party is capable of or willing to give), we must either change our goals or end the negotiation. Goals must be attainable. If my goal—to buy this car at a cheap price isn't possible because the seller won't sell the car cheaply, I'm going to either have to change my goal or find another car to buy (and perhaps from a different dealer).

(4) Effective goals must be concrete, specific, and measurable. The less concrete, specific and measurable our goals are, the harder it is to (a) communicate to the other party what we want, (b) understand what the other party wants, (c) determine whether any given offer satisfies our goals. "To get a car cheaply" or "to agree on a price so that the loan payment does not use all of my paycheck" are not very clear goals.

4.3 Strategy and Tactics

How are strategy and tactics related? Although the line between strategy and tactics may seem fuzzy, one major difference is that of scale, perspective, or immediacy (Quinn, 1991). Tactics are short-term, adaptive moves designed to enact or pursue broad (or higher-level) strategies, which in turn provide stability, continuity, and direction for tactical behaviors. For example, your negotiation strategy might be integrative, designed to build and maintain a productive relationship with the other party while using a joint problem-solving approach to the issues. In pursuing this strategy, appropriate tactics include describing your interests, using open-ended questions and active listening to understand the others' interests, and inventing options for mutual gain. Tactics are subordinate to strategy; they are structured, directed, and driven by strategic considerations. In Unit 2 and Unit 3, we outlined the strategies of distributive bargaining and integrative negotiation, along with the associated tactics that are likely to accompany each strategy.

4.4　The Planning Process of Implementing Strategy

Strategic planning is when business leaders map out their vision for the organization's growth and how they're going to get there. Strategic plans inform your organization's decisions, growth, and goals. So if you work for a small company or startup, you could likely benefit from creating a strategic plan. When you have a clear sense of where your organization is going, you're able to ensure your teams are working on projects that make the most impact.

A strategic plan is a tool to define your organization's goals and what actions you will take to achieve them. Typically, a strategic plan will include your company's vision and mission statements, your long-term goals (as well as short-term, yearly objectives), and an action plan of the steps you're going to take to move in the right direction.

The effective strategic plan document should include:
- Your company's vision;
- Your company's mission statement;
- Your company's goals;
- A plan of action to achieve those goals;
- Your approach to achieving your goals;
- The tactics you'll use to meet your goals.

The strategic planning process should be run by a small team of key stakeholders who will be in charge of building your strategic plan.

Your group of strategic planners, sometimes called the management committee, should be a small team of five to 10 key stakeholders and decision-makers for the company. They won't be the only people involved—but they will be the people driving the work.

Once you've established your management committee, you can get to work on the strategic planning process.

There are 5 steps in strategic planning (see Figure 4.1).

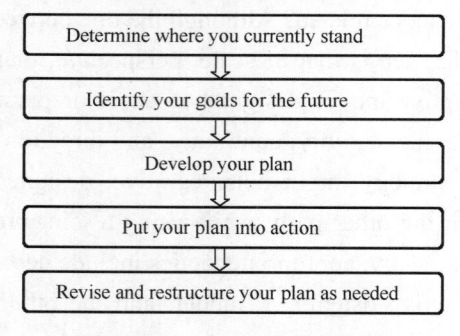

```
Determine where you currently stand
            ↓
Identify your goals for the future
            ↓
      Develop your plan
            ↓
   Put your plan into action
            ↓
Revise and restructure your plan as needed
```

Figure 4.1　Strategic Planning Steps

Step 1: Determine where you are.

Before you can get started with strategy development and define where you're going, you first need to determine where you are. To do this, your management committee should collect a variety of information from additional stakeholders—like employees and customers. In particular, plan to gather the followings.

Relevant industry and market data to inform any market opportunities, as well as any potential upcoming threats in the near future.

Customer insights to understand what your customers want from your company—like product improvements or additional services.

Employee feedback that needs to be addressed—whether in the product, business practices, or company culture.

Step 2: Identify your goals for the future.

This is where the magic happens. To develop your strategy, take into account your current position, which is where you are now. Then, draw inspiration from your original business documents—these are your final destination.

To develop your strategy, you're essentially pulling out your compass and asking "Where are we going next?" This can help you figure out exactly which path you need to take.

During this phase of the planning process, take inspiration from important company documents to ensure your strategic plan is moving your company in the right direction like:

● Your mission statement, to understand how you can continue moving towards your organization's core purpose;

● Your vision statement, to clarify how your strategic plan fits into your long-term vision;

● Your company values, to guide you towards what matters most towards your company;

● Your competitive advantages, to understand what unique benefit you offer to the market;

● Your long-term goals, to track where you want to be in five or 10 years;

● Your financial forecast and projection, to understand where you expect your financials to be in the next three years, what your expected cash flow is, and what new opportunities you will likely be able to invest in.

Step 3: Develop your plan.

Now that you understand where you are and where you want to go, it's time to put pen to paper. Your plan will take your position and strategy into account to define your organization-wide plan for the next three to five years. Keep in mind that even though you're creating a long-term plan, parts of your strategic plan should be created as the quarters and years go on.

As you build your strategic plan, you should define:

● Your company priorities for the next three to five years, based on your SWOT analysis and strategy.

● Yearly objectives for the first year. You don't need to define your objectives for every year of the strategic plan. As the years go on, create new yearly objectives that connect back to your overall strategic goals.

● Related key results and KPIs for that first year. Some of these should be set by the management committee, and some should be set by specific teams that are closer to the work. Make sure your key results and KPIs are measurable and actionable.

● Budget for the next year or few years. This should be based on your financial forecast as well as your direction. Do you need to spend aggressively to develop your product? Build your team? Make a dent with marketing? Clarify your most important initiatives and how you'll budget for those.

● A high-level project roadmap. A project roadmap is a tool in project management that helps you visualize the timeline of a complex initiative, but you can also create a very high-level project roadmap for your strategic plan. Outline what you expect to be working on in certain quarters or years to make the plan more actionable and understandable.

Step 4: Put your plan into action.

After all that buildup, it's time to put your plan into action. New strategy execution involves clear communication across your entire organization to make sure everyone knows their responsibilities and how to measure the plan's success.

Map your processes with key performance indicators, which will gauge the success of your plan. KPIs will establish which parts of your plan you want achieved in what time frame.

A few tips to make sure your plan will be executed without a hitch:

● Align tasks with job descriptions to make sure people are equipped to get their jobs done;

● Communicate clearly to your entire organization throughout the implementation process;

● Fully commit to your plan.

Step 5: Revise and restructure your plan as needed.

At this point, you should have created and implemented your new strategic framework. The final step of the planning process is to monitor and manage your plan.

(1) Share your strategic plan—this isn't a document to hide away. Make sure your team (especially senior leadership) has access to it so they can understand how their work contributes to company priorities and your overall strategic plan. We recommend sharing your plan in the same tool you use to manage and track work, so you can more easily connect high-level objectives to daily work. If you don't already, consider using a work management tool.

(2) Update your plan regularly (quarterly and annually). Make sure you're using your strategic plan to inform your shorter-term goals. Your strategic plan also isn't set in stone. You'll likely need to update the plan if your company decides to change directions or make new investments. As new market opportunities and threats come up, you'll likely want to tweak your strategic plan to ensure you're building your organization in the best direction possible for the next few years.

Keep in mind that your plan won't last forever—even if you do update it frequently. A successful strategic plan evolves with your company's long-term goals. When you've achieved most of your strategic goals, or if your strategy has evolved significantly since you first made your plan, it might be time to create a new one.

4.5 Case Study

A SWOT analysis to help you assess both current and future potential for the business (you'll return to this analysis periodically during the strategic planning process).

To fill out each letter in the SWOT acronym, your management committee will answer a series of questions as follows.

Strengths:
- What does your organization currently do well?
- What separates you from your competitors?
- What are your most valuable internal resources?
- What tangible assets do you have?
- What is your biggest strength?

Weaknesses:
- What does your organization do poorly?
- What do you currently lack (whether that's a product, resource, or process)?
- What do your competitors do better than you?
- What, if any, limitations are holding your organization back?
- What processes or products need improvement?

Opportunities:
- What opportunities does your organization have?
- How can you leverage your unique company strengths?
- Are there any trends that you can take advantage of?
- How can you capitalize on marketing or press opportunities?
- Is there an emerging need for your product or service?

Threats:
- What emerging competitors should you keep an eye on?
- Are there any weaknesses that expose your organization to risk?
- Have you or could you experience negative press that could reduce market share?
- Is there a chance of changing customer attitudes towards your company?

If you are the CEO of a technology company, analyze your company's SWOT.

4.6 Business Ethics

烛之武退秦师

晋侯、秦伯围郑，以其无礼于晋，且贰于楚也。晋军函陵，秦军汜南。

佚之狐言于郑伯曰："国危矣，若使烛之武见秦君，师必退。"公从之。辞曰："臣之壮也，犹不如人；今老矣，无能为也已。"公曰："吾不能早用子，今急而求子，是寡人之过也。然郑亡，子亦有不利焉。"许之。

夜缒而出，见秦伯，曰："秦、晋围郑，郑既知亡矣。若亡郑而有益于君，敢以烦执事。越国以鄙远，君知其难也。焉用亡郑以陪邻？邻之厚，君之薄也。若舍郑以为东道主，行李之往来，共其乏困，君亦无所害。且君尝为晋君赐矣，许君焦、瑕，朝济而夕设版焉，君之所知也。夫晋，何厌之有？既东封郑，又欲肆其西封，若不阙秦，将焉取之？阙秦以利晋，唯君图之。"秦伯说，与郑人盟。使杞子、逢孙、杨孙戍之，乃还。

子犯请击之，公曰："不可。微夫人之力不及此。因人之力而敝之，不仁；失其所与，不知；以乱易整，不武。吾其还也。"亦去之。

鲁僖公三十年（公元前630年），晋国和楚国大战于城濮，结果楚国大败，晋国的霸业完成。在城濮之战中，郑国曾协助楚国一起攻打晋国，而且晋文公年轻时流亡到郑国，受到冷遇，所以晋文公把新仇旧怨加到一块，于两年后联合秦国讨伐郑国。郑伯闻讯后，派烛之武面见秦穆公，劝他退兵。烛之武巧妙地利用秦、晋两国的矛盾表现出处处为秦国利益着想的样子，分析当时的形势，抓住利害关系，说明保存郑国对秦国有利，灭掉郑国对秦国不利的道理，终于说动秦国退兵。晋军失去盟军支持后，也被迫撤离了郑国。此文即记叙了这一历史事件。

讨论

请分析烛之武劝说秦国退兵的策略是什么。

4.7　Exercises

(1) Simulate business negotiations according to the strategic planning in the textbook.
(2) Explain the ways that goals affect negotiation.

Unit 5

Cross-Cultural Negotiation

✧ **Case-Lead-in**

On his first trip to Mexico, Harry, a US manager who intended to negotiate a contract with a Mexican firm, was invited to a dinner party by his Mexican counterpart. Since the invitation indicated that cocktails would begin at 7 p.m., Harry arrived promptly at that time. His host seemed surprised, and no one else had arrived. People began arriving about 8 p.m. Harry knew he had read the invitation correctly but felt he had gotten off a bad start. What advice would you have given Harry?

5.1　Learning Objectives

(1) To master the concept and nature of culture.
(2) To understand position taken during negotiation.
(3) To master steps in the negotiation.
(4) To understand the factors that facilitate successful negotiation.

5.2　The Nature of Culture

Any visitor to foreign parts is struck by the remarkable variety of customs, manners, and forms of social organization developed by people in their everyday affairs. In essence, the concept of anthropologists developed the culture as a way of accounting for this extraordinary richness. According to Raymond Cohen, a neat, one-sentence definition of culture can only mislead. More helpful is an ostensive definition intended to draw attention to the main features of the concept. Amid the welter of formulations put forward in the literature, three critical aspects of culture have gained general approval: that is a quality not of individuals but of the society of which individuals are a part; that it is acquired—through acculturation or socialization—by individuals from their respective societies; and that each culture is a unique complex of attributes subsuming every area of social life.

5.3　Dimensions of Culture

Beliefs and behaviors differ between cultures because each develops ways of coping with life. Hofstede defined culture as "the collective programming of the mind which distinguishes members of one human group from another". He devised four cultural dimensions that explained much of the difference between cultures. These dimensions are masculinity/femininity, uncertainty avoidance, power distance, and individualism.

(1) Masculine cultures typically value assertiveness, independence, task orientation, and self-achievement (traditional "masculine" characteristics), while feminine cultures value cooperation, nurturing, relationships, solidarity with the less fortunate, modesty, and quality of life (traditional "feminine" characteristics). Masculine societies tend to have a more rigid division of sex roles. Masculine cultures subscribe to "live-to-work" while feminine societies subscribe to "work-to-live". The competitiveness and assertiveness embedded in masculinity may make individuals perceive the negotiation in win-lose terms. Masculinity is related to assertiveness and competitiveness, while femininity is related to empathy and social relations. A more distributive process is expected in masculine societies, where the party with the most competitive behavior will likely gain more. The most masculine country is Japan, followed by Latin American countries. The most feminine societies are Scandinavian countries.

(2) Ambiguous (uncertain, unpredictable) situations. It favors conformity and safe behavior and tolerates deviant ideas. In high uncertainty-avoidance cultures, people tend to avoid uncertain situations, while in low uncertainty-avoidance cultures, people are generally more comfortable with ambiguous uncertain situations and are more accepting of risk. Low risk-avoiders require much less information, have fewer people involved in the decision-making, and can act quickly. High-risk-avoidance cultures tend to have many formal bureaucratic rules, rely on rituals, standards and formulas, and trust only family and friends. People in low uncertainty-avoidance societies dislike hierarchy and typically find it inefficient and destructive. In weak uncertainty-avoidance cultures, deviance and new ideas are more highly tolerated. Uncertainty avoidance may lead to focus on the apparent competitive and position aspects of negotiation and may hinder the exchange of information on interests and the development of creative proposals. A problem-solving orientation is likely found in cultures characterized by low uncertainty-avoidance and power distance. The United States, the Scandinavian nations, and Singapore all have low uncertainty-avoidance.

(3) Power distance refers to the acceptance of authority differences between people, the difference between those who hold power and those affected by power. One strives for power equalization and justice in low power-distance, while high power-distance cultures are status conscious and respectful of age and seniority. In high power-distance cultures, outward status forms such as protocol, formality, and hierarchy are considered essential. Decisions regarding reward and redress of grievances are usually based on personal judgments made by power holders. Power distance implies a willingness to accept that the party that comes out most forcefully gets a larger share of the benefit than the other party. A low power-distance culture values competence over seniority with a resulting consultative management style, and the Anglo-American, Scandinavian, and Germanic cultures are examples. Latin American, South Asian, and Arab cultures fall into high power-distance cultures. Low masculinity and low power-distance may be related to sharing information and offering multiple proposals and more cooperative and creative behavior. High masculinity and power-distance may result in competitive behavior, threats, and adverse reactions.

(4) In individualistic cultures, a tendency exists to put the task before relationships and to value independence highly. These individuals are self-actualized and self-motivated, and any relationships are defined by self-interest. Collectivism implies in group solidarity, loyalty, and strong perceived interdependence among individuals. Relationships are based on mutual self-interest and dependent on the group's success. Collectivist cultures emphasize honor and protecting others' self-image, while individualistic cultures emphasize protecting one's self-image and freedom from imposition. Collectivist cultures define themselves in terms of their membership within groups, sharply distinguishing in groups from out groups. Maintaining the integrity of in groups is stressed so that cooperation, conflict avoidance, solidarity, and conformity dominate the culture. Individualistic cultures value open conflict

and have linear logic, while collectivist societies stress abstract, general agreements over concrete, specific issues and tend to minimize conflict.

5.4　Why Culture Influences Negotiations

All human interactions are, by definition, intercultural. When two individuals meet, it is an intercultural encounter since they both have different (sometimes drastically different, if not opposite) ways of perceiving, discovering, and creating reality. All negotiations are, therefore, intercultural. Negotiations with a boss, spouse, child, friend, fellow employee, union representative, or an official from a foreign country are all interculturally loaded. Intercultural negotiations do not only exist because people who think, feel, and behave differently must reach agreements on practical matters such as how to produce, consume, organize, and distribute power and grant rewards, but because of the very nature of the challenging, unpredictable, and contradictory world where we live.

Negotiations involve two dimensions: a matter of substance and the process. The latter is rarely relevant when negotiations are conducted within the same cultural setting. Only when dealing with someone from another country with a different cultural background does the process usually become a critical barrier to substance; in such settings, process first needs to be established before substantive negotiations can commence. It becomes apparent when the negotiation process is international and cultural differences must be bridged.

When negotiating with someone from the same country, it is often possible to expedite communications by making reasonable cultural assumptions. The situation reverses itself when two cultures are involved. Making assumptions about another culture is often counterproductive since it can too often lead to misunderstandings and miscommunications. The international negotiator must be careful not to allow cultural stereotypes to determine his or her relations with a local businessperson. Needs, values, interests, and expectations may differ dramatically. It is like the proverbial fish out of water: when in water, a fish is unaware of any possible alternate environment; the water surrounding the fish is all it knows of the universe; hence, the whole universe must be made of water. It perceives a different environment only when the fish is removed from the water.

When one takes the seemingly simple process of negotiations into a cross-cultural context, it becomes even more complex, and complications tend to grow exponentially. That negotiation style used so effectively at home can be ineffective and inappropriate when dealing with people from another cultural background; its use can often result in more harm than gain. When working in another culture, heightened sensitivity, more attention to detail, and changes in basic behavioral patterns are required.

Nations have a national character that influences the goals and processes the society pursues in negotiations. This character is called culture. A cultural dimension exists in the way negotiators view the negotiation process. In international negotiations, the negotiators bring to the negotiating table the values, beliefs, and background interference of the culture and usually will unconsciously use those elements in both the presentation and interpretation of the data. Culture naturally influences members' negotiations—through their conceptualizations of the process, the ends they target, the means they use, and the expectations they hold of counterparts' behavior. Ample evidence exists that such negotiation rules and practices vary across cultures. Thus, cross-cultural negotiators bring into contact with unfamiliar and potentially conflicting sets of categories, rules, plans, and behaviors. The cross-cultural negotiator must take common knowledge and practices seriously. Difficulties sometimes arise from the different expectations negotiators have regarding the social setting of the negotiation. Culture influences negotiation through its effects on communications. Intercultural differences may cause misperceptions and misunderstandings.

National negotiating styles combine culture, history, political system, and economic status. Some cultures are likely to search for compromise, while others will strive for consensus, and still, others will fight until surrender is achieved. Some cultures prefer a deductive approach; they agree on principles, which can be applied to issues later. Other cultures think inductively: deal with problems at hand, and principles will develop.

Negotiation translates into anticipating culturally related ideas that are most likely to be understood by a person of a given culture. Negotiating means coping with new and inconsistent information, usually accompanied by new behavior, social environments, sights, and smells. The greater the cultural differences, the more likely barriers to communication and misunderstandings become. A few potential problems often encountered during a cross-cultural negotiation include (Frank, 1992).

(1) Need for more understanding of different ways of thinking.
(2) Pay attention to the necessity to save face.
(3) Need for knowledge of the host country—including history, culture, government, the status of the business, and the image of foreigners.
(4) Need for recognition of political or other criteria.
(5) Need for more recognition of the decision-making process.
(6) Need for more understanding of the role of personal relations and personalities.
(7) Need for more allocation of time for negotiations.

Culture forces people to view and value the many social interactions in fashioning any agreement differently. Negotiations can easily break down because of a need to understand the cultural component of the negotiation process. Negotiators who take the time to understand the approach that the other parties are likely to use and adapt their styles to that one will likely be more effective.

5.5 How Culture Influences Negotiations

The influence of ubiquitous cultural factors on international business negotiations is implicit and potential. Culture impacts negotiation in four ways: by conditioning one's perception of reality, by blocking out information inconsistent or unfamiliar with culturally grounded assumptions, by projecting meaning onto the other party's words and actions, and by impelling the ethnocentric observer for an incorrect attribution of motive. Culture affects the range of strategies negotiators develop and how they are tactically implemented. Cultural exchange is the catalyst and solidifying agent of economic cooperation, while cultural conflict is the "cancer" of economic cooperation.

1. Impact on the Composition of Negotiators

Different countries are primarily influenced by culture in determining negotiators' selection criteria, number, and division of labor. The US, for example, is a country with a relatively small power distance and tends to pay more attention to eloquence, professionalism, and reasoning ability when selecting negotiators. On the other hand, Japan is a country with a significant power distance, where status symbols are significant, and the principle of job matching is followed in the selection of negotiators. Americans have a deep-rooted concept of the legal system, and lawyers play an important role in negotiations. Whenever there is a business negotiation, they must bring their lawyers. In Japan, lawyers are generally not included in the negotiation team. Japanese people think that people who consult with lawyers every step of the way are untrustworthy and even think that bringing lawyers to negotiations is a deliberate attempt to create legal disputes later, which is an unfriendly act.

2. Influence on the Concept of Time

American negotiators attach importance to efficiency and like to make quick decisions. Because the US economy is developed, life and work are fast-paced, and Americans believe in time and respect negotiation progress and deadlines. In the negotiation, they want to minimize the red tape to reach the point as soon as possible. On the other hand, the Japanese are very patient and generally do not want to be the first to state their intentions but wait patiently and wait and see what happens.

3. Influence on Decision-making Style

Culture is an essential factor that influences the way of decision-making. Generally, there are two types of decision-making styles: top-down and bottom-up. In the US, top-down decision-making is adopted, and the main person in charge of the negotiation has all the authority to decide to complete the task. In Asia, decisions are usually made by the most senior figure or head of a family. In China, negotiators are highly trained in the art of gaining concessions. In Japan, on the other hand, joint participation and group decision-making are emphasized, with all members agreeing on bottom-up collective decision-making. Decisions can take a long time in Germany due to the need to deeply analyze information and statistics. In the U.K., pressure tactics and imposing deadlines are ways of closing deals; in Greece, this would backfire.

4. Influence on the Form of Agreement

Cultural factors also influence the form of the agreement reached between the parties. In general, Americans prefer a very detailed contract that explains the consequences of all possible scenarios because they believe that the deal itself is a contract and that negotiators should be able to explain what to do after any change in factors based on the contract, focusing on the tightness and completeness of the contract terms. In Japan, on the other hand, there is a preference for a generalized contract because they believe that the negotiation is about building a good relationship and that if an unexpected situation arises, the parties should resolve it based on the mutual relationship rather than the contract. As a result, sometimes, if Americans pursue too many surprises at the negotiating table, negotiators in other countries will perceive them as being in a position of distrust of the partnership.

5.6 Cross-Cultural Negotiation Strategies

In cross-cultural negotiations, differences in the cultural backgrounds of the negotiating parties lead to differences and conflicts in the negotiating styles of the negotiating parties. Based on recognizing the differences in negotiation styles between cultures, negotiators should make their negotiation strategies and tactics relevant and flexible to adapt them to specific negotiation targets, issues, and situations.

1. Be Aware of Cultural Differences and Have a Sense of Cross-cultural Negotiation

Andre Laurent, a French cultural studies expert, has pointed out that our own culture has become so much a part of ourselves that we cannot see our own culture, making us always think that other people's cultures are similar to ours. We often show surprise and even frustration when people influenced by other cultures behave in ways that are inconsistent with our own. This statement profoundly reveals that international business negotiators are often unaware of how cultural practices and values influence their behaviors and often use their standards to interpret and judge other people's cultures in international business negotiations, consciously or unconsciously, assuming that other people's behaviors are the same as their own. This "cultural myopia" can easily mislead negotiators to make wrong moves. In international business negotiations, negotiators must be sensitive enough to cultural differences and respect each other's cultural habits and customs. When in Rome, do as Romans do. Negotiators must cultivate cross-cultural negotiation awareness, recognize the differences in needs, motivations, and beliefs of negotiators in different cultural backgrounds, and understand, accept, and respect each other's cultures. The need for extensive study of the cultures must be addressed. It should include reading about the history and customs of the country in question and discussing with others who have had experience dealing with citizens of the foreign country. Negotiators should be good at seeing things from the other side's point of view and understanding the way of thinking and logical judgment the other side uses to see things. Negotiators should be flexible and adaptable so that their negotiation style applies to different cultural types of negotiations. Any negotiator in a cross-cultural negotiation activity must recognize that culture has no advantages or disadvantages. However, it is also essential to avoid the mindset of cultural stereotypes.

2. Respect for the Cultural Practices of the Other Party

Custom is a generally accepted and long-established way of life in a particular society characterized by constancy, variability, and spontaneity. It includes all the agreed and patterned ways of life in the long history of human beings, such as production customs, life, rituals, beliefs, and social customs. Different countries and regions in the world have different customs. In cross-cultural negotiations, it is crucial to be mindful of them and not to take them lightly. Otherwise, they may affect the negotiation process or make the negotiations unhappy. Different taboos are the psychological embodiment of different national cultures, so negotiators should grasp the rule of "ask forbidden questions when entering the country and follow the customs".

3. Prepare for the Negotiation Adequately

The focus of these preparations should be on the culture, not the language. Although a particular approach to negotiations with culture should be followed, sufficient flexibility should be available. Planning is crucial. Implementation is even more critical; the best-laid plans often must be corrected. The complexity of cross-cultural business negotiations requires negotiators to make more adequate preparations before the negotiations as follows.

On the macro level, it is necessary to understand the environment of business activities, including the international political, economic, legal, and social environment, assess the potential risks and their possible impacts, and formulate various measures to prevent them.

On the micro level, to thoroughly analyze and understand the negotiation counterparty, understand the cultural background of the counterparty, including customs, code of conduct, values, and business practices, and analyze the possibility of government intervention and the problems it may bring.

To arrange the negotiation plan reasonably.

Negotiation preparation includes negotiation background, assessment of people and situation, facts to be verified in the negotiation process, agenda, best alternative, and concession strategy. The negotiation context, in turn, includes:

- The negotiation location;
- Venue set-up;
- Negotiation unit;
- Number of participants;

- Audience;
- Communication channels;
- Negotiation time frame.

All of this preparation must take into account possible cultural differences. For example, cultural differences in venue layout may hurt cooperation. In a more hierarchical culture, a poorly arranged and casual room may cause unease or even irritation on the other side.

Also, negotiation styles vary by culture. The American culture tends to come together to finalize an agreement; while the Japanese culture likes to talk to each person individually first and then arrange a broader range of talks if everyone agrees; the Russians prefer a cumulative approach where they talk to one party first, reach an agreement, and then the two parties in front of them invite a third party and so on. The control of the negotiation time limit is also essential. Different cultures have different time concepts, such as North American culture has a strong time concept. For Americans, time is money; while the Middle East and Latin American culture have a weaker time concept, they believe they should enjoy the time. Therefore, one should be prepared for differences in time perceptions in international business negotiations.

4. Overcoming Obstacles and Misunderstandings in Communication

Communication barriers are the barriers to understanding the negotiating parties may encounter due to subjective and objective reasons in exchanging situations and views, negotiating cooperation intentions, and trading conditions. Language is an essential link between different cultures and negotiators but can also become a barrier to negotiation. Therefore, negotiators need to be able to use each other's language proficiently, or at least both sides can use the same language for negotiation and communication, to improve the efficiency of communication between the two sides in the negotiation process and to avoid obstacles and misunderstandings in communication.

Non-verbal communication is a significant factor in cross-cultural negotiations. Negotiators have to doctrine their body language and guess the meaning of the other party's gestures, intonation, silence, pauses, and facial expressions to avoid leading to ambiguity and misunderstanding. In international business negotiation, one should be good at observation, study carefully and summarize in time, and continuously accumulate and enrich the experience.

5.7 Case Study

On his first trip to Mexico, Harry, a US manager who intended to negotiate a contract with a Mexican firm, was invited to a dinner party by his Mexican counterpart. Since the invitation indicated that cocktails would begin at 7 p.m., Harry arrived promptly at that time. His host seemed surprised, and no one else had arrived. People began arriving about 8 p.m.

Harry knew he had read the invitation correctly but felt he had gotten off a bad start. What advice would you have given Harry?

5.8　Business Ethics

In every person's story of success, you will find experiences of them fighting big battles to achieve what they want. But yet for each personal story that involves fighting or hard effort, you will find yet others who had achieved the same thing almost without fighting and in the easier way. Since that is the case, realize that there are better and easier ways of doing things to the level where a person is able to achieve a whole lot more than the rest without any more effort. Highest strategies bring the greatest wins.

The highest victories come from winning without fighting. Achieving what you want with the least amount of energy expended enables you to achieve as much as you can. In order to expend the least amount of energy required in the accomplishment of any goal, you have to take the path of least resistance. Realize that there are many ways to reach the same objective. Choosing the best way will get you the best results. For the master, there are different levels of winning and he seeks the best possible kind.

Sun Tzu's Art of War says that the greatest generals acquire victory without even fighting any battles. The actual physical battle or confrontation of forces is the last resort that those generals use. They would use every other nonphysical means first and save on any unnecessary sacrificing of lives. They would use diplomacy, respect, reciprocity, fear, kindness or any other psychological means to get what they want. They would only resort to force to get what they want only when absolutely necessary.

Look at King Solomon's kingdom. He had everything he wanted through peace and not war. All the generals who won great victories through fighting many battles would feel ashamed when they look at King Solomon's achievement with his kingdom. All their victories seem like defeat in comparison with the victory of the wisest king ever. Therefore, it is possible to achieve everything you want with almost no fighting at all. Harmonize with the universal flow and the easiest and most effortless way will appear.

There are different levels of soldiers and generals on each side. The highest level generals and sovereigns gain victories without fighting. They can even steal from the enemy and shake his hand. An attack that doesn't appear as an attack is the best kind. It is only open attacks that create conflicts and opposition. But when you achieve what you want in a way that seems like no harm to the enemy, or even seems good to him, you face no opposition. Keep your friends close but keep your enemies closer.

The enlightened ones are those who win victories without fighting but by pure ingenuity and influence. You can create the appearance of fights to misdirect your enemy away from your true invisible strategies at work. Enlightened ones work by being successful in life instead of trying to fight against the whole world.

The purpose of any fight is to get what you want. In war, then, let your great object be victory, not lengthy campaigns. If you can get what you want without having conflict, then you can win without fighting. The more you are able to acquire what you desire through peace, the more powerful you will become without resistance. The more powerful you become, the less you will be attacked. Because others will rather submit to you and dominate weaker ones. That is when you can win more without fighting.

5.9 Exercises

Group presentation: topics involve comparative studies on some specific aspects between Chinese culture and English culture. When researching on the topics, students are suggested to include the following parts in the presentation.

(1) Find out similarities / differences on the given topic between two cultures.

(2) Provide adequate examples to show the similarities and differences you find.

(3) Explore on how different cultural values in each culture are reflected through your study.

Unit 6

Essential of Business Letter Writing

✧ **Case-Lead-in**

In 2008, an attorney in Philadelphia, the US, wanted to send an email to one of her colleagues. In the email, she suggested settling a lawsuit against pharmaceutical giant Eli Lilly and Company. The attorney typed her colleague's name into the "send" field of the email, but didn't notice that the email program had automatically filled in another name at that point.

Who received the email last? A reporter for The New York Times. A few days later, the New York Times published a front-page story about the 1 billion settlement. While it's not clear to what extent the mistake helped the Times get exclusive coverage of the settlement, it didn't stop people from talking about it with gusto and ranking it as one of the biggest email wrecks of all time.

With the unparalleled dominance of email in business communications, I'm sure we've all had embarrassing stories about accidentally sending the wrong email—luckily we probably didn't make the multi-billion dollar mistake. Email as a communication tool also creates another problem: reading and responding to new emails in your inbox can often wear you out.

6.1 Learn Objectives

(1) Understand the guidelines in business letter writing.
(2) Grasp letter format and layout of emails and business letter.
(3) Grasp how to the essentials of business letter writing。

6.2 Brief Introduction

A business letter is a type of letter which serves as a means of communication written for various commercial purposes. These purposes can include a business deal, complaint, warning, notice, invitation, declaration, information, apology and various other corporate matters. Business btters are the most popular and the most widely written types of letters. Business letters are also the oldest form of official correspondence and promoters of the mailing system.

6.3 Requirements for Business Letter and Email Writers

As a business letter or email writer, you need to master how to write good business writing.

First, understand the reader. It is necessary to consider who will read these documents, what position they are in, why they are reading these documents, and what they will know about this document to read.

Second, consider the questions the reader will ask. Good functional documents anticipate what questions the reader will have and give answers, usually these questions will be related to the reader's job and need to consider the questions they may ask.

Third, answer the reader's questions. Imagine the reader's various questions and answer them. This is a good way to organize the content of the document, to answer these questions clearly in the document, and to focus on the main issues.

Fourth, it allows the reader to find information in the document quickly. Important information needs to be highlighted in an eye-catching format so that the reader can find the information quickly.

Finally, the content should be clear and direct. Sentences should be simple and clear so that the reader can understand them at a glance.

6.4 Seven Guidelines in Business Letter Writing

Business writing is associated with formality, norms, rules, challenges, as well as certain opportunities. Overall, there are people who find it easier to write informal letters as there's more room for creativity, and there are those who prefer formal writing as it is more standardized and straightforward. Whether you like it or not, you should understand what effective business writing is, follow the rules, and understand how to compose a letter that conveys your message just right.

1. Clarity

Be clear when conveying your messages. Avoid using complex sentences—go straight to the point of your message, let your reader know what you are writing about. Nobody wants to spend minutes of their time on a message that is unclear or hard to comprehend. If your letter lacks that clarity, your reader will either ignore it or have a hard time comprehending what you are talking about. You are going to waste people's time and maybe even cost them their money. This is why you should always write with laser precision. Your clarity is the key factor in giving your audience the right meaning and conveying your intentions in a comprehensive manner, so you should really work on that aspect of your communication.

2. Simplicity

Use simple language and short sentences. Of course, it mustn't sound like you are writing to a first-grader, but you should also avoid complicated structures, flamboyant wording, and emotional expressions. "Your goal here is to get your message across to your audience, not to showcase your unique style. There is nothing difficult in business letters and you will often come across them in a working atmosphere"—says one of the chief managers at Papers Owl. "Without the ability to introduce business correspondence, you will be less in demand in the labor market."

3. Tone

Choosing the right tone of voice is one of the key tips for writing professional business messages. Forget about exclamation points, passive voice, and idioms—your writing has to be informative and kind of plain. You are here to provide a valuable piece of information in a written form, not to entertain the readers. The words you use have to be straightforward and bear no secondary meanings. You have to make sure your readers get your meaning, having no room for misinterpretation.

4. Goal

Know the goal of your messages and make sure the audience comprehends that goal too. State it at the beginning of your letter and use the right words to convey your meaning. One of the main tips here is to provide a short and precise statement of goal at the beginning of your letter. Say something like: "This letter is to inform you about…", and with that short and concise statement of purpose, you can move on to expanding the content of your letter. Unlike in creative essays, where you can just write for the sole purpose of writing, in business communication, messages have to bear meaning and purpose.

5. Friends and Co-workers

If you are having a business correspondence with a co-worker you consider a friend or confidant, you should not forget about formalities. You can swear and dish all you want in personal communication, but you should never allow any swear words into your official communication. There have been numerous cases of scandals in the large corporations where senior company executives used profane language in official communication, thinking nobody would ever read that. Such profanities might lead to serious outcomes, so you should not let that into your official written communication, even with people you trust.

6. Candor

Be candid with your audience. Of course, some diplomacy might be due when delivering bad news, though you should give things their names. Make sure you are saying things politely but frankly. The goal of official communication is delivering the right meaning without having to read between the lines. Being polite and a bit diplomatic is a good thing to do, especially when delivering not-so-good news within your company, but you must be sure you are saying things as they are when creating your piece of business communication.

7. Show Your Expertise

You want to sound like you know what you are talking about, and to achieve that, you have to use technical terms relevant to your topic. You should also know who you are writing for to be sure they comprehend the read. Be active when explaining your meaning to the audience and try to craft a piece of reading anyone would get. For instance, if your messages are going to be delivered to a broader audience via social media, you have to apply all of your skills to create a comprehensive note anyone would get.

6.5 Letter Format and Placement of Major Parts

A business letter is a formal document often sent from one company to another or from a company to its clients, employees, and stakeholders, for example. Business letters are used for professional correspondence between individuals, as well.

Although email has taken over as the most common form of correspondence, printed-out business letters are still used for many important, serious types of correspondence, including reference letters, employment verification, job offers, and more.

1. What to Include in the Letter

Make the purpose of your letter clear through simple and targeted language, keeping the opening paragraph brief. You can start with, "I am writing in reference to…" and from there, communicate only what you need to say.

The subsequent paragraphs should include information that gives your reader a full understanding of your objective(s) but avoid meandering sentences and needlessly long words. Again, keep it concise to sustain their attention.

2. Sections of a Business Letter

Each section of your letter should adhere to the appropriate format, starting with your contact information and that of your recipient's, salutation, the body of the letter, closing, and finally, your signature.

3. Contact Information

Your contact information should be included: your name, your job title, your company, your address, city, zip code, your phone number, your email address.

4. The Date

It should be the date you're penning the correspondence.

5. Recipient's Contact Information

It should be included: their name, their title, their company, the company's address, city, zip code.

6. The Salutation

Use "To Whom It May Concern", if you're unsure specifically whom you're addressing.

Use the formal salutation "Dear Mr./Ms./Dr. [Last Name]", if you do not know the recipient.

Use "Dear [First Name]", only if you have an informal relationship with the recipient.

7. The Body

Use single-spaced lines with an added space between each paragraph, after the salutation, and above the closing. Left justify your letter (against the left margin).

8. Closing Salutation

Keep your closing paragraph to two sentences. Simply reiterate your reason for writing and thank the reader for considering your request. Some good options for your closing include: Respectfully yours, Yours sincerely, Cordially, Respectfully.

If your letter is less formal, consider using: All the best, Best, Thank you, Regards.

9. Your Signature

Write your signature just beneath your closing and leave four single spaces between your closing and your typed full name, title, phone number, email address, and any other contact information you want to include.

6.6　The Layout of Emails

Your email message should be formatted like a typical business letter, with spaces between paragraphs and no typos or grammatical errors.
- Don't mistake length for quality—keep your email brief and to the point.
- Avoid overly complicated or long sentences.
- Make it easy for email recipients to quickly scan through your email and know why you're emailing.
- Proofread it, just like you would any other correspondence.
- If you're really concerned about typos, consider printing out the email draft. Often, it's easier to catch typos and grammatical errors on a hard copy than while reviewing on a screen.

1. Subject Line

Don't forget to include a subject line in your email. If you forget to include one, your message probably isn't even going to get opened. Use the subject line to summarize why you're emailing. Some examples of strong subject lines are as follows.
- Application for Marketing Associate—Jane Smith;
- Informational Interview Request;
- Thank You—Marketing Associate Interview;
- Referred by [Person's Name] for [Informational Interview, Discuss XYZ, etc.].

2. Salutation / Greeting

If you have a contact person, address your email to Dear Mr./Ms. Last Name. If possible, find out the hiring manager's name. This information is sometimes included in the job listing. If it's not, use sites like LinkedIn to determine the contact person, or check the company's website for information.

If there is a contact number, you can also call the company's front desk and see if the receptionist can provide information. Check your own network too: Do you know anyone who works at the company and might be able to share more information?

3. The Body of the Message

When you write your message, include a few short paragraphs as follows.
- Introduction (who you are) (first paragraph);
- The reason you're writing (second and optional third paragraph);
- Thanks for the consideration.

If you're applying for a job, copy and paste your cover letter into the email message or write your cover letter in the body of an email message. If the job posting asks you to send your resume as an attachment, send your resume as a PDF or a Word document.

When you're inquiring about available positions or networking, be clear about why you are writing and the purpose of your email message.

4. Closing

Include a formal closing, such as sincerely or regards, when you end your message.

5. Include an Email Signature

It's important to create an email signature and to include your signature with every message you send.

Include your full name, your email address, and your phone number in your email signature, so the hiring manager can see, at a glance, how to contact you. You can also include a link to your LinkedIn profile page or website so that recruiters and hiring managers can easily find out more information about you.

6. Don't Forget Attachments

Sending a job search email often involves attaching files, a resume, portfolio, or other sample work. Make sure to double-check that you have attached all the files mentioned in your email before hitting the "send" button.

7. Email Message Template

The following email message template lists the information you need to include in the email messages you send when job searching. Use the template as a guideline to create customized email messages to send to employers and connections.

6.7　The Layout of Business Letters

The layout of business letters should include the followings.

1. Letterhead

A letterhead is topmost heading printed on the letter. The heading consists of name, address generally accompanied by a logo of the organization. Most professional firms have their own pre-designed letterhead. Preprinted letterheads showcase the repute of a company. However smaller firms may not have it. They use their name and address in place of the letterhead.

2. Date

The date has to be written exactly below the letterhead. The date is an important part of a letter and is used for reference. The date is supposed to be written in full with day, month and year. Example—May 31st 2021 or May 31st, 2022.

3. Recipient

Recipient or receiver's name and address is the next part of a business letter. This part includes the name of the receiver, his designation and full address inclusive of phone and email.

4. Salutation

Salutation is the word of greeting used to begin a letter. It is a courteous gesture and shows respect to the receiver. Dear Sir/Madam etc. are specifically called opening salutations.

5. Body

It is the main part of the letter. The message of the letter is to be clearly mentioned in the first line, itself. The body has the relevant subject matter which is to be divided into several paragraphs, as need be. If there are instructions etc. these are to be in a bulleted or numerically listed in separate lines. The last paragraph should sum up the whole letter and offer any assistance or take a course of action as required or instructed.

6. Closing (Subscription)

Closing refers to the end of the letter. It is courteous and shows a mark of respect towards the recipient. Yours sincerely or sincerely etc. are commonly known as closings.

7. Signature

Signature follows after a few spaces. If the name is printed, then the signature is placed above it. An electronic signature can also be used. Scanned image of signature can also be used, if it is in accordance with the rules of the organization.

8. Sender's Name, Title and Contact Information

If these have not been incorporated in the letterhead, one can include name, title, address, phone, email etc. in separate lines.

9. Enclosure

If some documents have been attached, the word "Enclosures" should be typed/written a few lines after the signature of the sender. Thereafter, the number and type of documents attached e.g., "Enclosures (2): brochure, resume" is to be mentioned.

6.8 Addressing Envelopes

When sending a business letter to a person at a company, you'll need to maintain professional etiquette throughout the entire process. Follow the basic guidelines outlined above and then add a couple more pieces of information(see the Figure 6.1).

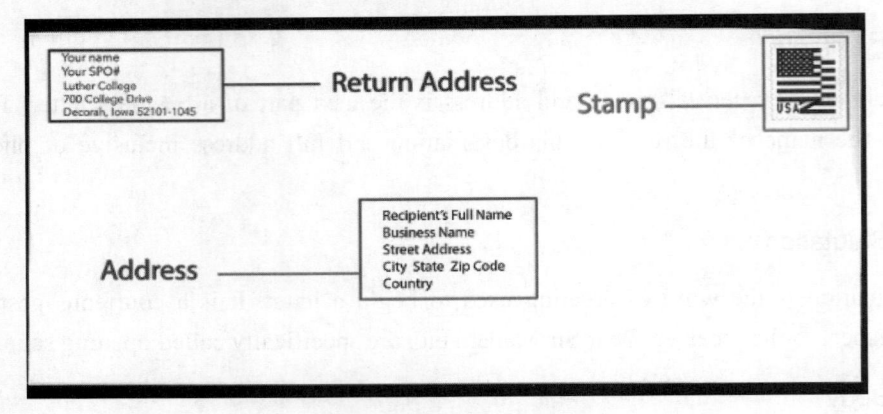

Figure 6.1　Envelope Example

- Place your name and address in the upper left corner of the envelope.
- Put the recipient's information in the center of the envelope.
- After the recipient's full name and on the same line if possible, add their position, such as "Director of Marketing". If the title does not fit on the same line, place it directly on the line underneath the name.
  - Underneath the person's name and title, add the full name of the company.
  - Add the company's street address on the line below the company's name.
  - Add the company's town, state, and zip code on the line below the street address.
  - The stamp goes on the upper right corner of the envelope.

6.9　Writing Procedure

It's easy to feel overwhelmed about a writing project—especially if the form of writing is new to you, or the topic is complex. Just break the task into manageable steps: Plan, Draft, Revise, and Edit.

1. Plan

Goal: Find your focus and prepare to draft.

Activities: Clarify your purpose, think about your reader, choose a format, and list the information you need to share. Then do any necessary research, review models, and develop an outline.

2. Draft

Goal: Get your thoughts on the page.

Activities: Expand your outline with sentences and paragraphs that use a fitting tone.

3. Revise

Goal: Fix any content problems in the first draft.

Activities: Test the quality and clarity of the ideas, organization, and voice. Also check words and sentences. Add, cut, and clarify as needed.

4. Edit

Goal: Fine-tune the piece before sending it out.

Activities: Review format and design. Edit and proofread by checking grammar, punctuation, spelling and mechanics.

6.10　The Outline of Business Letters

A business letter is a formal letter. Unlike a résumé or cover letter, it can be more than one page, and is likely to contain six parts.

1. The Heading

The heading contains the return address with the date on the last line. Sometimes it is necessary to include a line before the date with a phone number, fax number, or email address. Often there is a line skipped between the address and the date. It is not necessary to type a return address if you are using stationery with the return address already imprinted, but you should always use a date. Make sure the heading is on the left margin.

Example
Ms. Jane Doe
543 Washington St
Marquette, MI 49855
Tel:
Fax:
Email:
June 28th, 2011

2. Recipient's Address

This is the address you are sending your letter to. Be sure to make it as complete as possible so it gets to its destination. Always include title names (such as Dr.) if you know them. This is, like the other address, on the left margin. If a standard "8 ½ × 11" paper is folded in thirds to fit in a standard "9" business envelope, the inside address should appear through the window in the envelope (if there is one). Be sure to skip a line after the heading and before the recipient's address, then skip another line after the inside address before the greeting.

3. The Salutation

The salutation (or greeting) in a business letter is always formal. It often begins with "Dear (Person's name)". Once again, be sure to include the person's title if you know it (such as Ms., Mrs., Mr., or Dr.). If you're unsure about the person's title or gender, then just use their first name. For example, you would use only the person's first name if the person you are writing to is "Jordan" and you do not know whether they identify as male, female, or non-binary.

4. The Body

The body is the meat of your letter. For block and modified block letter formats, single space and left justify each paragraph. Be sure to leave a blank line between each paragraph, however, no matter the format. Be sure to also skip a line between the salutation and the body, as well as the body and the close.

5. The Complimentary Close

The complimentary close is a short and polite remark that ends your letter. The close begins at the same justification as your date and one line after the last body paragraph. Capitalize the first word of your closing (Thank you) and leave four lines for a signature between the close and the sender's name. A comma should follow the closing.

6. The Signature Line

Skip at least four lines after the close for your signature, and then type out the name to be signed. If you are printing this letter out and sending it by mail, you will sign your name in pen. This line will include your first and last name, and often includes a middle initial, although it is not required. You may put your title beforehand to show how you wish to be addressed (Ms., Mrs., Dr.).

7. Enclosures

If you have any enclosed documents, such as a resume, you can indicate this by typing "Enclosures" one line below the listing. You also may include the name of each document.

6.11　Case Study

Business Letter Example
Linda Lau
123 Main Street, Anytown, CA 12345-555-555-55555, linda.lau@email.com
March 5th, 2020

Oscar Lee

Managing Editor
Acme Graphic & Design
123 Business Rd.
Business City, CA 54321

Dear Mr. Lee,

I would like to invite you to attend our upcoming Liberal Arts department job networking event. The event will be held on the afternoon of May 1st, 2022. We wish to provide our graduating seniors with an opportunity to meet business leaders in the area who may be looking for new hires who hold degrees in the Liberal Arts.

The event will be held at the Cox Student Center at Northern State University and will last about two to three hours. If you have an interest in attending or sending a company representative to meet with our students, please let me know at your earliest convenience and I can reserve a table for you.

Thank for your time and I hope to hear from you soon.

Respectfully,

Linda Lau (signature hard copy letter)
Liberal Arts Department Chair

Email Message Sample

Subject Line of Email Message: Store Manager Position—Your Name
Salutation: Dear Mr./Ms. [Last Name] or Dear Hiring Manager
First Paragraph:

　　The first paragraph of your letter should include information on why you are writing. Be clear and direct—if you are applying for a job, mention the job title. If you want an informational interview, state that in your opening sentences.

Middle Paragraph:

　　The next section of your email message should describe what you have to offer the employer or if you're writing to ask for help, what type of assistance you are seeking.

Final Paragraph:

　　Conclude your cover letter by thanking the employer for considering you for the position or your connection for helping with your job search.

Closing:
Sincerely,
Your Name
Email Signature:
FirstName LastName

Email address
Phone

Analysis this business letter, review how to write a good business letter.

6.12　Business Ethics

　　书信文化是中国传统文化的一个重要组成部分。从"结绳记事"为代表的始于西周时期的实物信件算起，中国的书信文化迄今也已有 2000 多年的历史。1975 年，在湖北省云梦县城关镇西郊睡地虎一座战国末年秦墓出土的木牍家书（写于公元前 225 年），便是迄今发现的我国最早的文字书信。在中国广为流传的成语典故中，书信文化也留下了深深的印记，如青鸟传信、鱼传尺素、鸿雁传书、驿寄梅花等，不一而足。更有与书信文化相关联的邮驿、民信局和现代邮政等相关设施。古时，杜甫的"烽火连三月，家书抵万金"，张籍的"欲作家书意万重"，李清照的"云中谁寄锦书来，雁字回时，月满西楼"，春秋战国时期"三缄其口"，依然可以窥见书信在历代人们情感交流和商业活动交流中的重要地位。我国书信礼仪亦是源远流长的，如李斯《谏逐客书》、司马迁的《报任安书》等，从中可以领略规范的书信格式与礼仪，浓缩了人们对历史的记忆，也保留了我国传统文化的"原生态"味道。书信是富有神韵的中华优秀文化的载体，是中华悠久文明的历史见证。

讨论

我国古代书信的发展历史及作用。

6.13　Exercises

　　Review letter samples, including cover letters, interview thank you letters, follow-up letters, job acceptance, and rejection letters, resignation letters, appreciation letters, and more business and employment-related letter samples and writing tips.

Unit 7

Establishing Business Relations

✧ **Case-Lead-in**

One day, Sunshine Company learned from the Commercial Counselor's Office of the Australian Embassy in China that Nelson & Peterson Co., Ltd. (Postcode 94672), 56 Flushing Street, Sydney, Australia, intends to purchase mountain bikes and wants to find customers in China's mainland to establish long-term cooperative relations with it.

7.1　Learning Objectives

(1) Acquire how to obtain the channels to approach and information sources of foreign merchants.

(2) Master how to write a complete and satisfying letter for this purpose.

(3) Study some useful expressions and sentence patterns concerning the establishment of business relations.

7.2　The Significance of Establishing Business Relations

(1) To establish business relations is to choose prospective partners. It is the initial step and also an important undertaking in the field of foreign trade.

(2) The development and expansion of business depends on customers. If right partners are developed, new businesses will be started and enhanced, or else great losses will be incurred.

(3) In international trade, traders should first establish business relations with potential clients since they live in different countries.

7.3　The Channels of Establishing Business Relations

It is not easy to do business with customers in other countries because a foreign trade firm doesn't know them very well. For importers, they don't know where the sellers are and for exporters, they don't know where the buyers are. In doing international business, a foreign trade firm needs extensive business connections to open up, maintain and expand its business activities. Therefore, the establishment of business relations is one of the most important undertakings in the field of foreign trade.

Establishing business relations is the first step in international trade. Writing letters to new firms or customers to establish business relations is a common practice in foreign trade. If a newly established firm wishes to open up a market to sell something or buy something from firms in foreign countries or an old one wants to enlarge its business scope and turnover, the manager of the firm must first of all find out whom he is going to do business with. Usually, information like this can be obtained through the following channels.

(1) Banks with particular interest in this territory;

(2) Chamber of commerce at home and abroad;

(3) The economic and commercial counselor's offices of the embassy of the People's Republic of China in foreign countries;

(4) Fairs, exhibitions and expositions held both at home and abroad;

(5) Advertisement in newspapers, magazines or on TV;

(6) Trade directories of various countries and regions;

(7) Self-introduction or introduction from your business connections;

(8) Market investigation;

(9) Enquiries received from foreign merchants in the same line;

(10) Business website;

(11) Mutual visits by trade delegations and groups.

After getting the desired names and addresses of the firms from any of the above sources, the person in charge of the firm may send a letter to the firm concerned.

7.4 Writing Skills

When you write a letter for establishing business relationship, you should tell your customers:

(1) To state the source of information and the intention of the letter.

(2) Illustrate your purpose of writing.

(3) To introduce briefly one's own company, such as nature of company, business scope, financial standing, etc.

(4) Your expectation of entering into business relations and an early reply.

7.5 Typical Expressions for Letters Requesting for Establishment of Business Relations (See Table 7.1) and Replies (See Table 7.2)

Table 7.1 Typical Expressions for Letters Requesting for Establishment of Business Relations

Writing Steps	Typical Expressions
(1) Tell the receiver how you get his name and information.	Your company has been kindly introduced to us by…
	Having obtained your name and address from…, we are writing you in the hope of…
	Your name and address have been passed on us by…
	We learn through/from…that…
	On the recommendation of…, we have learned that…
(2) Make a self-introduction of your own company (such as nature of company, business scope and financial standing).	We take this opportunity to introduce ourselves as…
	Our lines are mainly…
	We write to introduce ourselves as a large dealer in…with good connections in the country.
(3) Express your expectation of establishing business relations.	We are willing to enter into business relations with you.
	We express our desire to …
	We are desirous of …

Writing Steps	Typical Expressions
(4) Express to the wish of setting up business relations and early reply.	We look forward to receiving…
	Hope to receive…
	Your early reply is appreciated.
	We are anticipating your answer.

Table 7.2 Typical Expressions for Replies

Writing Steps	Typical Expressions
(1) Express your appreciation for reader's interest in your company.	Thank you for…
	Thank you for your interest in…
	We have received…
	Your letter of August 8th has been received with thanks.
(2) Express your desire to establish business relations.	Your wish of establishing business relations coincides with ours.
	This is also our desire.
	We shall be very glad to enter into business relations with you.
(3) State the further action you will take, such as asking for information.	We are sending you our catalogue and price list…
	We shall be glad to have your specific inquiry.

7.6 Specimen Letters

Letter 1: Exporter's Request for Setting up Business Relations

Dear Mr. Peng,

We have learned from the Commercial Counselor's Office of our Embassy that you are in the market for 100% cotton women's jackets, which just fall into our business scope. We are writing to enter into business relations with you on the basis of equality and mutual benefits.

Our corporation is specialized in manufacturing women's garment, and we have got a lot of experience. Our own brand "Happiness" has won a high reputation at home and the abroad. They sell well in Russia, Occident, the Middle East and Southeast Asia area.

Our products are made of environmental-friendly material, 100% cotton, good in airiness, moisture absorption, fashion in design, and comfortable in wear.

Enclosed is our latest catalogue of women's jacket, which may meet your demands. It will be a great pleasure to receive your inquiries for any of the items again which we will send you our best quotations.

We are looking forward to your early reply.

Truly yours,

Fred Jackson

Unit 7 Establishing Business Relations

Letter 2: A Reply to the Above

Dear Mr. Jackson,

We acknowledge with thanks for the receipt of your letter of September 9th and take the pleasure of establishing business relations with you.

Your products are attractive and we plan to place large orders with you if your prices are competitive. We shall be obliged if you could send us sample books and best quotations on CIF New York basis.

Waiting for your reply.

Sincerely yours,

Xianjin Peng

Letter 3: Importer's Request for Setting up Business Relations

Dear Mr. Leeds,

We have seen your cotton garments displayed at Shanghai International Clothing & Textile Expo and have a pleasure to ask you to send us details of your goods with the lowest CIF New York price.

We are one of the largest dealers of garments in America and our annual requirements for cotton garments are considerable. We will place large orders with you if your price is competitive and your deliveries prompt. Meanwhile, we'd like to set up direct business relations with you after this transaction.

We are looking forward to hearing from you soon.

Yours faithfully,

Ping Wang

Letter 4: A Reply to the Importer

Dear Mr. Wang,

Thank you for your letter dated October 8th. We are glad to learn that you are interested in entering into business relations with our corporation in the line of garments.

As requested, we are now sending you by another mail our latest catalogues and latest price list.

If any of the items listed meets your requirement, please let us have your specific enquiry and we shall deliver the goods one month after receipt of your L/C.

We look forward to receiving your reply soon.

Sincerely yours,

John Leeds

7.7 Situational Conversation

A: Hello Sir/Madam, nice to meet you and glad to have the opportunity to establish business relations with your company.

B: Pleased to meet you too. I travel a lot every year on business, but this is the first time to come to your country. I must say I have been greatly impressed by your friendly people.

A: Thank you for saying so. Have you seen the exhibition halls? The things on display are most of our products, such as silk, woolen knitwear, cotton piece goods, and garments.

B: Oh, yes, I had a look yesterday. I found some of the exhibits to be fine in quality and beautiful in design. The exhibition has successfully displayed to me what your corporation handles. I have gone over the catalogue and pamphlets enclosed in your last letter. I have got some idea of your exports. I am interested in your silk blouses.

A: Our silk is known for its quality. It is one of our traditional exports. Silk blouses are brightly colored and beautifully designed. They have met with great favor overseas which are always in great demand.

B: Some of them seem to be of the latest style. Now I have a feeling that we can do a lot of trade in this line. We wish to establish relations with you.

A: Your desire coincides with ours. Concerning our financial position, credit standing, and trade reputation, you may refer to Beijing Bank, or to our local Chamber of Commerce or inquiry agencies.

B: Thank you for the information. As you know, our corporation is a state-operated one. We always trade with foreign countries on the basis of equality and mutual benefit. Establishing business relations between us will be to our mutual benefits. I have no doubt that it will bring closer ties between us. That sounds interesting. I'll send a fax home. As soon as I receive a definite answer, I'll make a specific inquiry.

A: We will then make an offer as soon as possible. I hope a lot of business will be concluded between us.

7.8　Useful Patterns & Examples

[Pattern 1] learn/obtain/have... from...

(1) We learned our company from the Internet that you are one of the leading manufactures in this line.

(2) We obtained your name and address from…

[Pattern 2] be in the market for…

(1) We are in the market for bed-sheet.

(2) We learned from China Council for the Promotion of International Trade that you are in the market for a communications satellite system.

[Pattern 3] establish/enter into/set up business relations with…

(1) We are willing to enter into business relations with your firm on the basis of equality, mutual benefit and exchanging what one has for what one needs.

(2) We wish to establish friendly business relations with you to enjoy a share of mutually

profitable business.

[Pattern 4] under separate cover/post

(1) Under separate cover, we have sent you two catalogues.

(2) We are sending by separate post a statement of account, from which you will observe that there is a balance in our favor of USD7000.

[Pattern 5] fall/come/lie within the scope of

(1) We note with pleasure the items of your demand just fall within the scope of our business line.

(2) Item of this kind fall within the scope of our business activities.

[Pattern 6] take the opportunity to…

(1) We take this opportunity to express our wish to enter into business relations with you.

(2) We take this opportunity to introduce ourselves as large exporter of leather goods in our country.

[Pattern 7] enjoy good reputation, enjoy great popularity

(1) The firm you enquired about is one of the most reliable importers in our district and has for many years enjoyed good reputation among the traders.

(2) The firm enjoys the fullest respect and great popularity in the business world.

[Pattern 8] deal in/deal with/trade in/specialize in/is in the line of…

(1) We are deal in the exportation of arts and crafts.

(2) They are anxious to deal directly with the actual producers.

[Pattern 9] avail oneself of (make use of)…

(1) We avail ourselves of this opportunity to express our thanks to you for your close cooperation.

(2) We avail ourselves of this opportunity to write you in the hope of establishing business relations with you.

[Pattern 10] take the liberty of doing sth.

(1) We take the liberty of writing you to establish direct business relations.

(2) We take the liberty of asking to send us a copy of your latest price list.

7.9   Case Study

Founded in 1980, Huaxin Trading Co., Ltd. is a comprehensive trading company authorized by the state to import and export. Its business scope includes mechanical and electrical equipment, metal materials, building materials, chemical raw materials, light industrial products, etc. The company has a fixed relationship with a number of suppliers, the supply of solid foundation at the same time, in the face of the changeable international market, the company also attaches great importance to the development of new products. For example, the commodity department has developed a new product, the HX series of porcelain, in conjunction with its hook factory. This series is made of fine porcelain clay, packed in exquisite gift box, and hand-drawn pattern, beautiful and generous, high quality, very competitive. In March 2020, the company's business personnel saw a message from a newspaper (the International Business Daily's echo column) that a Canadian company was seeking porcelain. Immediately got in touch with the Echo Station and learned that the Canadian customer was an import wholesaler in Toronto.

Based on the above background information, please write to James Brown & Sons in the name of the salesperson of the Commodity Department of Huaxin Trading Company, expressing the ardent desire to establish a trade relationship with it, and send the catalogue of the HX porcelain series along with it.

7.10 Business Ethics

在商业经营活动中，表现为商业经营行为的准则，"君子爱财，取之有道"便是其生动的表述。这里所说的"道"主要是指商业行为的根本法则，即道德追求和精神价值。依儒家的观点看，是说做一名儒家商人，经商要遵循商业道德规范，要光明正大地赚钱，不发不义之财，不做伤天害理的生意。

东汉时的王符说"商贾者以通货为本，以鬻奇为末。"他认为经商与务农、教书一样都应该以正业为根本，以邪辟为异端，不准贩淫奇，攫取暴利，这样才能使商业健康。

《谢家书》记载：东汉时公沙穆派人到市场代卖病猪，事先交代说："如售，当对买者言病，贱取其值，不可言无病，欺取其价也。"代卖者到市场后不说是病猪，高价卖出。公沙穆知道后，立即追上买主，退还多收的钱，并据实相告。买者说既已成交就不必退款，公沙穆坚决要退，"终不收钱而去"。

公沙穆经商"取之有义"成为四方美谈，因而大富。而令人沉思的是，据《郁离子》记载：赵国商人虞孚在吴国卖漆，本来可以稳获厚利，但因掺杂使假，失信于民，结果商品变质，本钱亏光，沦为乞丐，饿死他乡，这就是"取之不义"的应有下场。

讨论

经营者的行为与做人最基本的良心和道义之间的关系应如何？儒家"取之有义"的商业行为准则对市场条件下的企业经营有何指导意义？

7.11 Exercises

1. Write a Reply According to the Incoming Email

To: Jeannine@163.com
Date: June 15th, 2015
Subject: Establishing trade relations
Dear Sirs,

Having obtained your name and address from the Internet. We are writing you in the hope of entering into trade relations with you.

We have been one of the leading importers of Children's Wears in our country and enjoyed high reputation in European markets. At present, we are interested in your products and will appreciate it if you could send us your latest catalogues.

We are looking forward to your early reply.

Yours faithfully,

Douglas

2. Situational Writing

Situation:

Suncity Phone-house Inc. is an American sole distributor of mobile phones. They sell different models of Nokia phones and they ship worldwide. At present, you are in urgent need of 2000 sets of mobile phones.

Task:

Please write a letter to the American company to establish direct business relations and give the Bank of China, Liaoning Branch as your reference.

3. Case Practice

Taking the introduction case in this chapter as the background, as a salesperson of Sunshine Company, draft a letter to establish a business relationship for the company, introduce the company's information and product information in detail, and express the desire to establish a business relationship with it.

Unit 8

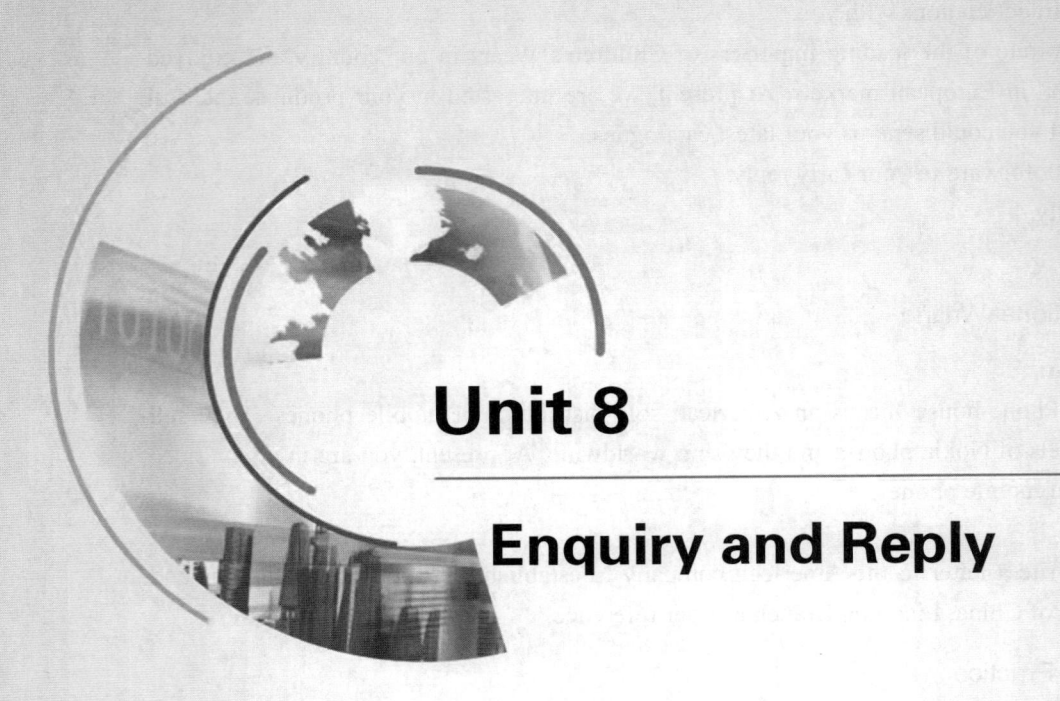

Enquiry and Reply

✧ **Case-Lead-in**

The Canadian Thomson Company is a company engaged in the import of handicrafts and is currently looking for high-quality brocade handbags. They learned from the Commercial Counselor's Office of the country's embassy in China that Ningbo Qianhu Trading Co., Ltd. can supply various brocade handbags in large quantities. So, Mr. Martin Crown of Thomson's Purchasing Department got in touch with the company and made an inquiry about brocade handbags.

Unit 8 Enquiry and Reply

8.1 Learning Objectives

(1) Understand the nature and characteristics of enquiries and replies.
(2) Get acquainted with the types of enquiries.
(3) Know how to write a satisfactory letter of enquiries and replies.

8.2 The Importance and Nature of Enquiry

Enquiry is the first step in international trade negotiation, which brings a would-be buyer and potential seller together. In international trade, an enquiry is usually (not absolutely) made by the prospective buyer without engagement, requesting for information on the supply of certain goods, which should be concise, specific and polite.

Sometimes, it can also be made by the seller, is a request for a reply informing an importer of prices, catalogue, samples and a quotation sheet, delivery date and usual payment terms before placing an order with a prospective exporter. It also is an invitation to bid.

Enquiries may be either dispatched by mail, cable telex, fax, or handed to the suppliers through personal contact, and even by telephone or face-to-face talk.

8.3 Categories of Enquiry

(1) General enquiries: If the importers want to have a general idea of the commodity, which the exporter is in a position to supply, they may make a request for a price list, a catalogue, samples and other terms.

(2) Specific enquiries (stronger intension to make an order than general enquiries): If the importers intend to purchase goods of a certain specification, they may ask the exporter to make an offer or a quotation for specific goods. That is a specific enquiry.

8.4 Writing Skills

Enquiry can be of two types: general enquiry and specific enquiry.
If you want to write a general enquiry, the following contents may be included.
(1) The source of information and a brief self-introduction.
(2) The intention of writing the letter (ask for a catalogue, samples or a price list).
(3) Stating the possibility of placing an order.
If you want to write a specific enquiry, the following contents may be included.
(1) The names and descriptions of the goods inquired for, including specifications, quantity, etc.
(2) Asking whether there is a possibility of giving a special discount and what terms of

payment and time of delivery you would expect.

(3) Stating the possibility of placing an order.

8.5　Typical Expressions for Letters Making Enquiry (See Table 8.1) and Reply (See Table 8.2)

Table 8.1　Typical Expressions for Letters Making Enquiry

Writing Steps	Typical Expressions
(1) Mention how to get the relevant information (name, address etc.) about the exporter.	Your name has been given to us by the Chamber of Commerce/ the … Embassy/ the … Bank in …
	Your firm has been recommended to us by Bayer AG, with whom we have done business for many years.
	Messrs …of … have given me your name as sole agents for …
(2) Tell the exporter the items you are interested in and express your initial intention for purchasing.	We are considering the purchase of …
	We are interested in importing snooker tables but we need to have further details of the costs before making a final decision.
	We are regular buyers of men's knitwear.
(3) Invite a quotation or an offer asking for details (pricelist, catalogue, sample etc.) of your desired commodities.	Will you please send us your illustrate/ latest catalogue and price list.
	We should like to receive a copy of your latest catalogue and full details of your export prices and terms of payment, together with samples.
	Kindly let me have a description of your electric hedge trimmers.
(4) State the possibility of placing an order and hope to receive an early reply.	Will you please let us know by 4th April so that we can place our order promptly.
	Please let us know by return of post whether you would be interested in such an order.

Table 8.2　Typical Expressions for Reply

Writing Steps	Typical Expressions
(1) An expression of thanks for the enquiry.	Many thanks for your enquiry of …
	Thank you for your enquiry and for your interest in our products.
	We thank you for your enquiry of …
(2) Take the opportunity to make a favorable comment on your products or services.	We are confident you will find our products the finest on the market and considerably better than those of our competitors who supply your market at present.
	The specimens sent will convince you of the excellent quality of our medical instruments.
(3) Cover all the details that your clients asked for, such as name of commodities, quality, quantity, and specifications, unit price, terms of payment, packing method, shipment, illustrated catalogues, samples, etc.	We are very pleased to have received your inquiry of March 15th, 2014 and enclosed our latest illustrated catalogue and price list with the details you ask for.
	With reference to your letter of May 5th and we are pleased to send /give/make you our best /lowest quotation for…
(4) Express your hopes of doing business with your clients.	We hope you will find our quotation satisfactory and look forward to receiving your order.
	We look forward to doing business with you.

8.6　Specimen Letters

Letter 1:　General Enquiry

Dear Sirs,

We have been informed by the Bank of US Commerce, New York, that you are one of the leading exporters of textiles in China, and that you wish to export pure silk garments to our market.

You will be pleased to note that our corporation is one of the leading importers of textile products, having over 30 years' history and high reputation.

We shall be able to give you considerable orders, if the quality of your products is fine and the prices are moderate. We would be obliged if you will send us some samples with the best terms at your earliest convenience.

Yours faithfully,

Suzanne

Letter 2:　A Reply to the Above

Dear Sirs,

We take pleasure to acknowledge receipt of your letter of January 20th, from which we learn that you are interested in bringing silk garments to the New York market.

We are enclosing our quotation sheet covering different sizes and colors of our pure silk garments that can be supplied from stock. We are also airmailing you two dozen sample garments in different sizes and colors. Delivery will be within 30 days after you placing an order to us. Payment of the purchase is to be effected by an irrevocable L/C at sight in our favor.

This offer is subject to your immediate reply which should reach us not later than the end of next month. The price will probably be changed once this particular offer has lapsed.

Yours faithfully,

Julia

Letter 3:　A Specific Enquiry

Dear Sirs,

We learn with pleasure from your letter of April 12th, 2004 that you are exporters of Chinese Blanket Cover and are willing to establish business relations with us.

At present, we are interested in Blanket Cover and shall be pleased if you will send us by airmail sample books and all necessary information on Blanket Cover, so as to acquaint us with material and workmanship of your supplies. Meanwhile, please quote us the lowest price CIF London, inclusive of our 3% commission, stating the earliest date of shipment.

Should your price be found competitive and delivery time acceptable, we shall place a large

order with you.
Yours truly,
Leon Allen

Letter 4: A Reply to the Above

Dear Sirs,

Thank you very much for your letter of April 28th, 2004, we are pleased to send you samples and all the necessary information on Blanket Cover under separate cover.

At your request, we are pleased to make you an offer, subject to our final confirmation, as follows:

Commodity: "Golden Cock" Brand Blanket Cover No.21

Size: 180cm×200cm

Color: All kinds of colors

Quantity: 1000 pieces

Price: GBP20 each piece CIF London inclusive of 3% commission

Shipment: During August/September

Payment: By 100% confirmed, irrevocable L/C in our favor payable by draft at sight to reach the sellers one month before shipment, and remain valid for negotiation in China till the 15th day after shipment.

As you will realize from the catalogue we sent you, our Blanket Cover is a perfect combination of warmth, softness and easy care. We are sure that you can get benefit from our products.

We look forward to your prompt reply.

Yours faithfully

8.7 Situational Conversation

Mr. Baker, an importer from Canada, is interested in the Flying Horse Brand bicycle and enquires for it.

Baker: We're interested in your Flying Horse Brand bicycle. Would you please quote me your price?

Zhang: But could you give us a rough idea of the quantity you require? You know, the price varies according to the quantity.

Baker: What's the minimum quantity of an order for your goods?

Zhang: The minimum quantity of an order is 1000 sets.

Baker: Well, then I'll order 1000 sets.

Zhang: In that case, our offer is USD80 per set.

Baker: Do you quote CIF or FOB?

Zhang: We usually quote on a CIF basis. The price is USD80 per set. CIF Vancouver with a commission of five percent for you. You will find our prices are very competitive.

Baker: What are your terms of payment?

Zhang: Our usual way of payment is by confirmed and irrevocable letter of credit available by draft at sight for the full amount of the contracted goods to be established in our favour through a bank acceptable to us.

Baker: Then could you tell me the earliest possible time of shipment?

Zhang: Within one month after your L/C reaches us.

Baker: Is your offer a firm one or one without engagement?

Zhang: Our offer is a firm one and remains valid for four days.

Baker: Thank you for your offer. I'll give you a phone call from my hotel tomorrow morning with my decision.

Zhang: Good. I expect you to accept our general trade terms and conditions. We believe through our cooperation, large transactions will be brought to speedy conclusion.

Baker: I hope so. Goodbye.

8.8 Useful Patterns & Examples

[Pattern 1] make enquiry for/enquire for…

(1) We would like to make an enquiry for your fashion shoes.

(2) Now that we've already enquired for your article, will you please reply as soon as possible?

[Pattern 2] at one's request

(1) At your request, we send you the newest samples and our revised catalogue and price list for your reference.

(2) At your request, we make you an offer for Soybean.

[Pattern 3] owing to/in view of…

(1) Owing to the increasing exchange rate, we have redrafted our sales forecasts.

(2) In view of the increasing demand for this type of our products, our stocks have run very low.

[Pattern 4] referring to/ with (in) reference to …

(1) Referring to payment, we cannot do otherwise than L/C at sight.

(2) We have made all possible inquiries with (in) reference to the integrity of the firm you mentioned.

[Pattern 5] due to…

(1) Our inability to entertain new orders is due to the heavy bookings of order.

(2) The delay of the steamer was due to a heavy storm.

[Pattern 6] We shall appreciate it if you…

(1) We shall appreciate it very much if you will give us your most favorable price.

(2) We shall appreciate it if you will send us your latest catalogue for our reference.

[Pattern 7] We regret to inform/note you that…

(1) We regret to inform you that the goods are out of stock for the time being.

(2) We regret to note you that your counter-offer is beyond what is acceptable to us, as we cannot meet your requirement of payment.

[Pattern 8] available

(1) We greatly regret that the goods you inquired about are not available for the time being.

(2) Complete catalogues as well as samples are available to all on request.

[Pattern 9] be obliged

(1) We should be obliged if you would kindly quote your best price and state your best terms and discounts allowable.

(2) We should be obliged to you for a prompt reply.

[Pattern 10] remain (be) valid/firm/open

(1) How long does your offer remain valid?

(2) We have received your L/C No.2825, valid for shipment on or before May 20th, 2016.

8.9　Case Study

Ningbo Qianhu Trading Company, established in 1986, is a comprehensive trading company with import and export rights approved by the former Ministry of Foreign Trade and Economic Cooperation. The company's products include handicrafts, rush products, wood products, artisan products, textiles, luggage and so on. Its products are exported to the United States, Australia, the United Kingdom, Japan, South Korea and other countries. After receiving the inquiry from Mr. Martin Crown, Mr. Chen from the handicraft department of the company approached Mr. Martin Crown and issued a firm quotation for the brocade handbag.

8.10　Business Ethics

This week, a customer placed an order for a certain hand tool. As a salesperson, you selected a more cooperative supplier and decided to place an order. However, the supervisor of this hand tool factory is your college classmate. In this case, do you need to report to the company?

This is required in accordance with the Code of Business Ethics. Because this may involve the receipt of benefits. Although you have a clear conscience, you didn't take a penny from him, and you didn't take special care of him, it is true that under the same conditions, their prices are very good, and their quality is also good. And because we know each other and have friendship, this supplier is more cooperative, isn't it a good thing? Need to think so much?

Even if you are upright yourself, according to the rules, it is indeed necessary. Even if you are open and honest, will anyone think that when an order is placed between such acquaintances, will the factory pay you a secret commission in private after the order is shipped? Nobody knows. Therefore, in such situation, it is necessary to actively inform the company of potential conflicts of interest, and it is up to the boss or executives to determine whether to continue to place orders for this factory. Conversely, if the client has a good relationship with you and has a particularly good impression of you, when he visits, he even prepares a personal gift for you. Do you need to declare it to the company? For example, a client brought me a box of biscuits, do I still have to hand it in? Do I have to report to the boss?

There is actually benchmark here. In many foreign companies, the definition of gifts is "accompaniment gifts", such as a box of biscuits, a pack of coffee, a can of candy, or even a box of chocolates, which is naturally no problem. But what if the customer gives you a mobile phone? Then you need to inform the boss of this situation. If the boss asks you to accept it, you can keep it yourself, otherwise it will be handed over to the company. If measured from an economic point of view, the value of "souvenirs", by our definition, is less than USD50. If it exceeds, in accordance with the standards of professional ethics, the company should be truthfully informed. Otherwise, once the evidence is in hand, the company will never be soft-hearted.

Always be vigilant and pay attention to business ethics as a benchmark for your integrity and character. Over time, this will be one of your core competitiveness in the workplace. Don't think about taking shortcuts and making quick money. Any "fast" often represents "unstable foundation" and "many problems". You must adhere to your own bottom line, be honest and upright, have a stand, and have principles. Resolutely do not touch things that should not be touched, and resolutely do not make money that should not be earned. Giving up a little bit of interest in front of you can make your future more stable. Don't believe in the so-called "successful" experience of others relying on cheating, infringing on the interests of the old company, and making money by unscrupulous means. Society is developing and thinking is progressing. Those who do this are destined to be marginalized and despised by mainstream views.

《礼记大学》言：修身、齐家、治国、平天下。Among them, self-cultivation is the foundation of everything. If this step is not done well, everything else is impossible to talk about. Be yourself, be worthy of your conscience, and the road will go farther and wider. Small success depends on wisdom, and great success depends on virtue.

8.11　Exercises

1. Write a Reply According to the Incoming Email.

United Textile Ltd.

York House: Lawton Street

Liverpool: ML3 2LL

England

Tel: … Fax: … Email: …

Our Ref: CT-GZ
Your Ref:
July 29th, 2015
Guangdong Textiles Import & Export Corporation
779 East Dongfeng Road,
Guangzhou
China
Dear Sir,

Messrs. Brown & Clark of this city inform us that you are an exporter of all kinds of cotton bed sheets and pillowcases. We would like you to send us details of your various ranges, including sizes, colors, prices, and also samples of the different qualities of material used.

We are large dealers in textiles and believe there is a promising market in our area for moderately priced goods of the kind mentioned.

When replying, please state your terms of payment and discount you would allow on purchases of quantities of not less than 100 dozens of individual items. Price quoted should include insurance and freight to Liverpool.

Yours faithfully,
United Textiles Ltd.
Manager

2. Write a Letter as per the Following Particulars.

You are asked to write a letter to a foreign company for a trial order of table-cloths. The letter should cover at least the following points.

(1) What have you got the information of the foreign company?
(2) What is your desire?
(3) What are the details of your want?

3. Case Practice

Taking the introduction case of this chapter as the background, in the name of Mr. Martin Crown of Thomson's purchasing department, make an inquiry about the brocade handbags of Ningbo Qianhu Trading Co., Ltd.

Unit 9

Quotation and Offer

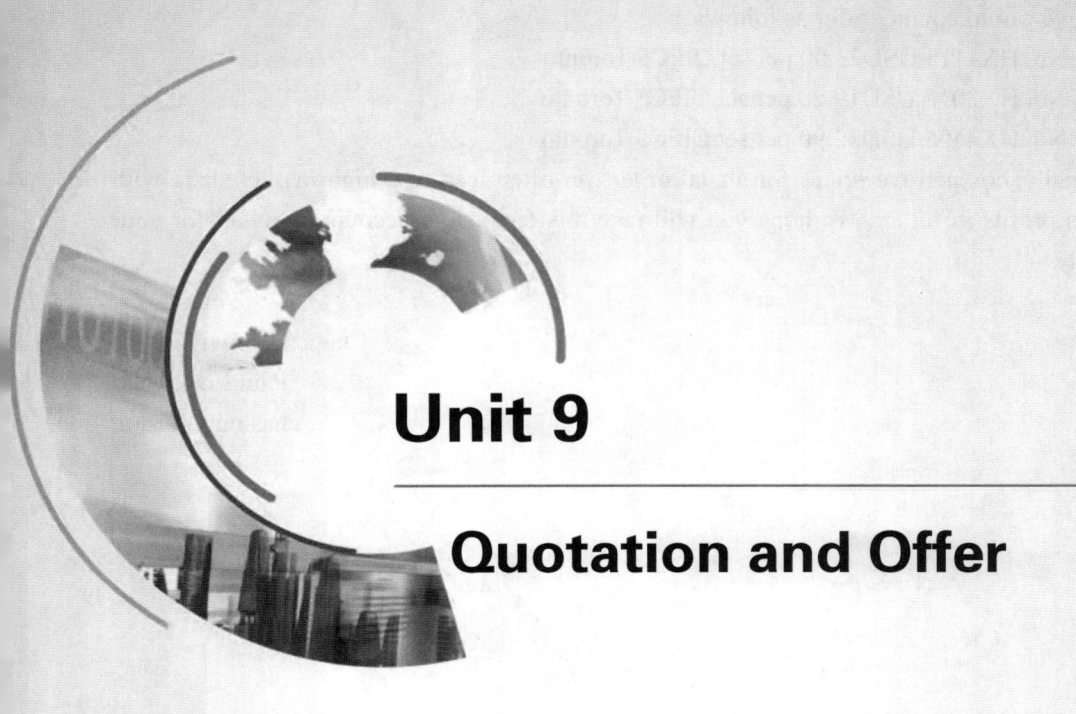

✧ **Case-Lead-in**

Founded in 1980, Huaxin Trading Co., Ltd. is a comprehensive trading company authorized by the state to import and export. Its business scope includes mechanical and electrical equipment, metal materials, building materials, chemical raw materials, light industrial products, etc. The company has a fixed relationship with a number of suppliers, the supply of solid foundation at the same time, in the face of the changeable international market, the company also attaches great importance to the development of new products. For example, the commodity department has developed a new product, the HX series of porcelain, in conjunction with its hook factory. This series is made of fine porcelain clay, packed in exquisite gift box, and hand-drawn pattern, beautiful and generous, high quality, very competitive. One day, the company received a counteroffer from the client James Brown & Sons as follows.

March 25th, 2021

Dear Mr. Huang,

Thank you for your email of March 16th, 2021 and your samples.

For your information, our customers are quite satisfied with the lab report of your samples, but they are still holding back.

After careful examining and comparison with similar products of other markets, we find your quotation is really much higher. Unless the prices could match with the market level, it is difficult to persuade customers to purchase from you.

So, we would counter offer as follows:

Art. No. HX1115 USD23.00 per set CIFC5 Toronto

Art. No. HX2012 USD19.20 per set CIFC5 Toronto

Art. No. HX4405 USD22.90 per set CIFC5 Toronto

Actually, competitive prices for a trial order can often lead to a high market share with enormous profits in future. We hope you will take this factor into account and wait for your early reply.

Yours truly,
James Brown & Sons
Paul Lockwood
Purchasing Division

9.1 Learning Objectives

(1) Understand some basic knowledge about quotation and offer.
(2) Can duly deal with the clients' inquiries effectively.
(3) Know the differences between the two types of offers.
(4) Acquire how to write a good and effective letter of quotation and offer.

9.2 The Importance and Nature of Offer

Making an offer or proposal is the most important step in negotiating the goods for export and import. Offer is conditions given by the seller or the buyer for making a contract. It can be given by both parties. If it is given by the seller, we call it a selling offer, but if it is given by the buyer, we call it a buying offer. The one, who volunteers to give conditions, is called offeror. The one, who accepts the condition, is called offeree.

The conditions mainly include the name of the commodity, Art. No., specification, quantity, price, packaging, terms of payment and delivery time. Therefore, whenever you received the inquiry, you must make an offer and provide all the detailed information the offeree requested.

Sometimes, if one hasn't received any inquiry letters, for expanding our export business, one can make an offer voluntarily. That's why one need selling offers.

9.3 Categories of Offer

There are two kinds of offers. One is firm, the other is non-firm offer or offer without engagement.

A firm offer is sent when the offeree accepts the offeror's terms and is ready to sign the contract. During the period of time stipulated in the firm offer, the offeror cannot withdraw or make any changes to the offer when the market is in declining. Once the offeree accepts his offer, the offeror must obey the terms and conditions he made. But after the valid time, the offer will become invalid. The offeror is no longer responsible for the obligations stipulated in the offer. Even if the offeree can accept the offer, the offeror has the right to refuse it. So when you make a firm offer, you must be careful of the following three points.

(1) The offer must be written clearly that the offer is firm.
(2) The offer must be clear, definite, complete and final and it must indicate all the main terms and conditions of the transaction.
(3) The offer must state the time of delivery.

Non-firm offer is the offer the offeror gives without any engagement with the offeror, and it does not necessarily contain all the things in a firm offer. It is not final, and often uses such words as "subject to prior sale" or "subject to our final confirmation".

9.4 Differences between Offer & Quotation

A quotation is a statement of the current price of an article you intended to sell. The distinctions between a quotation and an offer are the followings.

(1) A quotation is not legally binding on the seller.

(2) A quotation has no time of validity.

Offer not only includes the unit price of a commodity, but also contains other trade terms such as quality, quantity, delivery date, terms of payment etc. Unlike quote, price in an offer can not be changed easily after being offered.

9.5 Writing Skills

If you want to write a satisfactory offer, the following contents may be included:

(1) An expression of thanks for the enquiry.

(2) The details of offer, which includes: names of commodities, details of prices, quantity, packing, terms of payment and the date of delivery, etc.

(3) The promise on delivery date and the date of shipment.

(4) If it is the firm offer, state the validity of the offer.

(5) Hope of acceptance.

9.6 Typical Expressions for Letters Making Offer (See Table 9.1)

Table 9.1 Typical Expressions for Letters Making Offer

Writing Steps	Typical Expressions
(1) Thanks for the enquiry.	Many thanks for your inquiry of…
	Thank you for your enquiry and for your interest in our products.
	We thank you for your inquiry of…and are pleased to quote as follows.
(2) Provide the information required.	Please note our standard terms and conditions on the reverse side of this quotation…
	It is our usual practice to supply new customers with our goods for payment within one month from date of invoice, in the first instance, and later to extend this term to three months.
	Packing charges are included in the price, and we can make delivery whenever you wish.
(3) State the validity of the offer.	We must stress that this offer can remain open for three days only.
	Subject to being unsold/ to prior sale.
	This offer is firm, subject to your reply reaching us before 5 p.m. October 10th, our time.
(4) Hope of acceptance and await with the order.	We trust you will find our quotation satisfactory and look forward to receiving your order.
	We look forward to receiving your order soon.
	We will await with keen interest your formal order.

9.7 Specimen Letters

Letter 1: Request for Quotation for Crockery

Dear Sirs,

You have previously supplied us with crockery and we should be obliged if you would now quote CIF San Francisco for the items named below. The pattern we require is listed in your 2004 catalogue as No.8.

500 Teacups and Saucers,

200 Tea Plates,

100 2-pint Tea-pots

When replying, please state: (1) discounts allowable, (2) terms of payment, (3) earliest possible date of delivery.

Truly yours,

Fred Jackson

Letter 2: Exporter's Quotation

Dear Ms. Chen,

Thank you for your letter of April 5th, requesting for a further supply of our crockery, we are pleased to quote as follows:

Teacups……………USD500.00 per hundred

Tea Saucers………..USD200.00 per hundred

Tea Plates………….USD180.00 per hundred

Tea-pots, 2-pint …...USD3.00 each

Net CIF San Francisco

The above quotation is subject to our final confirmation. You are allowed a discount of 5% for items ordered in quantities of 500 or more. The terms of payment are by letter of credit at sight to be opened through the Bank of China and the shipment is to be made within four weeks upon receipt of the covering letter of credit.

We hope you will find these terms satisfactory and look forward to the pleasure of your order.

Yours faithfully,

Leon Allen

Letter 3: A Firm Offer from the Seller

Dear Sirs,

Your inquiry of April 21th asking us to offer you the subject article has received our immediate attention. We are glad to know that you are interested in our products.

We are making you an offer for 1500 sets of Aucma air conditioners of KFR-23GW at RMB3460 per set CFR Antwerp or any other European Main Ports for shipment during

June/July, 2012. As to the terms of payment, we require a confirmed L/C at sight in our favor.

Please be informed that this offer is valid for one week only because of the increase in the prices of raw materials.

We look forward to your prompt reply.

Sincerely yours,

Manager

Letter 4: A Non-firm Offer

Dear Sirs,

With reference to your enquiry of May 24th, we take pleasure in making the following offer.

5000 pieces of brocade handbags, at USD12.00/pc CIF Vancouver for shipment in August, 2003, for payment by irrevocable documentary L/C in seller's favor, which we hope you will find in order. Please note that this offer is subject to goods being unsold.

As we have received large number of orders from our other clients, it is quite probable that our present stock may soon run out. We would therefore suggest that you take advantage of this attractive offer.

We look forward to receiving your order.

Yours faithfully,

Manager

9.8 Situational Conversation

Making a Counter-offer

S: Ms. Yang, what's your idea of the price?

Y: The best we can do is USD820 per set.

S: I am afraid that's impossible. You can not expect us to reduce it to that extent.

Y: I think you are well informed about the prevailing market. Some Spanish firms are offering the same at much lower prices.

S: Price can not be taken separately from quality. A comparison of the quality of our products with that of rival goods will show you that ours is far superior.

Y: It is true that yours are of better quality. But your price is still on the high side even if we take the quality into consideration. How about meeting each other half way?

S: Well, I will have to think about it and give you a reply as soon as possible.

Y: OK, take your time please.

9.9　Useful Patterns & Examples

[Pattern 1] make/give/send sb. an offer for/on sth.

(1) Please make us an offer for 100 M.T. Of walnuts.

(2) We take pleasure in sending you an offer 50 sets of machine tools Model 70 as follows.

[Pattern 2] subject to

(1) This offer is subject to our final confirmation.

(2) This offer is firm, subject to your reply reaching here by 5 p.m. our time, Tuesday, August 6th.

[Pattern 3] in one's favor = in favor of sb.

(1) We have instructed our bank to issue an L/C in your favor for the amount of USD45000.

(2) Payment is by 100% confirmed and irrevocable sight L/C in favor of Longteng I/E Corp.

[Pattern 4] advise sb. to accept an offer

As the prices quoted are exceptionally low and likely to rise, we would advise you to accept the offer without delay.

[Pattern 5] send/give/make sb. one's best/lowest quotation for sth.

(1) Thank you for your enquiry of May 5th and we are pleased to send you our best quotation for walnut.

(2) Please make your lowest quotation for the lot on a CFR basis.

[Pattern 6] allow /offer/grant/give a special discount of…% on sth.

(1) We are prepared to allow you a 10% quantity discount if your order exceeds 200 cartons.

(2) In view of the longstanding trade relation between us, we grant a special discount of 5% this time.

[Pattern 7] in (out of) line with

(1) Our quotation always comes in line with the world market.

(2) The price you offered is out of line with the market, so it is beyond what is acceptable to us.

[Pattern 8] place a trial order with sb. for sth.

(1) Please place a trial order with us if you find our price competitive.

(2) We are prepared to place a trial order with you for fashioned shoes if your price is reasonable.

[Pattern 9] to entertain business at… price

(1) We can't entertain business at your price, since it is out of line with the prevailing market, being 20% higher than the average.

(2) It is impossible for us to entertain business at such price, since it is far below our cost price.

[Pattern 10] at /as per one's option

Our present rate of freight for cotton from A to B is USD10 per 40 cubic feet, at steamer's option.

9.10　Case Study

Michael has just received an inquiry on Oct.22nd from Johnson, purchasing Manager of Coast Co., Ltd., Republican of Ireland, which is one of long-term partners. As there is a big demand for half-sleeved cashmere sweater, He is making a prompt offer. Could you read this offer carefully and make a counter offer?

Dear Johnson,

We thank you for your letter of Nov. 3rd enquiry for 2000 pieces of half-sleeved cashmere sweater for shipment to Dublin.

Based on your demand of the items, we are making you, subject to your acceptance reaching us no later than Dec.20th, offer the followings.

Price: £198 per piece CIF Dublin.

Packing: In cartons.

Payment: Irrevocable letter of credit payable by sight draft.

Delivery: 15 days receipt of the L/C.

As you will have realized from the catalogue we sent you in October, our half-sleeved cashmere sweaters are perfect combination of warmth, softness and easy care. We are confident that you can do some profitable business.

Faithfully yours,

Michael

9.11　Business Ethics

Company A negotiates a procurement business with Company B. The salesmen of those two companies talked about the main purchase matters from the morning until 12 noon, both of them were tired and thirsty. The main reason why this negotiation was so delayed was that Company B wanted to pay by TT, which Company A had little contact with and therefore resisted. However, due to the long negotiation time, both parties in the negotiation were tired. The salesperson of Company B was in a hurry to leave, so the two parties signed a contract. A few days after the negotiation was completed, the salesman of Company A found that the contract did not specify the breach of contract, so he asked Company B to revise the contract, but Company B did not agree. However, Company A has not received the payment for the goods after sending the goods to Company B, so it called Company B. After inquiry, Company B found that although TT had been made, there was an error in the middle, and the payment was not sent to Company A. At this time, the seeds of distrust in the minds of the two parties had been planted, and Company A subsequently requested to renegotiate, but due to mutual distrust between the two parties, the negotiations were delayed.

Discussion:

(1) What makes the upfront negotiation process lengthy and contentious?

(2) What is the reason why the two sides cannot negotiate after the problem arises?

9.12　Exercises

1. Simulated Writing

Mr. Li received an offer from Mr. Smith, which lists the quotation for Phoenix Bicycles. Mr. Li thinks the quotation is on the high side. One reason is that the price of the same models dropped recently. Therefore, he asks for a 5% reduction of the quoted price. If ok, he will order 2000 items. Write a letter to Mr. Smith to state your opinion.

2. Problem Solving

Problem:

You represent Dongguan Mary Fashion Co., Ltd. Two days ago, Mr. Theo Kossowsky in Arcus Absorbents Inc., a new customer in Canada, sent an email to your corporation inquiring for Leisure Wear. How to deal with their specific inquiry?

Task:

Then make the Canadian client (Mr.TK@arcusabsorbents.com) a firm offer as per your own choice. The selling details are as follows.

- Product name: leisure wear.
- Model number: A0600105.
- Place of origin: China.
- Features.

(1) Deep V necked;

(2) With bead and embroidery;

(3) Composition: 85% cotton, 15% lycra;

(4) Price: USD24.6 per piece FOB Dongguan;

(5) Terms of payment: irrevocable L/C at sight;

(6) Inner packing: 1pc/polybag;

(7) Outer packing: 40pcs/carton;

(8) Shipment: within one month after receipt of the L/C;

(9) Remarks;

(10) No size and color limitation. Customized specifications are available.

3. Case Practice

The customer's counter offer constitutes a new offer. Based on the introduction case in this chapter, according to the above new offer, a counteroffer letter was written to James Brown & Sons Company of Canada in the capacity of Huangming, a salesman of Huaxin Company, requiring careful consideration. The counter-offer shall be made on the basis of not less than 10% of the profit.

Unit 10

Order and Acknowledgement

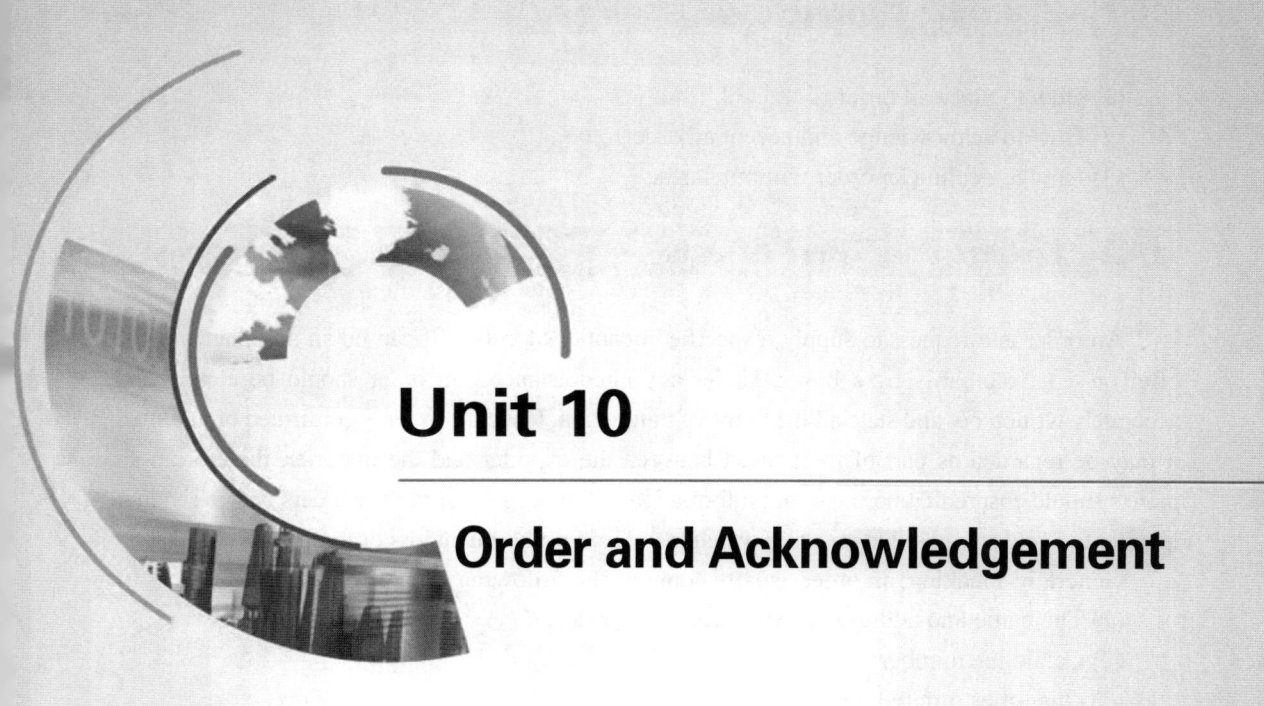

✧ **Case-Lead-in**

ABC Co., Ltd. is an import and export company of electronic computers and accessories, and has enjoyed a good reputation.

Clark, a foreign salesperson of ABC Co., Ltd. has got a repeat order of 500 sets of PC from BCD Co., Ltd. He will send an email to BCD Co., Ltd for thanking for regular orders from BCD Co., Ltd.

Requirements:

You are required to send an email to BCD Co., Ltd. as the role of Clark, according to the following tips.

Tips:
- Inform the customer of sending the ordered goods.
- Thank the customer for their regular orders.
- Satisfy the customer with fine quality goods at reasonable prices.
- Wish to get more further business opportunities.

10.1　Learning Objectives

(1) How to place an order.
(2) How to acknowledge and accept an order.
(3) How to decline an order without harm.

10.2　Orders and Their Effects

An order is a request to supply a specified quantity of goods. It can be an acceptance of an offer or sent voluntarily by a buyer. Under any circumstances, an order should be clearly and accurately written out and state all the terms of transaction. Once the order is confirmed or accepted, it may be regarded as part of the contact between the exporter and the importer, therefore both parties should ensure that no important information will be neglected in their orders before sending in order to avoid any possible mistakes which may lead to subsequent loss or trouble.

Generally speaking, an order usually contains the following information.
(1) The name and address of exporter and importer;
(2) Catalogue number;
(3) Quantities ordered;
(4) A full and accurate description of the commodities (such as name, type, size, color, specification, etc.);
(5) Price of the commodities, including unit price and total value;
(6) Packing and marking;
(7) Shipping company, shipping method, time of shipment, port of destination;
(8) Terms of payment;
(9) Other necessary information, including order number, order types, validity of the order, etc.

However, there are times when sellers cannot accept buyers' orders because the goods required are not available or prices and specifications have been changed. In such circumstances, letters rejecting orders must be written with the utmost care and with an eye to good will and future business. It is advisable to recommend suitable substitutes, make counter-offers and persuade buyers to accept them.

According to commercial law, the buyer's order is an offer to buy and the arrangement is not legally binding until the seller has accepted the offer. After that, both parties are legally bound to honor their agreement.

10.3　About Acknowledgement

Acknowledgement is a reply to an order, either to accept or to reject. When a seller receives his customer's order, he should acknowledge receipt of the order immediately.

A deal is concluded when the sell's offer is accepted by the buyer, or confirmed by the seller. In cases the buyer has made a counter-offer, or placed a firm offer, or confirmed a purchase with the seller, it should contain all necessary terms and conditions. After acceptance and confirmation, a Sales Contract or Confirmation made out by the seller is to be signed by both parties.

10.4 Writing Skills and Typical Expressions of Placing Orders (See Table 10.1)

Table 10.1 Placing Orders

Writing Steps	Typical Expressions
(1) Openings: make reference to the offer made by the reader and indicate that you are pleased to place an order.	Thank you for your quotation of … Please supply …
	We would like to confirm details of ordering the above mentioned goods.
	We have received your quotation and enclose our official order form.
	Please supply the following items as quickly as possible.
	We are pleased to place an order with you for the following goods.
	We confirm the order which was placed with you by telephone in this morning for the following…
	Please accept our order for the following items on our usual discount terms.
	Thank you for your quotation of July 5th. Our order number 123 is enclosed.
(2) State the details of your order.	Description of goods; Quantity; Price (unit price, amount, total …); Packing; Date and way of shipment; Payment terms and other terms.
(3) Closings: ask for confirmation of your order from your seller with the hopes of their attention.	We look forward to prompt delivery.
	Delivery is required not later than the end of this month.
	All these items are urgently required by our customer. We hope that you will send them as stipulated in the order.
	These items are urgently required. We understand that you are arranging for immediate delivery from stock.
	Please acknowledge receipt of this order and confirm that you will be able to deliver by …
	We hope to receive your advice of delivery by return of post.
	We hope that our handling of your first order with us will lead to further business between us and mark the beginning of a happy long time business relationship.

When you receive an order, you will ...

(1) Acknowledge the order (accepts the order), write a confirmation letter to acknowledge the order, or send a sales note to confirm the order (see Table 10.2).

(2) Reject the order.

(3) Offer substitute.

Table 10.2　Acknowledging Orders

Writing Steps	Typical Expressions
(1) Openings: express appreciation for the order received.	Thank you for your order dated …
	We thank you for your order number… and will dispatch the goods by …
	We are delighted to tell you that we have received your order No. … and will ship the goods by …
	We've received your order and will get started on it right away.
	Thanks for your order of No. …
	We were very pleased to receive your order of June 18th for cotton prints, and welcome you as one of our customers.
(2) Body: assurance of prompt and careful attention.	Assure the buyers the goods ordered will be delivered as requested.
	It is also advisable to take the opportunity to promote their products or to introduce other products.
(3) Closings: express your willingness to cooperate or suggest future business dealings.	It is our pleasure to serve you, and we hope you will give us that privilege again soon.
	We look forward to serving you again in the near future.
	We thank you so much for your order and look forward to being of service.
	We hope the goods reach you safely and that you will be pleased with them.
	We hope you will find the goods satisfactory and look forward to receiving your further orders.
	We are pleased to say that these goods have been dispatched today (will be dispatched in …/ are now awaiting collection at …).

The reasons for having to decline an order include that the goods required are not available; prices and specifications have been changed; the buyers and the sellers cannot agree on some terms of the business; the buyer's credit is not in good standing; or the manufacturer simply does not produce the goods ordered, etc.(see Table 10.3).

Table 10.3　Declining Orders

Writing Steps	Typical Expressions
(1) Positive openings: place the message in its correct communication context.	We were very pleased to receive your order of June 18th for cotton prints. Unfortunately, we are out of stock of the goods you ordered.
	We have carefully considered your counter-proposal of August 15th to our offer of wool sweater, but regret that we cannot accept it.
	We were pleased to receive your order of Nov. 2nd for vases. However, since you state the firm condition of delivery before Christmas, we regret that we cannot supply you on this occasion.
	Thank you for your letter of May 5th ordering … We regret to say that we can no longer supply this item.
	We are writing to let you know that we have to cancel your order No. dated … as the goods are out of stock at this moment.
(2) Body	Detailed and sensitive explanations or make counter-offers or offers suitable substitutes.
(3) A positive close—end the letter in the way that makes the reader aware	We are sorry not to be able to fulfill your present order immediately, but hope to hear from you soon that delivery at the beginning of next month will not inconvenience you unduly.
	We will always be happy to consider carefully any proposals likely to lead to business between us.

Continued

Writing Steps	Typical Expressions
of the writer's expectation for future business relations with him.	May I suggest you try … They usually carry large stocks and may be able to help you.
	If you decide to place an order for our recommended new stuff, please contact us.

10.5　Specimen Letters

1. Placing Orders

Complete information can be ensured by using the company's printed order that directly and clearly describes the items to be ordered.

Letter1: Printed Order Form

ABC Co., Ltd.
Address:
Telephone:

ORDER NO 123

DATE

CBA Co., Ltd.

Address:

Telephone:

Please supply

Quantity	Item(s)	Price(USD)
100	Cashmere blanket	340.00 each
100	Lambs wool blanket	100.00 each
100	Ladies lambs wool shawl	60.00 each

If you send an order by letter, make sure the information is complete and accurate. Note the following points to ensure that the letter order is accurate, complete and valid.

(1) List the necessary information in tabular form.

(2) List each item separately, with double space between paragraphs.

(3) State directly what you are ordering, not by implication. Use specific, direct words where appropriate, such as "we are writing you to place an order for XXX …" or "please ship XXX …" instead of vague language like "we are interested in XXX …" or "I'd like to …

(4) Provide complete information for each item, including the English name, quantity, catalog number, specification, unit price, total price, delivery time, packing requirements, transportation mark, etc.

2. Acknowledging Orders

If you accept an order, you need to confirm the acceptance of the order immediately. If possible, you can inform the buyer of the approximate delivery time, or you can also send a new catalog of the company's products to the customer for future purchase. Especially for the new customers of the initial order, it is better to express acceptance by letter, to show the importance and sincerity. If the delivery time cannot meet the customer's requirement, explain and give the earliest possible delivery time to see if the customer can accept it.

Letter 2: Acknowledge Regular Order
Dear Sirs,
Thank you for your order number 505 for Ladies Shawl.
As all items were in stock, they will be delivered to you in time.
We hope you will find these goods satisfactory and that we may have the pleasure of receiving further orders from you.
Yours sincerely

3. The Seller is Unable to Fully Accept the Order

If, upon receipt of an order, the seller fails to deliver the goods in full accordance with the terms and conditions set forth in the order, including time of delivery, price, quantity, specification, model, packing, payment method, etc., the seller may, depending on the specific circumstances, take the following measures:

(1) The seller may make a counter-offer and put forward its own terms and conditions to see if the buyer accepts them;

(2) The seller can provide substitutes to see if the buyer accepts;

(3) The seller may decline the buyer's order.

When a seller must decline a buyer's order, be sure to be careful about the wording and attitude of the letter so as not to jeopardize possible future business. A letter to decline an order is structured like a sandwich, with bad news in the middle rather than coming to the point. The letter to decline the order can be arranged as follows.

First, start to give a buffer, that is, thank the customer for the order, and repeat the following order. Instead of just saying no.

Second, explain why the order cannot be accepted and try to suggest alternatives, such as recommending other suppliers.

Then, clearly and definitely decline the order to avoid misunderstandings.

Finally, we can place our hopes on further business cooperation in the future.

Letter 3: Decline the Order as the Seller Can't Satisfy the Delivery Time Required
Dear Sirs,

We were pleased to receive your order of June 15th*. Unfortunately, we are out of stock of the model you ordered. This is due to the prolonged cold weather, which has increased demand considerably. The manufacturers have, however, promised us a further supply by the end of this month and if you can wait until then we will fulfill your order promptly.

We are sorry not to be able to meet your present order immediately, but hope to hear from you soon that delivery at the beginning of next month will not inconvenience you unduly.

Yours sincerely

Letter 4: Recommend Substitutes as Goods Ordered Are out of Stock

Dear Sirs,

Many thanks for your order of April 12th for sea breeze window air conditioners. You can be sure that your decision to buy them was a decision to buy the best in the market.

Unfortunately, your order cannot be filled as the line has been discontinued. However, we offer you, the latest range of split air conditioner. This latest model has several improvements and new features. This model has the following improved features and has been very popular with our other customers.

Remote controlled heavy-duty compressor noiseless is available in 3 sizes.

We are enclosing the illustrated catalogue including the above-recommended model, which we hope you will find satisfactory. They can be supplied from stock. If you decide to place an order, we can meet it within one week.

Please contact me if you have any queries.

Yours sincerely

10.6 Situational Conversation

Goods Unavailable

A: You've been doing a very good business with our green tea, I suppose.

B: Just so so, Mr. A, but today I'd like to find out if we can negotiate a contract for Menthol Crystal.

A: Menthol Crystal is in high demand these days. We are sorry, but nothing is available at the moment.

B: Unavailable? That's sudden. Last year you seemed to have a large stock. What's happened?

A: We've been flooded with orders. The goods are sold out.

B: You mean I'm late. What a shame! Mr. A, you know China is not the only exporter of Menthol Crystal. If you can't maintain the supply, buyers will look elsewhere. The market you have built up could be easily destroyed.

A: We are making efforts to enlarge output, but that can't be done overnight, demand is going up drastically. Production can't keep pace with it.

10.7 Useful Patterns & Examples

[Pattern 1] place an order with sb. for sth.

(1) We thank you for your quotation of September 20th and now place an order with you for the following items.

(2) In reply to your quotation of May10th, we are pleased to place an order with you for the products mentioned in the enclosed sheet.

[Pattern 2] book/give a trial order

(1) We shall book a trial order. If the quality is up to our expectation, we shall send another order in the near future.

(2) We thank you for giving us a trial order and promise that your order will be dealt with promptly and carefully.

[Pattern 3] to fill /execute/fulfill/work the order

(1) We regret that, owing to a shortage of stocks, we are unable to fill your order.

(2) We trust that you are able to fill the order at a low price.

[Pattern 4] confirm one's order

(1) We shall be grateful if you could confirm your order on the revised conditions.

(2) We confirm with you the following order for the pure cotton pillowcases at the prices in your letter.

[Pattern 5] to accept one's order

(1) Owing to heavy commitments, many orders haven't been completed. Therefore, we can only accept your order for October shipment.

(2) To our regret, we are unable to accept your order at the price requested, since our profit margin does not allow us any concession by way of price discount.

[Pattern 6] decline or cancel one's order

(1) While thanking you for your order, we have to explain that without supplies we have no alternative but to decline your order.

(2) After careful consideration on your request, however, we have come to the conclusion that we cannot but decline the said order.

[Pattern 7] order sth. at … price

(1) We have ordered 500 sets of milling machines at 1400 Euros per unit FOB Lisbon.

(2) We plan to order the following goods at the prices named after we received your catalogue and price list.

[Pattern 8] to sign and return a copy of … for one's file

(1) We have pleasure in informing you that we have booked your order No.123. We are sending you our Sales Confirmation No.632 in duplicate, one copy of which please sign and return for our file.

(2) Enclosed please find our S/C No.DF78 in duplicate. If you find everything in order,

please sign and return one copy for our records.

[Pattern 9] (handle the business)in this line

(1) Imes knows his business because he has been in this line for years.

(2) We have been in this line of business for more than twenty years.

[Pattern 10] supply from stock

(1) All the items in the catalogue can be supplied from stock.

(2) Can you supply from stock?

10.8　Case Study

B Co., Ltd. is an importer of foodstuff in Shanghai, China. Mary, a foreign salesperson of B Co., Ltd. has made a purchase order of 500 kgs first-class coffee from A Co., Ltd. She will send an email to A Co., Ltd. for confirming this order.

Requirements:

You are required to reply an email to A Co., Ltd. as the role of Mary, according to the following tips and attached purchase order.

Tips:

- Thank for email from A Co., Ltd.
- Confirm the details of the order.
- Enclose the purchase order.
- State the payment after receipt of the countersigned purchase order.
- Wish to get an early reply.

10.9　Business Ethics

Beechnut Deliberately Sells Adulterated Apple Juice

The product description says "100%" pure fruit juice, when it's actually a mixture of synthetic ingredients and is a "100% chemically synthesized fake cocktail".

The government notified the company of its unqualified inspection results and asked it to withdraw all products, but the company replied that the juice was not harmful to health and did not withdraw the product.

Ultimately, the company was convicted of adulterating and selling apple juice. Charges and scandals cost it an estimated USD25 million, with negative publicity causing the company to lose 20% of its market share, a huge loss.

Could a financial crisis be a reason for companies to sell adulterated juices?

Here comes the most vehement question of ethics, the relationship between the ends and the means of business activity.

In morality, ends and means are interrelated and mutually determined, ends determine means, and means serve ends. Business ethics emphasizes the consistency of ends and means. In pursuit of reasonable and legitimate interests, legitimate means must be chosen, not unscrupulous.

Beechnut believes that the company has fallen into a serious financial crisis, and the use of adulterated raw materials that are not easy to detect can save millions of dollars. Without looking ahead, what does it matter if the company does a little bit of a fake?

Beechnut believes that as long as the purpose of the company's survival is achieved, it doesn't matter what means is used. This practice seriously damages the ethics of business activities. Analyzing the dialectical relationship between moral purpose and means, we know that the unity of purpose and morality in means can ultimately achieve good results and embody and complete good motives. This is the ultimate standard for measuring good and evil.

Discussion:

(1) What lessons have been learned from Beechnut's approach?

(2) What are you going to do in the face of this moral dilemma if you're a Beechnut dispenser?

10.10 Exercises

1. Situational Writing

Write a letter based on the following situation.

Your company has accepted the buyer's order No.112 for Haier brand TV sets, please write and send the sales contract in duplicate. At the same time, the buyer is required to open a letter of credit immediately and guarantee that the goods will be shipped in time after receiving the letter of credit.

Steps:

(1) Accept order and send contract.

(2) Want to open L/C immediately and guarantee prompt shipment upon receipt.

(3) Concluding remarks.

2. Problem Solving

Problem: You are Zhao Qiang, the export manager in Zhuqing Graft & Gift Corporation. You have just received an order from Mr. Jari Kartano, the purchasing manager in IKEA, Norway Branch, as follows.

Commodity: Silicone Ice Tray

Model No. … : SIT002

Quantity: 1000 dozen

Color: red, pink, green, blue, yellow

Price: GB £19 per dozen

Payment: by confirmed and irrevocable L/C

Shipment: before the end of February

However, you find it very difficult for you to deliver the goods before the end of February. There are two main reasons: (1)you should produce the goods according to the buyer's design and it will need more time; (2)the Spring Festival is drawing near; it is difficult for you to arrange production during the holidays.

Task:

Then send a fax to Mr. Kartano to confirm the order.

3. Case Practice

Take the case-lead-in in this chapter as the background and send an email to BCD Co., Ltd. as the role of Clark, according to the listed tips.

Unit 11

Conclusion of Business

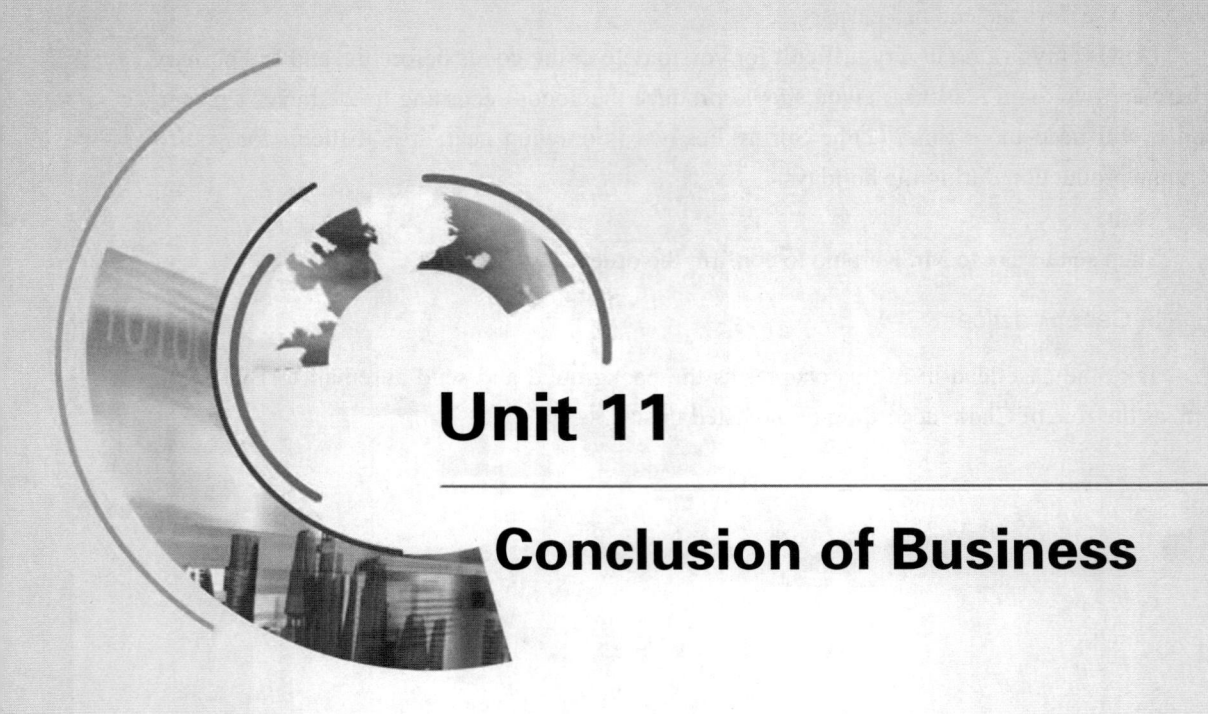

✧ **Case-Lead-in**

Ningbo Feiyang Home Appliances Co., Ltd. accepted the offer of 2000 fully automatic washing machines from Aston Canada, and sent a signing letter and a sales contract, asking the other party to sign it back as soon as possible, and looking forward to more cooperation in the future.

11.1 Learning Objectives

(1) Learn how to write letters of conclusion of business.

(2) Know the differences between sales confirmation and contract.

(3) Learn the structure, the components and the functions of sales confirmation and contract.

(4) Master the expressions and the words related to sales confirmation and contract.

11.2 Function of Contract

The main functions of an international business contract are as follows.

(1) It is an additional proof of rights and obligations, especially vital when the deal has been reached orally.

(2) It can act as guideline when both parties are implementing the whole deal.

A well-drafted contract spells out the rights and obligations of each party and protects you and your business to the most practical extent. It minimizes risks and protects the company in case of possible trade disputes, claims and/or legal actions. A good contract can increase your business, earn your respect, and let you make more money. A bad contract, on the contrary, can be disastrous.

11.3 The Contents of a Contract

After negotiations, both buyers and sellers agree with each other the terms and conditions they discussed. The buyer will write a letter to the seller to express his acceptance and readiness to place an order, and the seller usually sends an acknowledgement by letter after receiving an order. Once accepted and confirmed, the business is concluded.

A contract or a sales confirmation is made out, generally by the sellers, and signed by both parties. A contract is a formal agreement enforceable by law, which sets forth the rights and obligations for the parties involved in it. For smaller deals or transactions between regular business partners, a sales/purchase confirmation may be used instead of a formal contract. Though less detailed, a sales/purchase confirmation has the same legal effect.

The following contents of a contract are necessary in a contract.

1) Title of the contract
2) Preamble of a contract
(1) Contract No.
(2) Date of signing.
(3) Place of signing.
(4) Signing parties.

(5) Recitals of WHEREAS clause.

3) Body

(1) Definition clause: to give a specific explanation to the key words repeatedly appearing a contract, which have special meanings or easily cause misunderstanding and controversy.

(2) Specific conditions.

① Commodity
② Quantity
③ Unit price
④ Total value
⑤ Packing
⑥ Insurance clauses
⑦ Time of shipment
⑧ Port of shipment and destination
⑨ Shipping marks
⑩ Terms of payment

(3) General conditions.

① Duration
② Termination
③ Force majeure
④ Assignment
⑤ Inspection
⑥ Claims
⑦ Arbitration
⑧ Governing law
⑨ Jurisdiction
⑩ Notice

4) Witness clause

(1) Concluding sentence.

① Effecting date
② Applicable language and text
③ Number of original copies

(2) Signature.

(3) Seal.

11.4　Writing Skills

In writing letters talking about conclusion of business, the following points may be included:

(1) Thanking the senders for their offers/counter-offers or acceptance.

(2) Declaring that you accept the offer or confirm the acceptance from the senders and stating that you would like to conclude business with the senders according to the terms and conditions agreed upon (listing all the terms and conditions agreed upon in detail).

(3) Stating that you have enclosed an order form, a contract confirmation, or a sales confirmation and asking for the returning of one copy duly signed for your file (It may be not necessary, however, if a signed copy is not needed).

(4) Expressing your hope that the transaction would be conducted smoothly and successfully, and that business would be expanded in the future.

11.5 Typical Writing Steps of Conclusion of Business (See Table 11.1)

Table 11.1 Typical Writing Steps of Conclusion of Business

Writing Steps	Typical Expressions
(1) Thanks for the offers/ counter-offers or acceptance.	Many thanks for your offers/counter-offers and acceptance.
	Thank you for your cooperation on this negotiation.
(2) Declare your acceptance to the sender's offer and counter-offer as well as confirm the order with the certain terms and conditions.	We confirm having purchased from you 500 bicycles on the following terms and conditions.
	We are pleased to accept your offer and confirm this order with the following particulars.
(3) State that you have enclosed a contract confirmation.	We enclose our S/C No.10 in duplicate. Please sign and return one copy for our file.
	Enclosed are our 2 copies of Sales Confirmation No.145. Please send back one copy duly countersigned.
(4) Express your hope.	We are pleased to have finalized this business with you and expect that we can expand the trade between us in the future.
	We appreciate your cooperation and look forward to your early reply.

11.6 Specimen Letters

Letter 1: Letter of Request a Sales Contract

Dear Sirs,

Thank you for your letter of May 15th concerning our order No.09001.

As we have discussed all details in the past 2 weeks, we are pleased to accept your offer and confirm this order with following particulars.

Commodity	70gsm Copy Paper
Price	89RMB/Carton CFR Qingdao
Specification	500 pieces of A4 70gsm Copy Paper / Ream, 5 Reams/Carton; 100% wood-pulp made from Shandong Paper Mill
Quantity	10000 Cartons
Insurance	To be covered by the buyer

Please prepare the sales contract in English Version. After signing the contract we will apply for the issuing of the L/C in your favor at early stage.

We wish to thank you for your cooperation and hope that this transaction will pave the way for our long term business.

Yours faithfully,

Letter 2: A Reply to the Above

Dear Sirs,

We have received your letter of order confirmation dated October 4th with thanks.

Enclosed please find our signed Sales Contract No.09001 in duplicate. If you find everything in order, please counter-sign and return one copy for our file.

You may rest assured that your order will receive our best attention and the quality of our copy paper products will prove to be to your satisfaction.

Any comments kindly let us know.

Yours faithfully

Letter 3: Letter of Sending a Sales Confirmation and Discussing Related Clauses

Dear Sirs,

We are pleased to inform you that we were to receive your order of June 6th for our plush and stuffed toys.

We confirm supply of 5000 pcs of the plush toy elephant at the prices stated in your order No.66235 and will allow a 5% special discount on your order worth USD8000 or above. Our sales confirmation No.AK-312 in two originals was airmailed to you. Please sign and return one copy of them for our file.

It is particular to be noted that according to the stipulations of our S/C, your L/C should be confirmed, irrevocable as well as assignable, allowing 4% more or less both in amount and in quantity, gross for net. We wish to point out that stipulations in the L/C must strictly conform to those stated in our S/C so as to avoid subsequent amendments. You may rest assured that we will effect shipment without delay on receipt of your letter of credit.

We appreciate your cooperation and look forward to receiving further orders from you.

Sincerely yours,

Albert Jones

Export Manager

Letter 4: A Reply to the Above

Dear Mr. Jones,

Thank you for sending us the sales confirmation you prepared. We have checked the S/C and it is perfect. We will sign and return it to you before next week.

Regarding the requests you mentioned in your letter, you may rest assured that the L/C will strictly conform to your S/C, which is a confirmed, irrevocable, assignable L/C, allowing 4% more or less both in amount and in quantity, gross for net.

Thank you for your work and effort. We are looking forward to our next cooperation.

Sincerely yours,

James Green

Purchasing Manager

11.7 Situational Conversation

Miss Han: Mr. Green, before signing the contract, let's check the details again.

Mr. Green: OK. Let's do it now. On the whole, it seems perfect. But I think we need to further clarify the clause about packing. The clause doesn't mention the paper-divider used in packing.

Miss Han: Let me see. "Every 24 jars are put in a cardboard box after each jar is wrapped in tissue paper. The boxes are then put in wooden crates…"

Mr. Green: I remember we agreed that each jar is wrapped in tissue paper and then should be separated from each other by corrugated paper-dividers when packed in cartons.

Miss Han: Yes, that's right! I'll add that. Anything else?

Mr. Green: Yes, it's about the inspection clause. It only stipulates that the seller shall have the goods inspected by 15 days before the shipment. Can we add one more sentence that the buyer may have the goods reinspected by American General Administration of Quality Supervision, Inspection and Quarantine?

Miss Han: Of course. But it should be noted that you have the goods reinspected right after the goods' arrival at the destination, namely, the New York Port.

Mr. Green: OK, I agree. I have no more questions. Thanks for your friendly cooperation.

Miss Han: Same here! The revised contract will be ready for signing this afternoon.

Mr. Green: Great!

11.8 Useful Patterns & Examples

[Pattern 1] bring sth. to a conclusion

(1) Through mutual efforts, we have finally brought the business to a conclusion.

(2) Meetings can't go on forever so it's important to have a way to bring them to a conclusion.

(3) I'm sorry that I have not been able to bring our business to a more successful conclusion.

[Pattern 2] accept offer/confirm order/finalize the business

(1) We are pleased to accept your offer and confirm this order with the following particulars.

(2) We are pleased to have finalized this business with you and expect that we can expand the trade between us in the future.

[Pattern 3] in duplicate / in triplicate

(1) We enclose our S/C No.10 in duplicate. Please sign and return one copy for our file.

(2) Please draft the contract and note that the signed packing list in triplicate must accompany the original shipping documents.

[Pattern 4] to be noted that

(1) It is particular to be noted that the payment is to be made by confirmed, irrevocable L/C allowing partial shipments and transshipment, available by draft at sight.

(2) It is to be noted that T/T payment should be applied in our payment terms. Thus the L/C documents are no longer relevant and should be entirely removed from all clauses.

[Pattern 5] conform to

(1) Please note that the stipulations in the relevant credit should fully conform to the terms as stated in our S/C in order to avoid subsequent amendment.

(2) Should any inspected goods fail to conform to the specifications, the purchaser may reject the goods, and the supplier shall replace the rejected goods.

[Pattern 6] counter signed

(1) Enclosed are our 2 copies of Sales Confirmation No.145. Please send back one copy duly countersigned.

(2) As request, we return one copy of your Sales Confirmation No.145 completed with our countersignature.

[Pattern 7] rest assured

(1) You may rest assured that we shall effect shipment with the least possible delay upon receipt of the credit.

(2) You may rest assured that in our mutual interest, we shall do everything possible to give our full cooperation.

[Pattern 8] be up to

(1) We agree that the quality is up to the standard and the prices you quoted are satisfactory.

(2) We are very sorry to inform you that your last shipment is not up to your usual standard.

[Pattern 9] to enable

(1) Please amend the L/C immediately to enable the first shipment.

(2) I need to enable the order payment method to enable our clients call centre team to create orders in the system.

[Pattern 10] be enclosed

(1) A booklet including a general introduction, the scope of business and other topic is enclosed for your reference.

(2) We regret being unable to execute your order for silk to the pattern enclosed, which we now return.

11.9　Case Study

Mr. Anderson intended to sell a plane to Mr. Johnson. In his cable, Mr. Anderson offered: "Confirm sale of a plane… Please send 5000 pounds by telegraphic transfer." Mr. Johnson cabled back immediately: "Confirm purchase of your plane, terms and conditions same as your cable. I've sent the 5000 pounds to your Account Bank that keeps your money on your behalf until delivery of the plane. Please confirm delivery within 30 days from the date of this cable." Mr. Anderson did not reply and sold the plane to another buyer at a much higher price.

Disagreements occurred between the two parties about whether the contract was concluded effectively. In such a case, was the contract concluded? Why?

11.10　Business Ethics

Signing a Contract in Someone Else's Name Is Invalid!

On November 17th, 2021, consumer Wang complained to the Kaijiang County Consumer Rights Protection Committee, suspected of contract fraud, and asked the Consumer Council to deal with it.

After investigation, the Kaijing County Consumer Rights Protection Committee found that Wang's father was coaxed by others on March 25th, 2021, and signed a "model house move-in contract" with a household sales department in Kaijiang County in the name of Wang and paid a deposit. 20000 yuan. Wang said that the contract was not an expression of his true intentions, nor was it signed by his father, and asked for help returning the deposit of 20000 yuan and rescinding the decoration contract.

After investigation, the contract was signed by Lu Mou, a staff member of the sales department. Since the decoration contract only stipulates the price, but does not stipulate the quality of the decoration, it is an unequal standard contract and loses its fairness. Wang and his father did not authorize in writing or verbally authorize others to sign the decoration contract on their behalf, and the contract they signed was invalid.

After mediation, the sales department returned a one-time deposit of 20000 yuan paid by Wang's father.

11.11　Exercises

1. Situational Writing

Situation:

If one party is not satisfied with the sales confirmation, it can ask for amendment to it. Lanlu Import and Export Company mainly engaged in the silk products business. Silicoo Trade Company is the main importer of silk product in UK. It is the first time they cooperate with each other. After several rounds of business negotiation, they finally reach an agreement.

Task:

Suppose you work in Lanlu Import and Export Company. You have already made out the sales confirmation. Now you write a cover letter enclosed with the S/C No. LV-3901 in duplicate to Silicoo.

2. Problem Solving

Problem:

Suppose you work in Newstyle Trade Company. You did not get the import license for 1000 pcs of silk scarf which was agreed by both your company and your supplier before and this quantity has been stipulated in the S/C No.20111253. According to the current import license you've got, you can only import 800 pcs.

Methods:

On behalf of your company, write a letter to your supplier, and ask for amendment to S/C. Explain the reason with appropriate tone.

3. Case Practice

Work in pairs. Linda of Sunshine Electrical Company is checking the draft contract with Bland of Chicago Import and Export Company. Making a conversation practice with the help of the instructions below.

Linda of Sunshine Electrical Company
- Show the draft contract.
- Ask your partner to check the draft contract.
- Give your opinion on the inspection clause.
- Ask whether there are other parts that need to be revised.
- Tell your partner when the contract will be ready.
- Suggest the place.

Bland of Chicago Import and Export Company
- Express your appreciation for your partner's hard work.
- Check the draft contract and point out the inspection terms that need revising.
- Express your agreement on inspection terms.
- Tell your partner that you agree on other terms.
- Ask where the contract is to be signed.

Unit 12

Payment Methods

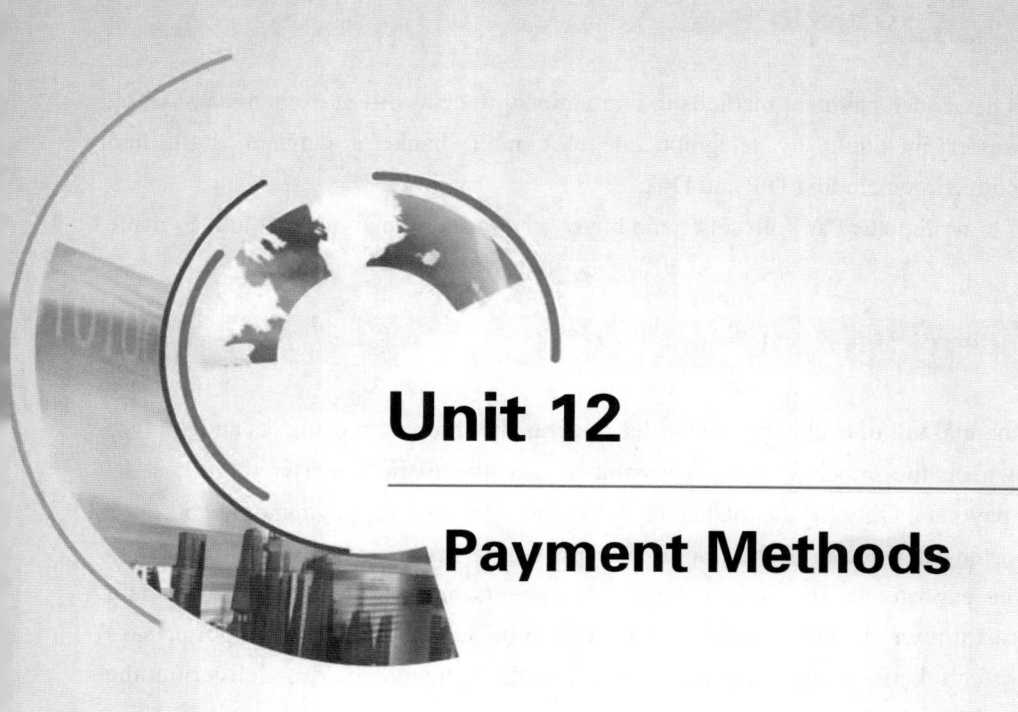

✧ **Case-Lead-in**

A Chinese company imported 200 metric tons of steel on FOB Vessel New York basis at the price of USD242 per metric ton. The importer established the L/C on time for USD48400, but the US exporter required the importer to increase the amount of the L/C to USD50000, otherwise, any export tariff and certificate fee should be paid by the importer separately by T/T.

Question: Is it reasonable for the US exporter to do so?

12.1　Learning Objectives

(1) Understand such payment methods in international trade as bill of exchange issued by the seller, transfer including by telegraph or telex mail, banker's demand draft, and documentary collection including D/P and D/A.

(2) Learn to write letters as both seller and buyer when using the above methods to make payment.

12.2　Modes of Payment

(1) Commercial bill of exchange. The seller presents the shipping documents and a bill of exchange drawn on the importer through a bank or directly to the importer to request its acceptance or payment. Only for the trusted buyer can the seller use this payment method.

The exporter often requires the importer to provide a bank for not very trustworthy customers. The exporter delivers the shipping documents only after that bank has paid against the draft drawn on them. In the case of a time bill of exchange, the exporter asks that the importer's bank accept and return the bill of exchange before delivering the documents.

(2) Bank transfer. It includes wire transfers (T/T, Telegraphic Transfers) and mail transfers (M/T). Payment by bank transfer means that the importing bank (remitting bank) transfers the funds in the importing party's bank account to the exporter's bank account by letter, telex, telegram, or the Internet through contact with the exporting bank.

(3) Banker's Demand Draft (BDD). The importer pays the local bank for the goods. The bank issues a demand draft on the exporter's bank with the exporter as the payee and gives it to the importer. The importer sends the bill of exchange to the exporter. The exporter presents the draft to the local bank for payment.

(4) Collection. The exporter draws a bill of exchange on the importer after the goods are shipped and entrust the bank of the exporting place (remitting bank) to collect the payment on their behalf through its branch or correspondent bank in the place of import. According to whether shipping documents accompany the bill of exchange, the collection is divided into a clean collection and a documentary collection.

According to the exporter's delivery conditions of the shipping documents, the documentary collection is divided into documents against payment (D/P) and documents against acceptance (D/A). D/P is divided into D/P at sight and D/P after sight according to the tenor of the bill of exchange.

12.3 Writing Skills and Typical Expressions (See Table 12.1—12.4)

Table 12.1 Exporter to Importer

Writing Steps	Typical Expressions
Openings	We have considered your letter of … and are pleased to grant the open account terms asked.
	We enclose your statement for the month of … showing an outstanding balance of USD …
	As requested in your letter of …, we have drawn on you for the amount of our April account at 3 months from…
	As agreed in our earlier correspondence, we have drawn on you for the enclosed invoice amount.
Closings	Please accept the draft and return it as soon as you can.
	We are willing to put your account on a documents-against-acceptance basis.
	We have instructed our bank to hand over the shipping documents against acceptance (payment) of our draft.
	Shipping documents and our acceptance draft have been passed to the… bank.
	As arranged, we have instructed our bank to surrender (hand over) the documents against payment (acceptance) of our draft.

Table 12.2 Importer to Exporter

Writing Steps	Typical Expressions
Openings	We have received your invoice number … and agreed to accept your draft 60 days after sight for the amount due.
	Thank you for your letter together with our November statement.
	We are sorry to have to ask for the term of your bill dated … to be extended for one month.
	We regret that we cannot meet in full our acceptance, which is due for payment on …
Closings	Please draw on us for the amount due and attach the shipping documents to your draft.
	Please let us know whether you are prepared to give us open-account terms.
	We want payment by bill of exchange at 60 days sight and would be glad if you agree.
	Our acceptance will be honored upon presentation of the bill at the branch of the… bank.

Table 12.3 Exporter to Remitting Bank

Writing Steps	Typical Expressions
Openings	We enclose our sight draft on … of … and the shipping documents.
	Please surrender the enclosed documents to … when they accept our draft.
	Please instruct your correspondence in … to release the documents only on payment of our sight draft for …
Closings	Please obtain acceptance of this draft before surrendering the shipping documents.
	Please present the bill for acceptance and then discount it for the credit to our account.
	Please present this acceptance for payment at maturity and credit us with the proceeds.

Table 12.4 Importer to Bank

Writing Steps	Typical Expressions
Openings	We enclose the accepted bill, drawn on me by …, and should now be glad to receive the shipping documents.
	Please accept and pay the following drafts for us and, at maturity, debit them to our account.
Closings	Please accept the above draft and debit your charges to our account.

12.4 Specimen Letters

Letter 1: The Direct Transaction with a Trusted Buyer

Dear Sirs,

We thank you for your order of June 25th for 5000 dozen of women's cashmere shawls at the quoted price of USDxxx CIF Tokyo per dozen.

The shawls are now ready for dispatch and will be shipped by the SS Golden Star sailing from Qinhuangdao on July 18th.

We are pleased to enclose shipping documents. Also enclosed is our sight draft drawn on you as agreed. Your immediate payment will be appreciated.

Yours sincerely

Letter 2: The Direct Transaction with an Unknown Customer

Dear Sirs,

We are pleased to inform you that we can supply the fancy leather goods included in your order No.123 of August 3th and by our draft at 30 days for acceptance by your bankers.

Immediately after we receive the accepted draft, we will arrange to ship the goods.

Meanwhile, we are holding them for you.

Yours faithfully

Letter 3: The Buyer Requests an Extension of Time

Dear Sirs,

You informed us on November 25th that you intended to draw on us at 60 days for the amount due on your invoice number ML525, namely UDS6800.54.

Until now, we have had no difficulty in meeting our obligations and have always settled our accounts promptly. We could have done so now had it not been for the bankruptcy of one of our most important customers. We would be most grateful if you could draw your bill at 90 days instead of 60 days. It would enable us to meet a temporarily difficult situation forced upon us by circumstances we could not foresee.

Yours sincerely

Letter 4: Seller's Reply Granting the Request

Dear Sirs,

We are replying to your November 30th letter asking for an extension of the draft's tenor from 60 to 90 days.

Given the special circumstances you mentioned and the promptness with which you have settled your accounts in the past, we are willing to grant the request. Our draft, drawn at 90 days, is enclosed. Please add your acceptance and return it to us.

Yours sincerely

12.5 Useful Patterns & Examples

[Pattern 1] agree with

(1) We have received our statement for the quarter that ended September 30th and find that it agrees with our books.

(2) This effectively means that the government does not agree with the proposal.

[Pattern 2] have no difficulty in doing sth.

(1) Until now, we have had no difficulty in meeting our obligations and have always settled our accounts promptly.

(2) If you can make headway this way, you will have no difficulty in ascending.

[Pattern 3] be left with no choice but to do sth. (have no choice but to)

(1) We have no choice but to vote it down.

(2) As a matter of stand, we have no choice but to ask you to accept our sight draft.

[Pattern 4] meet sb's obligations

(1) Never in the ensuing years had it failed to meet obligations.

(2) The builders failed to meet their contractual obligations.

[Pattern 5] take further proceedings

(1) We hope to receive a payment within the next few days to avoid our having to take further proceedings.

(2) The workers decided to take judicial proceedings against the company.

[Pattern 6] pass (hand over) the bill of lading (shipping documents) against payment (acceptance) of the draft

(1) The bank will instruct their correspondent in London to pass the bill of lading to you against payment of the draft.

(2) Please arrange for your correspondent in London to obtain payment of the amount due before handing over the shipping documents, and let us know when payment has been made.

[Pattern 7] take special care

(1) Take special care tonight because the road is icy.

(2) We have taken special care to include in the consignment only items suited to

conditions in the local place.

[Pattern 8] subject to

(1) Subject to satisfactory references and regular dealings, we would be prepared to consider open-account terms with quarterly settlements.

(2) Egypt had agreed to a summit subject to certain conditions.

[Pattern 9] take up

(1) Please hand the documents to ABC Co. as soon as they are ready to take them up against payment due.

(2) Increasingly, more wine-makers are taking up the challenge of growing Pinot Noir.

[Pattern 10] place the transaction on a cash basis

(1) We had no choice but to follow our standard practice of placing the transaction on a cash basis with new customers.

(2) We will conclude the business (transaction) on a cash basis.

12.6　Case Study

Company A from China exported to Company B of the Republic of Korea. Payment was to be made by D/P at 90 days after sight. After the shipment of goods, draft and shipping documents were sent to the foreign collection bank through the remitting bank in the exporter's country. Company B had accepted the draft. After the arrival of the goods at the port of destination, Company B presented the trust receipt and took delivery of the goods for resale in advance against the borrowed shipping documents from the local collecting bank, because Company B was in urgent need of the goods. When the draft was falling due, Company B became insolvent because of poor management. The collecting bank informed the remitting bank that the drawee rejected the payment and suggested Company A to collect the money back directly from Company B. There was another 30 days left before the draft was due.

Question: Please analyze the possibilities of getting back the money when the draft is on due, and provide your suggestions of how to solve the problem.

12.7　Business Ethics

Chinese philosopher Confucius emphasized creating an ethical society based on human interaction rather than the belief in an afterlife. Although Confucianism doesn't deny the existence of God or an afterlife, Confucius held that humans are incapable of knowing or understanding such things, so they should focus on creating an ideal society in this life.

According to Confucianism, correct behavior is more about developing the greater good than acting in one's own self-interest isn't inherently bad, but Confucius and his followers considered acting for the good of society to be a more righteous path.

The Confucian theory of ethics also teaches that circumstances can determine what's ethical and what isn't. So although lying may be unethical in most situations, it can be ethical when doing so serves the greater good when a lie can prevent a murder, for example.

In business, Confucian ethics are similar to the golden rule. In one translation of his works, Confucius is credited with saying: "What one does not wish for oneself, one ought not to do to anyone else; what one recognizes as desirable for oneself, one ought to be willing to grant to others".

12.8 Exercises

1. Situational Writing

Luck &Joy Company in New York intends to import some products from China Cloths Imp. & Exp. Corp. The importer suggests D/A payment because the order is small and the profits are little. But the exporter insists L/C payment because it is the first order from the Luck & Joy Company and it needs the protection from the bank.

Task:

(1) Suppose you are the representative of the Luck & Joy Company, please write a letter advising the payment by D/A on the basis of your company's benefits.

(2) On behalf of China Cloths Imp. &Exp. Corp., you write a reply, insists that the payment should be effected by L/C instead of D/A payment and explain the reasons.

2. Problem Solving

Problem:

Sullivan Brothers Co. is one of the largest producers in pharmaceutical industry in Canada.

Their product SWEET SNOW BRAND ANTIVIRAL ORAL LIQUID is warmly accepted in European market for years. On the light of the excellent reputation and high-quality products, Sullivan Brother Co. only accept terms of payment by L/C in any circumstances and consider L/C as their usual practice.

Task:

Xuehua Pharmaceutical Co., Ltd. is a fast developing Chinese company in line of pharmaceutics for three years. This company intends to import a large amount of SWEET SNOW BRAND ANTIVIRAL ORAL LIQUID. After settling on price, quality and quantity, you suggest payment by half L/C and half D/P for the following reasons.

- Chinese market has not been opened up;
- Your order is substantial;

- You're a new customer of the exporter;
- Your credit is trustworthy.

Solutions:

Sullivan Brothers Co. refuses to make payment by half L/C and half D/P, but agrees to allow a 3% commission and early shipment to help with the turnover of the Xuehua Pharmaceutical Co., Ltd.

Unit 13

Packing

✧ **Case-Lead-in**

Our company has imported a batch of gloves. According to the contract, there will be 100 cartons, 60 pairs per carton. After the goods arrived Dalian, we found the packing had been changed to 120 cartons, 50 pairs per carton. The seller made the changes without a previous notice to us. So is it reasonable for us to refuse the goods and file a claim against the seller?

13.1 Learning Objectives

(1) To master the packing way, understand the packaging link's role in foreign trade.

(2) Understand the international trade of goods packaging material types, considering the characteristics of the commodity and mode of transportation to determine different packaging requirements.

(3) Grasp the vocabulary of packaging, can write an email about packing.

13.2 Types of Packing

In international trade, goods can be bulk, bare, and packaged.

- Cargo in Bulk refers to goods that can be loaded on transportation without packaging, such as coal, grain, ore, and oil. The loading and unloading of such goods require the corresponding terminal handling equipment.
- Naked cargo (naked cargo/without outer packing) refers to goods naturally formed into pieces without packaging or a little processing and tying. Generally, the quality does not receive external influence, such as wood or steel, the natural number of pieces.
- Packed cargo refers to the goods that must be packaged to protect the integrity of the quality and quantity of goods in the circulation process to facilitate the transportation, storage, and sales of goods.

13.3 Function of Packing

Packing can be divided into two types: the transport packing (outer packing) and sales packing (inner packing). As we know, the former is for protecting the goods against damage or losing while the latter is for prettifying the goods.

13.4 Writing Skills

When writing letters concerning packing, we should observe the following rules.

(1) Requests should be concise and clear.

(2) Reasons should be persuasive.

(3) Give necessary information or description.

(4) Determine any changes in packing mutually before shipment.

13.5 Typical Expressions for Letters of Packing (See Table 13.1) and Replies (See Table 13.2)

Table 13.1 Typical Expressions for Letters of Packing

Writing Steps	Typical Expressions
(1) Pleasant opening/ To inform the receiver that you would like to discuss packing.	We appreciate your letter of ...
	We are now composing this letter to discuss the packing of ...
	We wish to order ... if you can meet the following packing requirements.
(2) To express detailed requests such as packing materials and costs.	The relative clause should be ... packing: In addition, directive marks should be ....
	We write to you regarding the packing of ..., and we would like you to have the goods packed in ...
	On the outer packing, please mark the ..., and directive marks like ... should also be indicated.
(3) Express the wish that the receiver can accept this packaging requirement and early reply.	Please let us know whether you can meet these specifications and whether you will increase your prices.
	We should be grateful if you accept these requirements.
	Please let us know whether you can meet these requirements.
	We look forward to your early confirmation.

Table 13.2 Typical Expressions for Replies

Writing Steps	Typical Expressions
(1) Express your appreciation for receiving the letter and your main idea.	We have received your letter of ... concerning packing details.
	We regret our inability to agree to your requirements for packing the goods in ...
	Thanks a lot for your packing instructions, but we regret our inability to comply with your request for special packing.
(2) Write your opinions or solutions to the packaging?	We shall pack .. .in ... instead of in ... as...
	To ..., we would like to make the following suggestions for your consideration.
(3) Express the hope of confirming your proposal and a pleasant ending.	We would like your confirmation on the packing.
	We hope you will accept our packing and assure you of our sincere cooperation.

13.6 Specimen Letters

Letter 1: Buyer's Request for Making the Specific Requirement for Packing

Dear Sirs,

We are glad to inform you that our clients are quite satisfied with the packing of their previous order.

As for the packing of 2400 bicycles under your S/C No. K-L-23, we suggest you have them packed each in a corrugated cardboard pack and 10 in a wooden case and then 240 in a container.

We hope these requirements can be met and look forward to your confirmation.

Yours faithfully

Letter 2: Reply to the Above

Dear Sirs,

We have received your letter of August 1st and are glad to inform you that we will pack 2,400 bicycles under our S/C No. K-L-23 if required, namely each in a corrugated cardboard pack and 10 in a wooden case, and then 240 in a container. The whole cargo would therefore comprise 10 containers.

Dispatch could be made within 30 days after receiving your irrevocable L/C at sight.

We are looking forward to your L/C.

Yours faithfully

Letter 3: Buyer's Request for Shipping Marks

Dear Mr. Alexander Wax,

Greetings.

We are writing regarding the packing of Order No.121 (Hardness Tester RH-150).

Regarding the packing of testers, we would like you to have the testers packed in plastic carry cases against moisture individually, and cases are packed in boxes of 100 each. The goods' outer packing must be seaworthy and can stand rough handling during transit. In addition, directive marks should be "Fragile". And the name of the country of origin of the goods must be marked on every package, weight, and dimensions.

Yours faithfully

Letter 4: Reply to the Above

Dear Ms. Fenny,

Thank you for your packing requirements. We will make sure to meet all the requirements.

Pictures of plastic carry cases and specifications are attached. All cases shall have an inner lining of waterproof paper against moisture. The goods will be outer packed in strong wooden cases suitable for export with directive marks "Fragile". And the official mark required by authorities will be marked on every package, as weight and dimensions.

We are very grateful to have your opinion about packing. We hope you will accept our packing and assure you of our sincere cooperation.

Best Wishes,

Alexander Wax

13.7　Useful Patterns & Examples

[Pattern 1] be packed in ...

(1) The goods are packed in strong export wooden cases.

(2) The chemical fertilizer is packed in plastic drums of 25kg net each with sealed double PVC plastic bags inside.

[Pattern 2] in ... of...each

(1) The book is packed in plastic in lined waterproof cartons of ten copies each.

(2) Piers are packed in boxes of 2 dozen each.

[Pattern 3] in bulk

(1) Nowadays, more people buy coffee in bulk and brew at home instead of purchasing pricey solo drinks.

(2) The transport system for coal, crude oil, grain in bulk, and cement in bulk has been continuously improved.

[Pattern 4] be protected against

(1) The Hardness Testers must be well protected against dampness, moisture, and rust.

(2) These cartons are well protected against moisture by plastic lining.

[Pattern 5] to be lined with

(1) The cartons for packing eggs are lined with the shake-proof corrugated paper board.

(2) The packing should be double bags lined with Kraft paper.

[Pattern 6] be secured

(1) We do not object to packing in cartons, provided the flaps are glued down, and metal bands secure the cartons.

(2) Each carton is lined with a shake-proof paper board and secured by overall strapping.

[Pattern 7] to be wrapped in ...

(1) The goods will be wrapped in Kraft paper and packed in wooden cases.

(2) The strawberries are wrapped in plastic gift boxes with fashion patterns suitable for gifts and self-consumption.

[Pattern 8] in ... condition

(1) The goods arrived in good condition.

(2) If the goods should arrive in a damaged condition, please inform us at once.

[Pattern 9] ... proof (waterproof/ shake-proof/leakage-proof/sound-proof)

(1) I can assure you that all the cartons are lined with plastic sheets, so they're waterproof.

(2) The storage place shall be clean, hygienic, high temperature and leakage-proof, and far away from the source of pollution.

[Pattern 10] be marked/stenciled/printed with ...

(1) All the goods exported should be marked with "passed-equality" by the local

commodity inspection bureau.

(2) Per our usual practice, every case should have a stenciled shipping mark with our initials on a diamond.

13.8　Case Study

British Moore Company with the condition of CIF, bought from LanTuo Company 300 cases of canned fruit in Australia. The contract with a provision reads: "Packed in carton, 30 tins in each carton." It was found that 150 cases that the seller delivered were 30 tins in each carton, the rest were 24 tins per box. The buyer refused the goods while the seller argued that 30 tins per box is not an important part of the contract, and with the quality, no matter it was 30 or 24 tins per box, it was correspond to the contract's quality requirement, therefore, the buyer should accept.

Question:
Please analyse the case.

13.9　Business Ethics

New Ways to Pack

There are many exciting new biodegradable packaging solutions coming along.

Plant-Based: this is made from biological sources—everything from mushrooms and seaweed to corn and food waste.

Edible: this also comes from biological sources, going one step further by being safe to eat!

Plantable: these have seeds embedded in them, a fun idea for customers. They work well for containing small, lightweight items such as cosmetics or jewellery, and can also be used as fillers or product wraps.

Compostable and biodegradable plastic alternatives: these are made out of materials that can be composted at home and commercially. They're often made from plant-based polymer that can break down in compost.

The basic idea of packaging is not just to appeal to the consumer, but at the same time ensure that the content inside is intact. Sustainable packaging materials are made up of products that are recyclable and reusable, but they may not be as efficient as plastic and other thicker packaging materials that ensure product safety.

13.10　Exercises

1. Write a Reply According to the Incoming Email

Suppose you are a staff in Hangzhou Silk Knit Export Corp. Write an email to T.G.

Cooper advising the new mode of packing for its order of shirts.

Your company has made a comparative study between carton and wooden case and found that packing in carton has many advantages. For example, it is fairly fit for ocean transportation; it is well protected against moisture by plastic liner; it is light in weight and easy to handle.

2. Situational Writing

Situation:

An import company in the United States would like to import 50 metric tons of China Black Tea from a Chinese export company. Your supervisor has assigned you to request that the export company send the product design together with the quotation, and the inner packing should use window packing so that the tea packed in the cartons/boxes can be seen directly. Also, your supervisor requested that the country of origin and indicative mark "Keep Dry" appear on the outer packages.

Task:

Follow your supervisor's request, please write a letter to the Chinese export company.

Unit 14

Shipment

✧ **Case-Lead-in**

Fior Co., Ltd trades in the garden furniture which is designed and made in the UK. Cheng Yin, a salesperson of Fior Co., Ltd. has got the early shipping email from Mike of Amber Co., Ltd. She will send an email to Mike for refusing the early shipment.

14.1 Learning Objectives

(1) Learn to write inquiries for sailing schedules and freight rate.
(2) Learn to write a reply to the above inquiry.
(3) Learn to write shipping instructions.
(4) Learn to write shipping advice.

14.2 About Shipment

The assumption of responsibility for transport in international trade varies depending on the trade terms used in the trade contract or the contract's provisions. Using Incoterms 2020 Group F trade terms for the transaction, transportation is the importer's responsibility. The exporter has to prepare the goods, and importers are responsible for chartering a ship, booking shipping space, and nominating means of transport, so the two sides must do a good job of the interface.

If the transaction is concluded with the trade terms of Group C, transportation is the exporter's responsibility. The exporter is responsible for chartering a ship or booking shipping space and should send the shipment advice to the importer in time so that the importer can be ready to receive the goods.

Due to the complexity and professionalism of international cargo transportation, traders often charter ships, book ship space, pick up goods, and store warehouses through freight forwarders on their behalf.

International cargo transportation link correspondence generally involves flight and freight rate consultation and reply, charter booking, the importer to the exporter issuing shipping instructions, and the exporter to the importer issuing a shipping notice.

14.3 Method of Shipment

In international trade, shipment can be made by sea, air, rail, truck and parcel post. In order to deliver goods more efficiently, we also have multimodal transport and land bridge transport.

14.4 Writing Skills and Typical Expressions

Writing skills and typical expressions are as follows (see Table 14.1—14.4).

Table 14.1 Inquiry for Sailings and Freight Rates

Writing Steps	Typical Expressions
(1) Openings.	Please let us know the current rates of freight for the following:

Continued

Writing Steps	Typical Expressions
(1) Openings.	Please quote an inclusive rate for collection and delivery of … from …
	Please quote the rate for freight and send us details of the sailings and the time usually taken for the voyage.
(2) Descriptions of the goods to be shipped.	We shall shortly have ready for Shipment from … to …, 4 wooden cases of …
	We have a consignment of … now waiting to be shipped to …
	We shall shortly have a consignment of …, weighing about …

Table 14.2　Reply to Enquiry

Writing Steps	Typical Expressions
(1) Express your appreciation for the future potential business.	Thank you for the inquiry of … we are pleased to quote as follows for the shipment of … to …
	Thank you for the inquiry regarding sailings to … in August.
	We shall gladly book 4 cases for either of these vessels and enclose our shipping form. Please complete it and return it as soon as possible.
(2) Freight and schedule.	The attached schedule shows all our charges, including freight, bill of lading (airway bill, railway bill), fee, insurance, and commission.
	The S.S. … will be loading at the number 2 dock from July 4th to 9th. Following her is the SS …, loading at number 5 dock from July 18th to 23rd inclusive.
	The freight rate for … in wooden cases is USD …

Table 14.3　Letters of Pressing Shipment or Instructions by the Buyer

Writing Steps	Typical Expressions
(1) Refer to the Contract.	We refer to Contract No. …, which stipulates for shipment to be effected not later than …
	We are referring to our Contract No. … Up until now, we have not heard anything concerning the Shipment.
	It is over two months since we sent in an order for …, yet we are still awaiting delivery.
(2) Closes.	If you should fail to effect shipment before …, we would have to lodge a claim against you for the loss and, at the same time, reserve the right to revoke the contract.
	Any further delay in shipment would be detrimental to our future business.
	Your failure to deliver the goods within the stipulated time has greatly inconvenienced us.
	As our customers urgently need the item …, we hope you can assure us of punctual shipment.
	Please take the matter up immediately and ensure the goods are delivered immediately.
	We would appreciate it if you would ship the goods as soon as possible, thus enabling the goods to arrive here in time to catch the brisk demand.

Table 14.4　Shipping Advice (S/A)

Writing Steps	Typical Expressions
(1) Advise the consignee or their forwarding agent of the details of the shipment.	Please note that we have shipped the following goods to you by S.S. … which left … yesterday and is due to arrive at … on…
	We are pleased to inform you that all goods ordered on your above indent have now been shipped by S.S. … which sailed from … yesterday and is due to arrive in … on….
	We are glad to inform you that we have loaded … on S.S. …, which is due to sail on … by … with the stipulations in your L/C No. …
	We hereby inform you that the goods under the credit mentioned above have been shipped. The details of the shipment are as stated below.

Continued

Writing Steps	Typical Expressions
(2) Closes.	The consignment is urgently required, so we appreciate your prompt attention.
	We hope to hear from you soon that the goods have arrived safely.
	We trust the above shipment will reach you in sound condition and expect to receive further orders from you.
	We hereby certify that the above content is true and correct.

14.5 Specimen Letters

Letter 1: Inquiry for Sailings and Freight Rates

We shall shortly have ready for shipment from xxx to xxx, 4 cases of xxx. The cases measure xxx, each weighing 80kg.

Please quote your rate for freight and send us details of your sailings and the time usually taken for the voyage.

Letter 2: Shipping Company's Reply to the Above Inquiry

The S.S. xxx will be loaded at the number 2 dock from July 8th to 13th. Following her is the SS XXX, LOADING AT NUMBER 5 DOCK FROM July 20th to 24th inclusive.

The voyage to XXX normally takes 14 days. The freight rate for xxx packed in wooden cases is xxx per tonne.

We shall gladly book 4 cases for either of the vessels and enclose our shipping form. Please complete and return it as soon as possible.

Letter 3: Inquiry for Air Freight Rates (Through an Agent)

We shall shortly have a consignment of electric shavers weighing about 20kg for a customer in Damascus. We wish to send this by air from Beijing.

Please let us have details of the cost and any formalities to be observed. The invoice value of the consignment is USD3580, and we should require insurance coverage for this amount plus the costs of sending the consignment.

Letter 4: Forwarding Agent's Reply

Thank you for your inquiry regarding your consignment to Damascus. The attached schedule shows all our charges, including freight, airway bill fee, insurance, and commission.

We need the information requested in the enclosed form to prepare your airway bill. Three copies of the certified commercial invoice and a certificate of origin will also be necessary.

Your consignment should be in our hands by 10 a.m. on the morning of the departure day. Please telephone us when you are ready to deliver the consignment to our airport officer so we can prepare to receive it and deal with it promptly. Alternatively, we can make arrangements to collect the goods.

We hope to receive instructions from you soon.

14.6　Useful Patterns and Examples

[Pattern 1] call (draw) attention

(1) A publicity campaign has been launched to highlight the problem.

(2) Good advertising is vital to call attention to a product and introduce new products.

[Pattern 2] in urgent need

(1) The earthquake victims are in urgent need of medical supplies.

(2) These people are in urgent need of relief.

[Pattern 3] without further delay

(1) We trust you will now attend to this matter without further delay.

(2) Please settle this long outstanding account without further delay.

[Pattern 4] advise (inform) … of …

(1) I will advise you of the dispatch of the goods.

(2) We were advised of the dangers before we began this work.

[Pattern 5] press for

(1) The rent collector is pressing for payment again.

(2) Many parents have been pressing for an inquiry into the problem.

[Pattern 6] book shipping space

(1) We can book the shipping space on the direct steamer to your port.

(2) Please book the necessary shipping space in advance to insure the timely despatch of the goods ordered.

[Pattern 7] be liable to

(1) If the cartons are not strong enough, most will be liable to go broken on arrival.

(2) If the carrier issues a bill of lading for which there are no goods, the carrier will likely be liable to the holder.

[Pattern 8] in sound conditions

(1) We trust the shipment will reach you in sound condition.

(2) We trust the above shipment will reach you in sound condition.

[Pattern 9] take out

(1) We shall arrange to take out cover on your purchases of leather goods against TPND in addition to W.P.A.

(2) Please take out insurance on this lot for the invoice value plus 10%.

[Pattern 10] call at

(1) As the only direct steamer which calls at our port once a month has just departed, the goods can only be shipped next month.

(2) Under F.O.B. terms in a bulk purchase, the buyers shall nominate a carrying vessel to call at the port of shipment and lift the contracted goods.

14.7　Case Study

Mondo Co., Ltd which is an importer of leather briefcases and travel bags is going to exhibit at a trade fair later this year. So it is badly in need of the Italian leather products from Berkshire Co., Ltd which is purchased previously.

Ding Qi, a salesman of Mondo Co., Ltd. will send an email to Berkshire Co., Ltd for urging early shipment.

You are required to send an email to Berkshire Co., Ltd as the role of Ding Qi, according to the following tips.

Tips: point out the Contract No.
◆ Express desire of receiving goods early;
◆ Explain the reasons for urging goods;
◆ Express regret of causing inconvenience;
◆ Wish to get an early reply.

14.8　Business Ethics

Everyone knows that the purpose of business is to make money. Business earns more to the national capital flow more favorable of the staff at the same time also brings many benefits. But the business must abide by business morality to make money. Lack of business morality will bring great harm, for example, damage the interests of consumer. Destroy the fair competition order. Damage the interest of the other competitors, at the same time, serious damage to the enterprise's own interests. So a lack of business morality of the enterprise is difficult to survive in the society. If students want to become a successful entrepreneur, to follow the business ethics under the conditions, maximize the benefits, is a marvelous man. While good ethics often equates to good business, sometimes it doesn't. Sometimes being truly ethical means giving up something you want in exchange for doing the right thing. That's why we worry about ethics in the first place—if it didn't cost us anything, everyone would be ethical all the time.

14.9　Exercises

1. Problem Solving

Suppose your company has ordered 2000 sets of machines under CIF from Union Tech Co. Write a shipping instruction to that company.

Before shipment, the buyers generally send their shipping instructions to the sellers, informing them of the packing and mark, mode of transportation, etc. In this dealing, you should include the following details in your email.

(1) The seller is supposed to send the machinery to Guangzhou by the end of August;

(2) The goods should be packed in seaworthy cases to withstand rough handling;

(3) Looking forward to shipping advice from the seller.

2. Skill Training

Suppose you are person in charge of corresponding in an importing company, now your company has a great deal with a British exporting company, and that company fails to inform you the shipping situation. Please write a letter asking for the current situation about your goods and urge that British company to effect the shipment in time.

Unit 15

Insurance

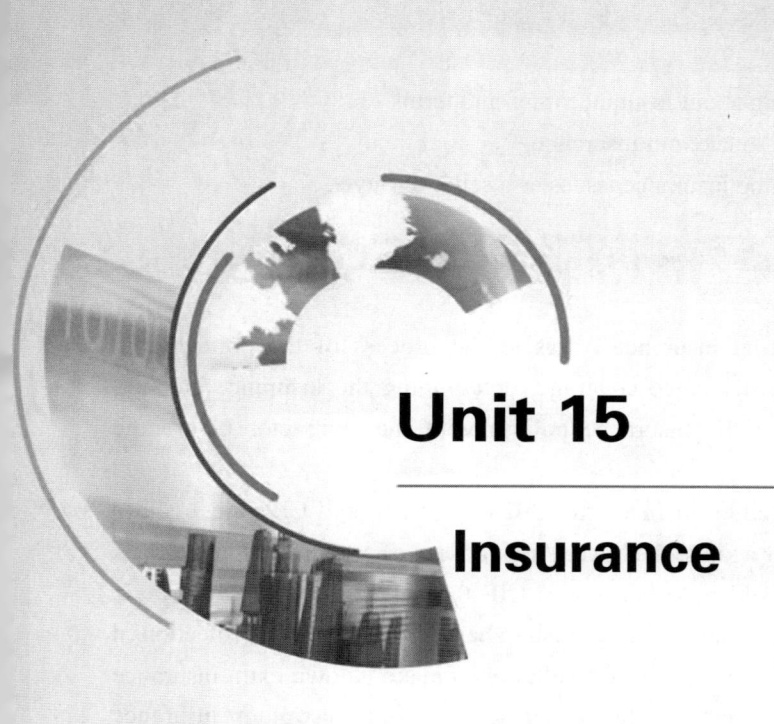

◆ **Case-Lead-in**

Suppose you are China National Garments Imp. & Exp. Corporation, and at the buyer's (Fashion Trading Company in UK) request, you have made an offer for 3000 dozen of Silk Blouses at ￡4500 CIF London per piece. Upon receipt of your offer, the buyer sent you a letter as follows. How will you write to your buyer?

15.1 Learning Objectives

(1) How to write inquiries asking about insurance rates and terms.
(2) How to write a letter asking to take out insurance.
(3) How to write a letter regarding insurance issues as a seller or buyer.

15.2 About International Cargo Transportation Insurance

International cargo transportation insurance refers to the process of the policyholder taking out insurance (choosing the insurance coverage, determining the insurance amount, paying the premium, and receiving the insurance policy) with the contractor before the shipment of the goods.

Among the 11 trade terms specified in Incoterms 2020, only CIF and CIP rules require the seller to take out insurance cover against the buyer's risk of loss of or damage to the goods during the carriage. The buyer should note that under CIF the seller is required to obtain insurance only on minimum cover. Should the buyer wish to have more insurance protection, it will need either to agree as much expressly with the seller or to make its own extra insurance arrangements. While the CIP rule requires the seller to take out maximum insurance coverage—the Institute Cargo Clauses (A) or (Air) or similar for at least 110% of the value of the goods. It is, however, still open to the parties to agree on a higher (for CIF) or a lower (for CIP) level of cover.

The risk of damage or loss of goods en route is borne by the buyer, so the seller takes out the insurance for the buyer's benefit and the premium is included in the price of the transaction. Under other trade terms, the seller is not obliged to handle insurance. The seller must present to the buyer with any insurance document the buyer will need in case it may claim under that insurance.

15.3 The Field of International Cargo Insurance

In the field of international cargo insurance, the world's most influential insurance policy is the Cargo Clause of the Institute of London (ICC), which includes ICC (A), (B), (C), ICC (A) being the most extensive and ICC (C) being the most limited. In addition, the insured can also take out separate insurance policies including ICC War and ICC Strike. The insurance coverage under the Marine Cargo Insurance Policy of PICC includes FPA (Peace Insurance), WPA (Water Damage Insurance), and AR (All Risks Insurance), with FPA having the smallest coverage, followed by WPA and AR having the largest coverage.

15.4 Writing Skills and Typical Expressions

Writing skills and typical expressions are as follows (see Table 15.1—15.3).

Table 15.1 Enquiry and Applications For Cover

Writing Steps	Typical Expression
(1) Openings: provide information about the consignment you wish to insure.	We will shortly have a consignment of ..., valued at ..., to be shipped from ... by ... Liners Ltd.
	We regularly ship a consignment of ... to ... by ... Liners Ltd.
	We wish to insure the following consignment against All Risks for the sum of ... These goods are now held at No.3 dock, ... (port), waiting to be shipped by S.S. ... due to leave for ... on ...
	Thank you for your letter of June 9th quoting your rate for an open policy of USD ... covering consignment on the routes named.
	We thank you for your reply to our inquiry of June 5th. The terms you quote, namely ... are acceptable.
	Please arrange to insure the following consignment ...
	Please hold us covered for the consignment below (on the attached sheet).
	We should be glad if you would provide cover of USD ... on ..., in transit from ... to ...
	Please quote your lowest All Risks rates for shipments of ... to ...
	We wish to renew this Policy for the same amount and on the same terms.
	We will shortly be making regular shipments of ... to ... by ...
(2) Body: state what cover you want to take out for your consignment.	We wish to cover the consignment against All Risks from our warehouse at the above address to the port of ...
	We would be glad if you issued an All Risks open policy for, say, USD ... to cover these shipments from our warehouse at the above address to the destination port.
	We want to know whether you can issue a WPA plus breakage risks policy for these shipments and, if so, on what terms.
(3) Closings: emphasize what you expect the insurance company to reply, e.g. confirmation of your request, terms, and conditions for the insurance and policy.	Please let us know on what terms you can cover the risks mentioned.
	Please quote your rate for the cover.
	In particular, we would like to know whether you can give a special rate in return for the promise of regular monthly shipments.
	Please send me particulars of your terms and conditions for the Policy and a proposal form if required.
	I look forward to receiving the Policy within the next few days.
	Please arrange cover in this sum for the risks mentioned in your letter and on the terms quoted, namely 1%.
	Please let us have the Policy, and one certified copy, by June 30th. The charge should be billed to our account.
	Please arrange the necessary cover and send us the Policy soon.

Table 15.2 Replies to Requests or Applications for Cover

Writing Steps	Typical expressions
(1) Openings: express your appreciation for the inquiry or application for a cover.	Thank you for your letter of... We shall be glad to provide cover in the sum of ... at ... for the consignment mentioned in your application.
	Thank you for your inquiry of June 14th regarding insurance to cover your consignment mentioned in the letter.

Writing Steps	Typical Expressions
(1) Openings: express your appreciation for the inquiry or application for a cover.	Thank you for your letter of … We quote below our terms for arranging cover for …
(2) Body: answer the questions regarding the rate and terms and conditions for the insurance required.	You will see that we offer three types of cover for the international sale of goods, which are FPA, WPA, and AR.
	We enclose a leaflet describing the insurance terms and conditions for the consignment you mentioned in your letter.
	The premium for this cover is at the rate of … of the declared value of USD …
(3) Closings: inform the reader that the business is being taken care of and when the reader can receive the offer or Policy.	The Policy is now being prepared and should reach you in about a week.
	Please let me know if I can provide any further help.
	I enclose a proposal form. Please complete and return it by 7 days before the date the Policy is to run.
	Please complete and return the proposal form by June 23rd, so we can be sure of issuing the Policy in time.
	We undertake all classes of insurance and would welcome the opportunity to transact further business with you.
	It is an exceptionally low rate, and we trust you will allow us to handle your insurance business.

Table 15.3 Letters Between Seller and Buyer Regarding Insurance

Writing Steps	Typical Expressions
(1) Openings: make references to the order No. or S/C No. or L/C No.	We wish to refer you to our order No.123 for …
	Please refer to our order No.123 for …
	We thank you for your June 23th letter requesting us to effect insurance on the captioned shipment for your account.
(2) Body: express what you ask the reader to do in terms of cover, insurance value, and Policy or let the reader know whether you will grant what they require you to do.	As we now desire to have the shipment insured at your end, we shall be very pleased if you kindly arrange to insure the same against AR for 110% of the invoice value USD …
	We are pleased to confirm covering the above shipment with … against AR for USD… We will send you the Policy and our debit note for the premium to you in a day or two.
	We know that according to your usual practice, you insure the goods only for 10% above the invoice value; therefore, the extra premium will be for our account.
(3) Closings: make it clear how to settle the extra fees.	We shall refund the premium to you upon receipt of your debit note.
	For your information, this consignment will be shipped by S.S. … sailing on or about the 5th of next month.
	We sincerely hope that our request will meet with your approval and await your reply with keen interest.

15.5 Specimen Letters

Letter 1: Enquire About Insurance Rates

Dear Sir,

We will shortly have a consignment for xxx, valued at UDSXXX CIF XXX, to be shipped from xxx by a vessel of xxx Liners Ltd.

We wish to cover the consignment against all risks from our warehouse at the above address to

the consignee's warehouse at the port of xxx. Please quote your rate for the cover.
Yours sincerely

Letter 2: Request for a Special Rate
Dear Sir,

We regularly ship consignments of bottled sherry to Australia by liners of the XXX Shipping Line. Can you issue an ICC (A) policy for this shipment? And, if yes, on what terms? In particular, we would like to know whether you can give a special rate in return for the promise of regular monthly shipments.

We hope to hear from you soon.
Yours sincerely

Letter 3: Applications for Insurance Cover
Dear Sir,

We thank you for your reply to our inquiry of June 6th. The terms you quote, namely 1%, less 5% special discount for regular shipments, are acceptable. We understand that these terms will apply to all our shipments of bottled sherry by regular liners to Australian ports and cover ICC (A), including breakages and pilferage.

Our first shipment will be on July 2nd for 20 cases of sherry, valued at USD9000.00. Please arrange open account terms with quarterly settlements.

We look forward to receiving the Policy within the next few days.
Yours sincerely

Letter 4: Request for an ICC (A) Policy
Dear Sir,

We wish to insure the following consignment against ICC (A) for USDXXX.

Four c/s Fancy Leather Goods, marked XXX.

These goods are now held at No 2 Dock, xxx, waiting to be shipped by S.S. XXX, due to leave for Bombay on Friday, June 23rd.

We require immediate cover as far as Bombay. Please let us have the Policy as soon as it is ready. In the meantime, please confirm that you hold the consignment covered.
Yours sincerely

15.6　Useful Patterns & Examples

[Pattern 1] in return
　　(1) Give without the expectation of getting something in return.
　　(2) "Well, then, in return for your story,"continued Noirtier,"I will tell you another. "
[Pattern 2] apply to

(1) The Convention does not apply to us.

(2) Underline the following that applies to you.

[Pattern 3] insure … against … for the sum of …

Or take out (effect) insurance against … for the sum of …, arrange to insure for … against …

(1) Please effect insurance for 120% of the invoice value against All Risks and War Risks, as requested by the buyer.

(2) For transactions concluded on a CIF basis, we usually take out insurance with the People's Insurance Company of China against All Risks.

[Pattern 4] hold … covered

(1) Meanwhile, we confirm that we hold the consignment covered as of today.

(2) Would you please confirm that you hold the consignment covered?

[Pattern 5] meet with your approval

(1) We sincerely hope our request will meet with your approval.

(2) We are sure our product's quality and quality will meet your approval.

[Pattern 6] on our behalf

(1) You can prepare the Bills of Lading and Customs Entry Forms on our behalf.

(2) We hope you will cover insurance on our behalf for the consignment mentioned below.

[Pattern 7] charge/record … to one's account

(1) Please charge the samples to our account this time.

(2) The extra premium will be for your account.

[Pattern 8] file a claim with the insurance company

(1) Since the goods have been covered by insurance, you should lodge your claim against the insurance company concerned.

(2) We have filed a claim against you for the short delivery of 15 cases.

[Pattern 9] as per

(1) As per the contract, the seller should effect shipment not later than May 15th.

(2) We usually insure our goods with the PICC as per their Ocean Marine Cargo Clause, January 1st, 1981 revision.

[Pattern 10] in excess of

(1) Commodity Weight in excess of 30 kilos is charged at a higher rate.

(2) The insurance policy should be in triplicate, covering All Risks and War Risk including W.A. and breakage in excess of 5% on the whole consignment.

15.7　Case Study

The export 50 metric tons rice was insured against all risks and war risk on a "warehouse to warehouse" basis. The rice was lost during transportation from the exporter's warehouse to the quay at the port of shipment. If the contract was concluded on a CIF basis, would the seller get the compensation from the insurance company? What about under CFR or FOB? Why?

15.8 Business Ethics

Valuing Your Inventory versus Valuing Your Employees

Assume you are the owner of a small apparel manufacturer with approximately fifty employees. Your business is located in a blighted area of town where the jobs you provide are important, but the insurance costs of doing business there are significant, too. Recently, fire and theft coverage has escalated in cost, but it is essential to protect your premises and inventory, and local ordinances require that you purchase it. You have customarily provided health coverage for your employees and their families, which many of them would not be able to afford if they had to bear the cost themselves. You would like to continue providing this coverage—though, due to your small employee base, you are not legally obligated to do so—but these costs have risen too. Finally, you would prefer to stay in this location, because you feel an obligation to your workers, most of whom live nearby, and because you feel welcomed by the community itself, which includes some longtime customers. Still, you may be forced to choose between paying for your employee health care costs and moving to a different area of town where fire and theft coverage would not cost as much.

Critical Thinking:
- How will you make the decision within an ethical framework?
- What will you, your business, and your employees gain and lose based on what you decide?
- What, if anything, do you and your business owe the community of which you have been a part for so long?

15.9 Exercises

1. Simulated Writing

Situation:
V.T. Impex (Shandong) Limited is one of the leading suppliers and exporters of agricultural products, including spices, fresh and frozen vegetables, dehydrated vegetables, fresh and dried fruits, nuts, and kernels.

Task:
You are on behalf of V.T. Impex (Shandong) Limited. Write a letter to discuss the insurance terms with your business associate Mitasi Trade Company and finally come to an agreement.

2. Problem Solving

Problem:

HIPPO Trade Company is a Canada based company dedicated in importing and exporting electrical products. Shenzhen Betop Electronics Co., Ltd. is an integrated high-tech company specialized in researching, producing, selling and serving LED products. At present, HIPPO is going to purchase 500 rolls of waterproof LED rigid light bar BT-5050 from Betop. Betop usually covers All Risks subject to China Insurance Clauses (CIC) for their goods, but HIPPO wish to get TPND and Breakage of Packing Risk except All Risks. This transaction is on CIF basis.

Solutions:

You work for HIPPO Trade Company. Write a letter to request for addition risks. Make your point about the extra insurance costs.

Unit 16

Claim and Settlement

✧ **Case-Lead-in**

When you purchase a product that is defective or doesn't perform properly, how do you lodge a complaint that will get results? Discuss with your partner to work out as many tips as you can for effective complaints.

16.1　Learning Objectives

(1) Understand the disputes may occur in the international trade.

(2) To be able to write relevant letters with regard to claim and settlement.

(3) Master some negotiation strategies.

(4) Grasp some words, expressions and typical sentences on this topic.

16.2　Brief Introduction of Complaints and Claims

Business transactions do not always run smoothly. Regardless of how careful or efficient business organizations are, things go wrong occasionally. Merchandise may be shipped to a wrong address or arrive in less than perfect condition; details for an order may be confused; payment may be incorrect; badly needed goods may be delayed; quality may be different from the standard expected. When troubles and conflicts in trade happen between the importer and exporter in different countries, the letters of complaint or claims are commonly used in practice.

If the loss is not serious, the party suffered the loss may write a complaint letter to call the other party's attention to avoid this matter happening again. If the loss is serious, the party suffered the loss may lodge a claim for compensation.

On receiving complaints or claims, the seller should make investigations and settle the problem.

On the contrary, sellers may also raise claims against buyer for non-establishment of L/C or a breach of contract, etc.

16.3　The Different Types of Claims

There are three types of claims: trade claims, transportation claims and insurance claims.

1) Under the trade claims

(1) The buyer is likely to file a claim against the seller for:

- The loss caused by non-delivery or delay of delivery;
- Inferior quality of the goods and improper packing.

(2) The seller might also claim the compensation from the buyer for:

- Failure of opening an L/C;
- Delay in booking the vessel (FOB);
- Delay in payment.

2) Under the transportation claims, shipper/consignor or owner of the shipped goods raise a claim against the carrier for:

- Damage or imperfection of goods;
- The delivery of short weight or shortage of quantity.

3) Under the insurance claims the insured would file a claim against the underwriters. The insured goods are damaged or lost due to the factors which are called risks.

16.4 Writing Skills

The claim from the buyer is usually about the quality, quantity, packing or time of delivery, the seller may claim on the buyer for the damages caused by problems involved in payment. Response to such letters may be positive and negative dependent on concrete situations.

(1) Claim letters always express the regret about the loss with the clear and complete evidence. Give your suggestions and hope for an early reply/settlement.

(2) Settlement letters always make clear explanation or promise to take actions.

(3) Both claim and settlement letters should express to maintain a good business relationship.

16.5 Typical Expressions for Letters Requesting for Claim and Settlements

Typical expressions for letters requesting for claim and settlements are as follows (see Table 16.1 and Table16.2).

Table 16.1　Typical Expressions for Letters Requesting for Claim and Settlements

Writing Steps	Typical Expressions
(1) Beginning with the statement of the problem and expression of sorrow.	We regret to say that we have just found the goods have been broken …
	We have just received the Survey Report from the third party evidencing that …
	We deeply regret to inform you that the … is not in accordance with the samples.
	On opening the containers, we found that the goods were short by …
	The loss was due to… which you should be responsible.
(2) Suggestion solutions clearly based on the actual loss.	This problem has caused us … with much inconvenience.
	We must request you to arrange for the dispatch of replacement at once.
	We are therefore suggesting replacing the entire quantity as soon as possible in order to meet the deadline.
	We require you to replace the damaged goods and grant us a discount of 10% to compensate for our loss.
	We have lost considerable business because of the delay of shipment, thus we request your compensation for the loss.
(3) Regretting the need to settlement and closing with a hope to get a favorable reply.	We are looking forward to your settlement at an early date.
	We are obliged to thank you for your kind attention in this matter.
	We would like to know your decision to do regarding to our losses.
	Hoping you will find a way to give us prompt settlement.

Table 16.2 To Agree/Reject a Claim

Writing Steps	Typical Expressions
(1) Express the regret for the loss.	With reference to your letter dated … we would like to express our regret over the unfortunate incident.
	With reference to your claim for ..., we are very sorry for our mistake.
	We are very sorry for the trouble caused by the delay of shipment.
	We apologize for the inconvenience caused.
(2) Explaining the reason and suggestion: the solution or rejecting the request.	We agree to accept all your claim.
	We regret the loss you have claimed and agree to compensate you …
	We would like to present two explanations for this issue.
	We will make you a compensation of ... and offer the preferential terms in our next cooperation.
	The fact is that our worker sends wrong goods into your container and we are now sending you a replacement.
	Apparently, we shall not be responsible for the loss.
	Our suggestion is that you should file a claim against the insurance company.
	We will get this claim resolved soonest and hope to compensate you for your loss to your satisfaction.
(3) Closing the letter with expression of sorrow and promising to take action soonest.	We are prepared to make you a reasonable compensation.
	We hope this will not affect our long-term relationship.
	We apologize in advance for any inconvenience it might bring to you.
	Your cooperation and forgiveness are appreciated.

16.6 Specimen Letters

Letter 1: Claim on Damage Packages

Dear Sirs,

We regret to say that when inspecting the goods from No.987 shipments in our port, totally 150 cartons were found with broken inner packages which we could not sell to our customers. We presumed that the damage was made because you used the cartons for outer packing which are not strong enough. An international honored surveyor already has been instructed to inspect the goods and to issue a survey report.

As we need the goods to deliveries to our customers next month, we require you to replace the damaged goods at once with compensate for our loss.

We are very depressed about this claim and we are looking forward to your settlement at an early date.

Yours faithfully

Letter 2: A Reply to the Claim on Damage Packages

Dear Sirs,

Thanks for your letter of November 15th. We would like to express our regret over the unfortunate incident.

On going into this matter we find that the mistake was indeed made in the packing, and we are very sorry about the quality of carton we used on the outer packing. We have arranged for the 150 sets of goods with reinforced the packing and ready to delivery to you next week. Relative documents will be mailed as soon as they are ready. Please keep the current 150 sets of goods as free samples and we will offer the preferential terms in our next cooperation.

Please accept our apologies for the trouble caused to you.

Yours faithfully

Letter 3: Claim on Wrong Goods

Dear Sirs,

We bought 1,000 Oli Brand, Model T602 Umbrella from your company with 5% discount of listing price. The goods were delivered on July 10th.

Unfortunately, when we opened the case we found it contained raincoats which we have not ordered. We presume that a mistake was made in assembling the order.

As we need the umbrellas to complete deliveries to our own customers, we must ask you to arrange to dispatch the correct items at once.

We attached the contract of our order and please recheck soonest. In the meantime, we are holding the case at your disposal, and please let us know what you wish us to do with it.

Yours faithfully

Letter 4: A Reply on Wrong Goods

Dear Sirs,

We are sorry to learn from your letter of wrong goods. We have looked into this matter and found that we did make a mistake in putting the wrong orders.

We have arranged for the correct goods to be dispatched to you at once. And we shall be grateful if you will keep the case of raincoats until called for our local agents who have been instructed accordingly.

We apologize for the inconvenience caused by our error.

Yours faithfully

16.7　Useful Patterns & Examples

[Pattern 1] claim … for …

(1) We have received your fax of May 10th, claiming for inferior quality on the consignment of 10000 pieces of valves.

(2) We reserve the right to claim compensation from you for any damage.

[Pattern 2] claim on …

(1) Your claims on this cargo have been settled.

(1) Claim on delayed shipment is that sellers fail to make the delivery according to the time schedule.

[Pattern 3] to lodge/file/put/make/submit/forward/raise/register a claim for …

(1) We reserve the right to lodge a claim for loss.

(2) The customer lodged a claim on this shipment for USD1000 on account of short weight.

[Pattern 4] at one's disposal

(1) Should we return the damaged goods to you for replacement or hold them at your disposal?

(2) The money is at the disposal of the committee.

[Pattern 5] due to …

(1) Based on the immediate investigation we made, it is believed that the loss is due to the fact that the shipment has been delayed.

(2) Due to increasing competition, many insurance companies have said they would increase investment this year in product quality, technology and customer service.

[Pattern 6] settle /settlement

(1) I am writing this letter to you in order to settle the claim for inferior quality on the 10 tons of sands.

(2) We have received your compensation in settlement of our claim.

[Pattern 7] replacement / to replace sth. by/with sth.

(1) Based on the survey report, we request your company to arrange the full refund or send replacement of those damaged tea sets immediately.

(2) We request you send a replacement of 1200 cartons of 70gsm copy paper by the end of this month.

[Pattern 8] make compensation

(1) I am sure you will be satisfied with the replacement, if not, we will make compensation for you.

(2) As a result of your fault, you should make compensation for our loss.

[Pattern 9] be obliged to do

(1) Since we have failed to settle the disputes through friendly negotiation, we are obliged to refer them to the arbitration committee.

(2) They are obliged to pay the compensation to us according to the contract.

[Pattern 10] a survey report issued by …

(1) We should require a survey report issued by your local insurance agent, with which we may know the event of the damage.

(2) According to the survey report issued by CCIB, we regret to tell you that the quality of your shipment for our order No.990630 is far from the agreed specifications.

16.8　Case Study

　　Messrs. Westcott & Co. complain that 500 tins of condensed milk ordered by them arrived dented and punctured; they attribute the damage to improper packing and emphasize the need for greater care. Write a letter on behalf of Westcott & Co. to the above effect.

16.9　Business Ethics

　　中国古代先有圣人"无讼"之教，后有君王"无讼"之谕。对于封建官员阶层而言，他们大都是无讼法律思想的信奉者和实践者。一方面是因为他们自幼接受儒学教育，儒家经义早已烂熟于心；另一方面，中央政府考核地方行政官员的一个重要指标，就是官员辖区内民、刑事案件的发案率。发案率低，表示该地区民风淳厚、以礼为治，足以证明主政官员施政有方。因此，官员在处理辖区案件时，必然努力贯彻无讼法律思想。至于如何贯彻，则属于无讼法律思想的实践问题。实践大体有两种形式：一是通过宣传教化将可能发生的讼案消解于民间。官员多以"告示"形式宣讲无讼思想，告诫治下百姓不要因细故妄打官司，如南宋著名思想家朱熹《劝谕榜》言："劝谕士民乡党族姻所宜亲睦，或有小忿，宜启深思，更且委曲调和，未可容易论诉。盖得理亦须伤财废业，况无理不免坐罪遭刑，终必有凶，且当痛戒。"二是以"息讼"的方式处理已经提起诉讼的案件。无讼的最终意义在于人与人之间不存在纠纷和争端，但这只是一种理想的社会状态，纷争在现实中是难以避免的。无讼的实现更可能做到的是将发生的纷争以非诉讼的方式解决，也就是息讼。

16.10　Exercises

　　(1) Suppose you are Jimmy Brown from UT Co. Write an email to Swift Communication Company to lodge a claim for the inferior quality of the digital camera.

　　(2) Situational writing.

Situation

Suning Electronics Import&Export Company sells water heaters to a business person from Holland. He ordered 2000 sets of the water heaters. When the goods arrived, he refused to accept them and make the payment. The reason was that 200 water heaters were heavily damaged.

Task

　　(1) Suppose you are the businessperson from Holland, please write a claim letter for the problem mentioned above. You may ask for the replacement of the damaged goods by showing the copy of the survey report by the related authority.

　　(2) On behalf of Suning Electronics Import&Export Company, after the research, you reply to accept the claim and agree to replace the damaged goods at once and show the sincere apology to the business person.

Unit 17

Telephone Etiquette

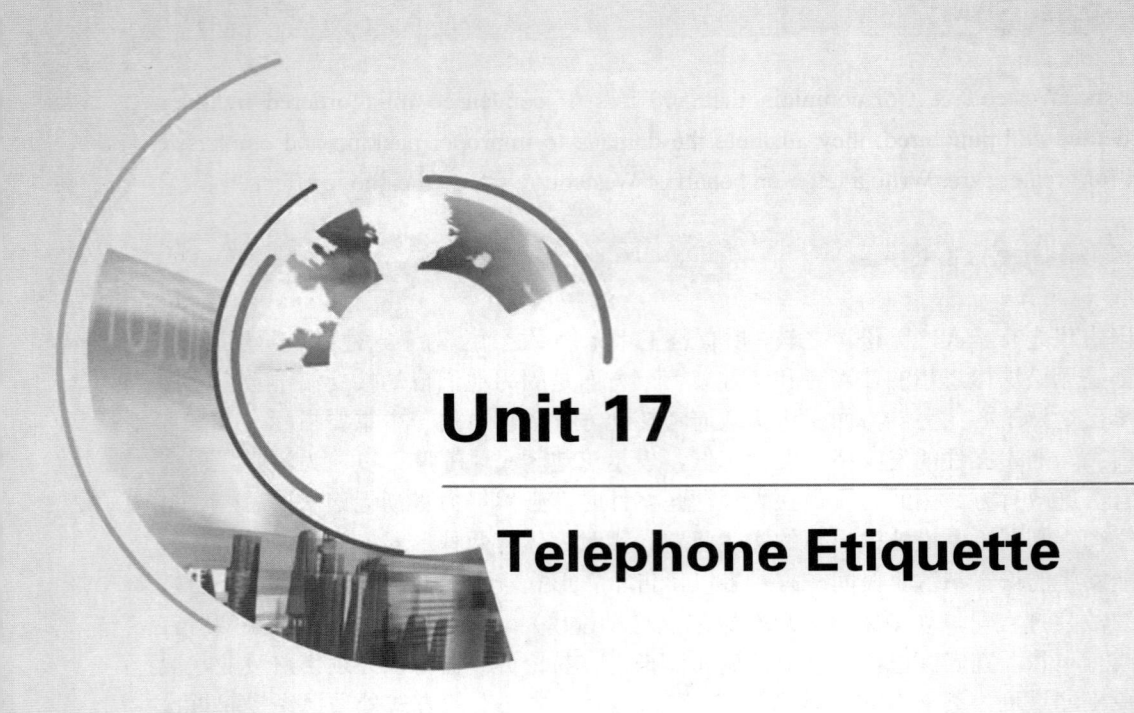

◆ **Case-Lead-in**

It may be hard to imagine what our life would be like without cell phones right now, but in fact, the telephone was invented only a few decades ago. Now we can not only make phone calls and send text messages, but also post photos and share our life with cell phones. As we increasingly rely on these functions provided by cell phones, we seem to engage in cell phone too much. During the process, we become ignoring people and phone manners. It could be an international issue, and we cannot find a way out in a short time, what we can do is to pick up some telephone etiquettes now.

17.1 Learning Objectives

(1) Acquire how to prepare make outgoing calls.
(2) Acquire how to receive incoming calls.
(3) Develop good telephone manners and techniques.
(4) Understand other useful abilities in dealing with social media in business.

17.2 The Significance of Telephone Etiquette

Communicating with your business partners on the phone is still an important way to conduct business, especially in recent days. Making a phone call is different with emailing or texting your partners, since you can still use vocal expression to convey emotions without showing facial expression. You can receive feedback promptly and allow you to have a more in-depth conversation than writing communication.

Therefore, even we have multiple online communication technologies, the phone is irreplaceable till now. It is necessary to equip yourself with some telephone etiquettes.

(1) Before engaging with your cell phone, remind yourself you are here to communicate with people, don't miss this opportunity.

(2) When you make a phone call, please do consider others who surround you. Keep your voice down and try not to interrupt other people.

(3) Respect the law or regulation for using the phone, i.e., while driving or flying.

(4) Don't keep trying.

(5) Use a normal ringtone.

17.3 The Guidelines for Handling Outgoing Calls

If you want to make a phone call, make sure this is a necessary call and there is no better way to communicate the problem you want to talk about. Then you need to consider follow tips to keep a good telephone behavior.

(1) To prepare an agenda, if necessary, a list will be good. This will help you to convert all important issues at the first time.

(2) Start by using a greeting, then give your name, affiliation, and a brief summary of the purpose of your call.

(3) To remind yourself that you might interrupt something the person is working on, to be succinct, or asking whether that person is convenience to receive a lengthy conversation.

(4) To use the speakerphone cautiously and courteously.

(5) To consider the speaker in a teleconferencing.

(6) To make your voice more influential.

(7) To leave a complete and desensitized message if you reach their assistance or colleague.

(8) To be accurate and professional.

(9) To be aware of offline chats.

(10) To leave a voice mail like a briefing.

(11) To end the call judiciously

17.4　The Guidelines for Receiving Incoming Calls

Receiving phone call requires much similar behavior as making a phone call, only you cannot project who is going to call you and what for. But you still can build a professional image and practicing your technique.

(1) To answer promptly and courteously, but make sure you speed clearly, if it is possible, speak slowly than usual. We all might experienced that when you make a phone call to reception of any hotel, it is hardly to pick up their words.

(2) To be cheerful, and give your name and your affiliation.

(3) To be concern when you receive a phone call. Try to be helpful even it is not for you.

(4) To take notes, especially when you are taking phone calls on behalf of others.

(5) To explain what you are doing when you are looking for information, responsible person or transferring phone calls.

(6) To notice the phone call is a signal for in-depth communication.

(7) To make your voice more influence.

(8) To be accurate and professional.

(9) To be aware of offline chats.

(10) To end the call judiciously.

17.5　Typical Expressions for Handling Outgoing and Incoming Calls

Typical expressions for handling outgoing and incoming calls are as follows (see Table 17.1 and Table 17.2).

Table 17.1　Typical Expressions for Outgoing Calls

Behaviors	Typical Expressions
Greeting and introduction.	Hello, Weldon, this is Mary from marketing department.
	Good morning, May I speak to Mr. Francis? This is Jordan of AI Intelligent, and I'm following up the offer I sent him yesterday.
To be succinct.	Hello, Mrs. Berkley, I have only to minutes, but I really want to have the quarterly sales numbers.
To be accurate.	I have checked and our total price is 300 million yuan.

Continued

Behaviors	Typical Expressions
To end the call judiciously.	It is my pleasure to talk with you.
	I have gotten what I need, thanks for your help.
	I must go now, should I call you again if there still are something missing?

Table 17.2 Typical Expressions for Incoming Calls

Behaviors	Typical Expressions
To give your name and affiliation.	Mrs. Berkley, sales department. How can I help you?
To be helpful.	We don't have the quarterly sales numbers, let's see what I can find for monthly data.
	Mr. Francis is out of office/away from his desk, may I take a note for him?
To explain what you are doing.	Please hold the line, I will check the number for you.
To be accurate.	May I repeat your name, affiliation and offer to make sure that I got right?
To end the call judiciously.	Would you prefer to hold a while, or would you like Mr. Francis to call you back?

17.6 The Guidelines for Teleconferencing

In recent years, teleconference has become a part of our life. Due to the covID pandemic, traveling internationally for business become difficult, sometimes, even impossible. So, teleconference fills the gap and provides the world a new opportunity for development of technology, market, and business etiquette. With the increasing number of online meetings which we have participated in, some business etiquette related to teleconference should also be paid attention to.

(1) To be prepared.

Although participants do not go to conference room in person, there still are many issues which need to be concerned.

As any offline meeting, teleconference needs to be noticed in advance. Attendees need to be informed a reason time before to make sure there is no conflict of time.

Documents also need to be prepared and distributed to attendees in advance for their reading before the conference.

In recent years, there are many apps which provide service in teleconference market, you can easily mean them, like Zoom, Microsoft team, and Tencent Meeting. If you want to conduct online training, there are some other apps available as well.

Before attending a teleconference, you need to check fitness of your equipment and software to make sure stability. If you prepared visual documents, it would be better to test before you start your conference, microphone and webcam need to be checked too.

The organizer should choose a suitable place to ensure a reliable network and independent quiet environment.

If you are organizer, you shall initiate the meeting at least 15 minutes earlier, in case some participants are early birds. You could play some background music or video for entertainment purpose, or conference related material will do too.

A plan B is always necessary, because nobody can tell what would happen during the teleconference. If any unpredictable terms arise, alter option is available.

(2) To use mute mode except you are the speaker.

(3) To use a headphone, if you don't have a qualified microphone.

(4) To dress properly, teleconference is still a business environment. Pajamas or home dress are not good choice.

(5) To choose a virtual scenery if you are not satisfied with yours.

(6) To take notes, if the visual documents will not be shared according to intellectual property reason.

(7) To take the initiative.

During teleconference, participants are not seating in the same room, so body posture, nonverbal language, and facial expression will not work. So, if you want to join in their discussion, the earlier the better.

Normally interrupting other person's speaking is rude, but sometimes in a teleconference, you need to interrupt to get your chance to speak out.

(8) It is your duty as a host to make sure the agenda is followed.

17.7　Case Study

Case One

The 36th International Fair for Trade in Services will be held in country K in November. The Organizing Committee sent an invitation for your company's participation. However, the November is your company's 150th anniversary. The whole company is busy with celebration related matters, so your company decided not to participate in the fair. Then the organizing committee conducted multiple phone calls and try to persuade your company to change your idea. Finally, your company was persuaded and agree to participate in the fair.

After receiving the relevant information and booth arrangement sent by the organizing committee, your company found that because your decision to participate in the fair was late, most of the booths have been arranged, and the location given to your company is relatively remote. Your company was very dissatisfied with this, so you called the Organizing Committee as the representative for several rounds to negotiate booth arrangement, and finally a new arrangement of your booth was agreed and it was considered as satisfactory to both parties.

Requirements: Design the plot by yourself, and act as the company manager and the organizing committee member with your partner. Design several rounds of phone calls regarding about two topics.

In this process, you can design conflict, persuasion and finally reach an agreement. The key question here is that how you can ensure that your phone calls are efficient.

Tips

The party who expresses their views should try to clearly state their views, while the other party should consider being a good listener.

Case Two

Sky-blue Co., Ltd is an advertising company originally from country H. In recent years, development of their business has been slowdown. To solve the problem, they hired a new director of customer department. As an important department of advertising business operation, the customer department is directly responsible for business negotiation with customers, contacting customers' specific advertising requirements, communicating with functional departments within the company, and organizing functional departments to complete various advertising implementation plans on time.

After taking office, George, the new director of the customer department, fired some employees in the department and recruited a group of new members internationally. But one year later, things do not seem to have improved.

One day, George received a phone call from his boss Ben: "George, why is your team so fragile? It's only a year since the new team was just established. Why have all the core members wanted to resign? You must remember, all of them were hired after you arrived. Besides, why does the major customer of your team complain about your design again? I don't want to hear any complaints from the customer again!" Ben's voice sounds angry and frustrated.

George explained to Ben, but it didn't seem to satisfy him.

Finally, Ben said: "I think you should solve the problem as soon as possible!"

"I know!" George didn't explain any more.

If you are George, you are going to organize a teleconference to talk with your employees about current problem all of you are facing. Your task: to hold a teleconference with your group members (4—5 members will be fine).

In the process, your group needs to do the followings.

(1) Make an advance announcement for the meeting to ensure all members are noticed;

(2) Book an online conference room;

(3) Plan an agenda;

(4) Prepare required documents and visual documents if needed;

(5) Test your equipment and solve any problems raised;

(6) Attend the conference and host the conference;

(7) Observe group members' performance and note any behavior which is not etiquette;

(8) Discuss all behaviors you have noted, and provide improvement suggestions.

17.8　Situational Conversation

Exercise One

List ten behaviors that you think are the most impolite/annoy when people communicate on the phone.

Exercise Two

Acting as the role of telephone caller and receiver in following case, to improve your technique in practice.

Your task: read background information and then play the role you are assigned. During the process, please take notes on your counterpart's behavior and exchange opinions after you complete the process.

Step One

Caller	Receiver
You, David, are the marketing manger of Hana Co., Ltd, called Lee, the director of purchasing department in G&S Inc. to make an offer about your products.	You are the director of purchasing department in G&S Inc., received the call. But you don't know the company as well as their products before, so you promised to look through this offer and if it is necessary, you will consult your colleagues who are working in operation department.
Called Mr. Lee again to follow up and provide more information about your products and feedbacks from your current customers.	You are assistance of Mr. Lee, and he is away from the office. You took notes for him and suggested that Mr. David should call him again later today.
Called Mr. Lee again in the afternoon.	Mr. Lee received the phone call but he still had no idea about your products. He said that he already talked with director of operation department, and he will call you soon.

Step Two

Receiver	Caller
You provided more information about your products and feedbacks from your current customers.	Christina, director of operation department, called you ask for more information about your product. She took some note and checked with some details.
You received the offer.	She made an offer again.

Exercise Three

You are working in Goldfish Co., this morning you made a phone call to a supermarket and want to purchase 13 boxes of drinking water. But the call was directed to voice mail. So, you left a voice message.

Q1: what information you are going to leave in the message?

Q2: how can you define a good voice message? And why. If you want to leave an effective voice message, what information must be included?

The supermarket delivered drinking water to your company on time, instead of sending 13 boxes, they sent 30 boxes. You make a phone call to their sales manager.

Q3: what do you plan to say this time?

Q4: What preparations will you make to make this phone call?

17.9 Business Ethics

《上去密韩太尉书》苏辙

太尉执事：辙生好为文，思之至深。以为文者气之所形，然文不可以学而能，气可以养而致。孟子曰："我善养吾浩然之气。"今观其文章，宽厚宏博，充乎天地之间，称其气之小大。太史公行天下，周览四海名山大川，与燕、赵间豪俊交游，故其文疏荡，颇有奇气。此二子者，岂尝执笔学为如此之文哉？其气充乎其中而溢乎其貌，动乎其言而见乎其文，而不自知也。

辙生十有九年矣。其居家所与游者，不过其邻里乡党之人；所见不过数百里之间，无高山大野可登览以自广；百氏之书，虽无所不读，然皆古人之陈迹，不足以激发其志气。恐遂汩没，故决然舍去，求天下奇闻壮观，以知天地之广大。过秦、汉之故都，恣观终南、嵩、华之高，北顾黄河之奔流，慨然想见古之豪杰。至京师，仰观天子宫阙之壮，与仓廪、府库、城池、苑囿之富且大也，而后知天下之巨丽。见翰林欧阳公，听其议论之宏辩，观其容貌之秀伟，与其门人贤士大夫游，而后知天下之文章聚乎此也。太尉以才略冠天下，天下之所恃以无忧，四夷之所惮以不敢发，入则周公、召公，出则方叔、召虎。而辙也未之见焉。

且夫人之学也，不志其大，虽多而何为？辙之来也，于山见终南、嵩、华之高，于水见黄河之大且深，于人见欧阳公，而犹以为未见太尉也。故愿得观贤人之光耀，闻一言以自壮，然后可以尽天下之大观而无憾者矣。

辙年少，未能通习吏事。向之来，非有取于斗升之禄，偶然得之，非其所乐。然幸得赐归待选，使得优游数年之间，将以益治其文，且学为政。太尉苟以为可教而辱教之，又幸矣！

Appreciation

In ancient times, we didn't have such a convenient way of communication like cell phone, so if people want to exchange feelings and transmit information, the only way is to write letters. Mr. Su Zhe, as a young office, wrote this letter to Mr. Han Qi, who was a well-known military general at that time. To write the letter, Mr. Su expected to get a chance to visit Mr. Han. Therefore, the beginning of the letter, Mr. Su showed his respect Mr. Han, and introduces himself. Then he expounded his opinions on literary issues. The language he used is vivid and his views are unique. After attracting reader's interests, finally he put forward his request, and politely ended the letter.

We believe that if Mr. Su had a cell phone, his phone call would also be phenomenal. Because no matter which medium is used, the methods of effective communication and transmission of ideas are always similar. Not only we can learn relevant etiquette from modern works, but also gain experience from the wisdom of the ancients.

Unit 18

Job Application and Interview

◆ Case-Lead-in

Stevens, a middle-aged man, had worked as a programmer in a company for 8 years. However, the company went out of business. At that time, Stevens' third son had just been born, and the enormous financial pressure made him breathless. Stevens began a long career looking for a job. One day, Stevens saw in the newspaper that a software company was hiring programmers, and the pay was very good. He rushed to the company immediately, ready to apply for the job. The competition was fierce. After a brief conversation, the company informed him to take the written test a week later. In the written test, Stevens once again passed, left final interview two days later.

However, in this final interview, Stevens was not selected. Instead of resentment, Stevens wrote a letter to the company to express his gratitude for providing him the opportunity of written test and interview. After the company received the reply, they were all moved by such a letter, and finally the president also knew about it. One week later, Stevens receives a beautiful New Year's card, offer from the company.

Unit 18　Job Application and Interview

18.1　Learning Objectives

(1) Master how to write resume and recommendation letter.
(2) Understand how to prepare for an interview.
(3) Mastering interview skills.

18.2　Brief Introduction

In today's world of rapid economic development, economic development brings high standards of talent requirements, and with it, the "pressure" and "fear" of job seekers. But employment has always been a hot topic of discussion in society. The difficulty of employment is not "comparative", the possibility of employment itself is extremely low. Over-ambitious, unable to find a way out, or take the wrong path may be the cause of employment difficulties.

In this chapter, we will explain the recruitment process from a company's perspective and give students strategies and skills to deal with it, focusing on English resume creation, application and submission, interview and final acceptance of the offer.

18.3　Resumes and Application Letters

A resume is a summary of your education, job experience, and job-related skills that you send to potential employers. An application letter, sometimes called a cover letter, is a special kind of business letter that accompanies a resume for a job. From it and the resume, potential employers learn about you and decide whether to interview you for a job.

Remember that a potential employer's first impression of you will be based solely on this initial application letter and resume. If the application letter and resume are sloppy, the employer may conclude that you do not care, you do not look after details, and you are not focused. Do your best to make sure your application letter and resume are free of errors and present you in the best possible light.

1. Resumes

Resumes can be written in various formats, but all resumes have certain elements in common. Your name, address, phone number, and e-mail address should be displayed at the top of the resume, usually in boldfaced text. Be sure your email address sounds somewhat professional. You can never go wrong with a simple email address made up of your full name or just your last name. Try to keep your resume to one page. Place references on a second page.

Other common components to include are education, work experience, and a brief description of honors and awards. In the "education" section, include your major academic interests. Include your grade point average only if you believe it will increase your chances of getting an interview. In the "work experience" section, list any work or major volunteer experience you have done in chronological order, putting the most recent work first. Use verbs that describe what you did. Do not use "worked" as a verb, if at all possible. For example, do not say "worked as a waiter". Instead, say "waited tables". If you are currently working, the verbs for your current job should be in the present tense. For any previous work, verbs should be past tense. All resumes should be objective and factual. False information misrepresents you.

Components that are optional include a professional objective statement, which is usually near the top of the resume. A professional objective statement tells what you hope to achieve and is usually written this way: "to be employed as a customer service representative for a major agricultural business" or "to use my agricultural mechanics skills in a farm implement dealership". The objective statement is optional because everyone's real objective is to get a job interview. Sometimes an objective statement is helpful to the person reading your resume. Including a professional objective statement is up to you. Just make sure that it enhances your resume and does not detract from it.

Another optional section is "interests and activities". Only include interests and activities that you know will enhance your resume. Do not include information that may hinder your chances of getting an interview. In this section you may wish to include volunteer and school activities.

You may want to list contact information (name, phone number, email address) for references on a second page. List three references who can discuss your work experience, educational qualifications, and your character. Examples of references may include a former employer or coworker, a teacher, or a member of the clergy. Do not list family members as references.

Just like the application letter, the resume should be free of misspellings, typographical errors, and grammatical errors. As for the look of the resume, do not use unusual typefaces; use a traditional-looking type style. Also use basic white or off-white paper. Avoid bright or unusual paper colors.

The common formats for resumes are the chronological resume and the functional resume. The chronological resume is probably the more common format. A chronological resume is written in reverse chronological order, with headings grouped by what a person has done, such as "education", "employment experience" and "interests/activities".

The functional resume classifies the experiences that demonstrate your skills and capabilities into categories, such as "professional" "technical" "communication" "leadership" "management" and "sales". A functional resume usually finishes with a reverse chronological listing of your job experiences. Until you have a lot of experiences that you can group together by skills and capabilities, you may not wish to use a functional resume.

2. Application Letter

A resume is important, but the application letter is equally important. Most prospective employers read not only a resume, but also the letter—if not initially, then on the second pass. The application letter is a great opportunity to sell your unique credentials. It provides the employer with a first impression of you.

Writing an application letter is similar to writing any other business letter. However, the emphasis in an application letter is on promoting your abilities, qualities, and characteristics so that the prospective employer believes that you are the right person for the job. The letter details specific experiences that show what you can do for the employer if you are hired. An application letter also gives you the opportunity to demonstrate your writing skills.

Customize your letter for each job application. Such items as including the correct company name and employer name, job title, and contact information are important and make a good first impression. If possible, do not send an application letter to "To Whom It May Concern" or "Dear Sir or Madam". Find out the employer's name and spell the name correctly. Also, make sure you get the employer's gender correct if the name, such as "Chris" "Ashley" or "Jamie", could be either for a male or female. Match the job requirements and desired qualifications with your skills and credentials.

The letter should include an opening paragraph that explains which job you are applying for and how you found out about the job. The body of the letter provides specific examples of activities or courses you have been involved in that make you right for the job. One way to match up your qualities with the mission of the organization is to find out what the company does and some of its recent activities, and then write about how your specific experiences can support that. Much of this information can be found on a company's website. If you are applying for a job at a local company, you may be able to get information about the company by asking people in your community. In addition, the application letter connects the content of your resume to the facts of the specific company and job description. In the letter, do not ask about salary and benefits. Those topics should be covered in the job interview, not in the application letter.

The end of the application letter should include information on how the employer can contact you, and you should request a job interview. Also, you can state that you will follow up after a designated period of time (usually two to three weeks) if you have not heard from the employer. This shows that you are interested in the job, and it provides a time frame for the employer to get back with you.

Remember that you are not asking for a job in the application letter; you are asking for a job interview. During the interview is when you "push" for a job. The application letter is your foot in the door. In order to get your foot in the door, the application letter must look appealing. Otherwise, you may get your foot slammed in the door.

Also, thank you letters are important components of the job search. Thank you letters can distinguish you from the crowd because so few people write and send them. After a job interview, send a thank you letter. Send the letter within three days following a job interview and tell the interviewer something new about you (possibly something you learned after the interview), relate your skills more clearly to the job you are seeking, and let the employer know why you want to work for the company. In the first paragraph, thank the person for the interview. In the second paragraph, reiterate two or three of your strong points. In the last paragraph, close with another "thank you".

18.4　The Job Interview

The job interview is when the employer meets with you to determine if you have the right qualifications to do the available job. It is also an opportunity for the employer to identify whether or not you fit the company culture. Are you a team player? Do you have the same values and work ethics as other employees?　It is also a chance for you to show evidence that you have the right qualities needed.

1. The S.T.A.R Method

Your job as an interviewee is to promote your brand (THE BEST YOU). Share concrete examples of ways in which you have excelled in class and in the workplace using the STAR method.

For the S—briefly describe a situation most relevant to the question.

For the T—briefly, describe a challenge you faced.

For the A—describe specific steps you took to solve the problem.

For the R—the result is always positive. Even when a learning experience.

If you follow these steps, you will be a star at every interview!

2. Pre-Interview Research

Research and analyze the position and the company before the interview in effort to determine whether or not there is a fit. Take the time to prepare your own thoughtful questions for interviewers to respond to during the interview so that you are able to better determine whether or not the position and company are a fit for you. Glassdoor—a job-search app, can be a useful tool for your research.

Things to consider in your research are as follows.

Is this where you want to go to work every day?

Does the job description interest you? Are their values well aligned with your own?

Know how long they have been in business.

What their major product is.

Know why you would want to work there and what you will contribute to the company.

What are they known for?

Who are their customers/clients (profile)?

What is the "culture"?

3. Be Your Best Self

Should you be yourself during the interview? Yes! Your very BEST self! Don't sit in the waiting room with your legs stretched out, phone in hand, with a chilled out demeanor. Leave your phone in the car! Stand up and greet the interviewer with a firm handshake, and certainly not a limp handshake which might suggest a weak character. Smile and make eye contact. Remember that those first few seconds are a great opportunity to create a great impression.

Avoid the classic negative body language traits; don't cross your arms as this can be interpreted as defensive and try to sit forward and make direct eye contact to demonstrate your enthusiasm for the position.

The first traits hiring managers look for in candidates is a positive attitude. SHOW them that, if you work for them, you will be a team player who will follow directions and take initiative. That you can do the work!

4. The Interview

Most interviews have a schedule—which makes it easier to follow along and prepare. The employer will talk about their organization, ask about your skills and experience and what you have to offer. A sample problem or situation may be offered for you to offer a solution. Think through it and analyze it like a class problem. Teamwork is important to offer as are concise answers. A timeline will usually be offered. If not, ask for one.

When asking a question during an interview, remember to keep your answers short. While it is true that you should answer many of the questions in a precise manner, there are also instances where you have to give detailed and somewhat longer answers. If you are asked about a specific task in your previous job that you performed really well, be sure to elaborate on your answer. Providing too short of a response to a question requiring an example means you're not selling yourself well enough. That said, be sure not to ramble. Generally, limit your more detailed responses to 2-3 minutes. You can practice this by rehearsing verbal presentations of key qualifications in your resume.

Be ready to convey your relevant skills, interests, and goals. Practice explaining your strengths and accomplishments ahead of time and have your elevator pitch ready. If they ask you what your salary expectationis, it is a good idea to know the starting salary range for your major so that you are able to provide realistic information. Indeed.com or glassceiling.com are good internet sites to use when checking into general salary ranges. Generally, salary is not discussed during the interview. The key objective for you and the employer is to determine the mutual fit and how you can add value. Compensation talk comes last—after they're sold on you.

18.5　Case Study

How to answer common interview questions.

(1) Question: Tell me about yourself.

How to answer: This is your opportunity to discuss who you are as a professional. Be sure to mention your education, experience, skills, possibly even why you choose this career path. Keep your response focused on who you are as a professional.

(2) Question: What are three of your greatest strengths?

How to answer: Be thoughtful and honest in your response. Describe the skills you have that are most relevant to the position. Be prepared to back up your response with an example. You can provide examples of how your strengths have worked for you in the past and discuss the ways the skills could benefit you in the position you are interviewing for.

(3) Question: What are three of your weaknesses?

How to answer: Be honest, but be cautious of stating that your weakness is what they are looking for an employee … Think about the job duties described in the job postings and try not to point out weaknesses that would be a major obstacle should you be hired. It is also wise to discuss how you are working on the weakness. Do not respond with "I can't really think of anything".

(4) Question: Why should we hire you?

How to answer: Be sure to point out qualities/skills/attributes that you possess that may set you apart from other candidates. Do you have certifications that others may not? Demonstrate confidence without sounding conceited. Illustrate your worth as an employee by talking about what past and present supervisors would say about you. Make sure you highlight your uniqueness to show you would be the best candidate for the position.

(5) Question: Describe a leader you admire.

How to answer: You do not have to know the person in order imitate their leadership, but it may be more realistic if you do. Be sure you list someone that you believe has effective leadership and know why you feel they are successful in leading. Refrain from choosing a controversial leader. Discuss why you admire this person, what is it about their leadership that made you choose them. What are some of the lessons you learned from this person and how could you incorporate that into your life.

(6) Question: Tell me about a time when you had to extend a deadline.

How to answer: You do not want to give a negative view of your accountability. Your answer should not indicate that you have poor time management skills or poor work ethic. Discuss your willingness to adjust a deadline if you think it will add to the overall quality of the project. What could happen if you had not adjusted the deadline? What steps did you take to extend the deadline?

(7) Question: Where do you see yourself in five years?

How to answer: This is one question you would not answer specifically. If you would like to see yourself in management, it is fine to say so, but you may not want to list a specific title you would like to hold. Be realistic. Consider the company you are interviewing with, their opportunities for advancement and how that will fit into your five year plan.

(8) Question: Why are you leaving your current job?

How to answer: Give two or three reasons why you are looking for a new position. Regardless of your feelings towards your supervisor and co-workers, refrain from talking negatively about them. This is a good opportunity to discuss the fact that you will be obtaining (recently obtained) a degree and you are looking for an opportunity to use the knowledge you gained through your education.

(9) Question: Why do you feel you would be a good fit for this position?

How to answer: Consider the skills and characteristics that you possess that could help you succeed in the position you are interviewing for. Think about the kind of person that would be perfectly compatible with the job duties. Discuss how you stay current in the field.

(10) Question: What do you look for in a good supervisor?

How to answer: Be sure to discuss the qualities, traits, characteristics that you look for in a supervisor. Discuss the characteristics, do not just list them.

(11) Question: If you were hired how could your supervisor help you do the best on the job?

How to answer: Discuss what you would want to see from your supervisor in the first weeks of your new position... Training, what type of supervision would you expect as you begin, things they could to do assist you in getting acclimated to the position, etc.

(12) Question: Tell me about your relationship with your current and past supervisors.

How to answer: This question will give the interviewer a sense of your personality and how it relates to the prospective supervisor. How you discuss your past supervisors will give insight to the way you work and any potential problems that may arise. AVOID being negative! Be honest, but try to put a positive spin on it. If you didn't get along well, discuss what you learned about yourself, etc.

(13) Question: Talk about a work environment that you think would be ineffective for you.

How to answer: What do you need to have a positive work environment, or things that could have been better at a previous environment? Discuss how it would be ineffective without those things. You could consider the importance of: communication, feedback, ability to infuse a personal touch on projects, etc. Would having these items make the work place more or less effective?

(14) Question: In your previous experience, would you say you were known for taking the initiative? If so, provide an example.

How to answer: If you are known for taking the initiative, be sure to provide a good example of what you did and why it was taking initiative. If you have not been known to take initiative in the workplace, provide an example of why.

(15) Question: Do you prefer a stable day-to-day routine or a dynamic constantly changing environment?

How to answer: Be sure to consider the position you are interviewing for. If you prefer consistency, will this job provide that? If you prefer dynamic constantly changing, will this position provide that?

(16) Question: How well do you handle criticism?

How to answer: You may consider responding that constructive criticism allows you to grow as a professional.

(17) Question: Tell me something about yourself that I will not find in your resume.

How to answer: This is your opportunity to discuss experiences that you may have omitted from your resume to keep it at one page. Be sure the information you provide is relevant and not found in your resume. You want to give them something new. If you have won awards that weren't noted, if you are currently working on a certificate, but didn't include it on the resume because it is not finished… Now is the time to bring those things up.

(18) Question: Tell me about a time when you showed real determination.

How to answer: Talk about a time when you persevered to accomplish a goal. Choose something that will reflect an interest in developing new skills, demonstrates your ability to gather resources and manage stressful situations. Discuss the results you obtained.

(19) Question: How do you manage stress in your daily work?

How to answer: The interviewer is attempting to gain information to see if you have a tendency to crack under pressure. Be sure you show that you can manage high-pressure situations. Think of ways you manage your stress throughout the day. Stay professional, and be sure not to give an example of something that would display you are unproductive during work hours because of stress.

(20) Question: What do you bring to this job that is unique and would make us want to hire you?

How to answer: Your answer should demonstrate confidence in your abilities without sounding conceited. Consider what past and present supervisors or co-workers would say about you. What specific skills do you have that relate to this job? What specific tasks do your current co-workers/supervisors come to you to complete and why? Be sure to answer the question, do not just list the same skills that are displayed on your resume.

(21) Question: What would your ideal job be like?

How to answer: Discuss the qualities of your ideal job in broad strokes: fair pay, good people, company stability, etc. Touch on your qualifications and relevant skills to illustrate why you're a good fit for the job. Talk about learning of the job opportunity and why it spoke to you — why the position intrigues you.

(22) Question: Do you prefer working alone or in a group?

How it works: Be honest, but also appear flexible. Consider the values and mission of the company… is teamwork something they strive for? If you are best at completing tasks alone, you can honestly say that, but also state that you can work in a group setting, and if you are better working in a group, that is okay, but be sure to mention you can also complete tasks individually. Be sure that you consider the typical work day in this position and if you would normally be working alone or in a group…

(23) Question: Why do you want to work here?

How it works: Be sure to consider what you know about this company, their mission, values, reputation, etc. (be aware of these, but do not recite them in the interview.) Discuss the reasons why a position in this company is appealing to you. Be sure to be insightful.

You can exercise interview with your partner according to the above questions.

18.6　Business Ethics

《史记》记载："平原君已定从而归，归至於赵，曰：'胜不敢复相士。胜相士多者千人，寡者百数，自以为不失天下之士，今乃於毛先生而失之也。毛先生一至楚，而使赵重於九鼎大吕。毛先生以三寸之舌，强於百万之师。胜不敢复相士。'遂以为上客。"

平原君归赵后，对毛遂赞叹不已，赞叹毛遂一人比百万大军还要厉害，毛遂从此被赵胜尊为上宾，毛遂家族在之后也得以成为望族。据《清漾毛氏族谱》记载，毛遂因定楚有功，置守之地，入于荥阳，后以为望族。现今也建有相关纪念建筑，以示对毛遂的纪念和尊重。

毛遂作为平原君的门客，在自荐前已成为平原君食客三年之久，但毛遂并没有得到平原君身边的近臣举荐，如果毛遂没有自荐，即使毛遂富有一生才华，也因没有他人举荐而在平原君门下众多食客中平淡无奇，很难有出头之日，毛遂也会留有遗憾。后来用毛遂自荐表示推荐自己，将自己的能力和才华充分展示，实现自己的目标。

讨论

毛遂自荐成功的原因，再分析一下一个人如何发现自荐机会及如何有效自荐？

18.7　Exercises

(1) Finish one qualified resume.

(2) According to STAR method, please simulate that you are going to a high-tech company, how to use STAR method.

(3) Exercise interview with your classmates.

Unit 19

Business Travel Etiquette

✧ **Case-Lead-in**

Most of us spend most of our time working in domestic office. The rest may travel all the time. No matter which one, business travel is a part of our job, and your company counts on you to handle things well when you present your company in partners' or counterparts' places. But travel could be annoyed and tired, you still need to keep positive and active all the time. That won't be easy.

Unit 19　Business Travel Etiquette

19.1　Learning Objectives

(1) Acquire how to prepare your business trip before your departure and after your arrival.
(2) Be prepared with a travel list.
(3) Acquire some knowledge about foreign holidays.
(4) Understand different kinds of greeting and be able to apply the proper greeting in right region.
(5) Acquire basic etiquettes attending conference, seminar, and training program.
(6) Acquire basic etiquettes attending trade fair.

19.2　The Significance of Business Travel Etiquette

Travel becomes easier than before with the help of airplane and high-speed train, even though, thinking about carrying a huge luggage, getting to the airport or railway station, confirming the right terminals, making check-in and security check, boarding plane, and the last but not the least, departure on time. None of these will be easy for a traveler. Besides, you might have unpredictable neighbor, crying baby, person with too much luggage, or using their cell phone loudly. All this will be the last straw to crush your fragile nerves, meanwhile, you must keep your business etiquette during the whole process.

19.3　Basic Etiquette of Business Travel

Before departure

(1) To check your passport and visa if you travel internationally, ID for domestic. If it is possible, make a photocopy of your passport and visa, in case you need them occasionally.
(2) To book your accommodation.
(3) To prepare some local currencies, and to be aware the total amount you are allowed to carry with you.
(4) To carry reasonable carry-on luggage, it is better to check total weight in prior.
(5) To decide what to bring with you
(6) To bring some small gifts for your hosts.
(7) To put stuff which you might use in the air in a separated bag, then you won't need to open the bin often during the flight.
(8) To be prepared for delays, it happens all the time.
(9) To be prepared for cultural shock.
(10) To be aware of your health condition.
(11) To have a good sleep before your flight.

Here is a check list, you might use when you prepare a business trip.
- Passport and visa
- ID
- Plane ticket (if you have a hard copy)
- The name, address, and telephone number of your hotel
- The name, address, and telephone number of your visiting places
- Taxi- information or car rental- information
- Credit cards
- Foreign currency
- Clothing (business and casual) and comfortable shoes
- Glasses or contacts
- Gifts
- Umbrella
- Power bank
- Medicines
- Business documents and cards
- Pen

After arriving

(1) To be sure that you comply with local laws, not carry on any illegal goods, no matter the goods are legal in your country.

(2) To look after your property and self-safety.

(3) To respect local customs, people, city, culture, and country.

(4) To make sure your visit is not scheduled on their holiday or weekend.

(5) To call the front desk, if you have any problems with your room and equipment.

(6) To deal with jetlag.

(7) To make sure you have small bills with you.

(8) To meet your counterpart in lobby, coffee corner, or meeting room.

(9) To give tips, like a dollar.

(10) To dress conservatively.

(11) To make sure you have international driver's license or a license recognized by local authority.

(12) When you are in a foreign country and you find yourself is in a kind of trouble, you might need to remember: if you are in any kind of severe trouble, do remember to go to your embassy or consulate for help.

If you travel with your boss

Traveling with your boss is an opportunity to let the boss know you more, and to demonstrate your abilities on planning, implementing, handling uncertainty and risk. Firstly, you must show your respect to your boss by taking things in your hand.

Before your departure, you need to make adequate preparation in advance and communicate schedule with your boss, to check whether your boss has any suggestion. During the trip, you should take charge of process to make sure things go in the right path.

19.4 Foreign Custom and Holiday Etiquette

As we have been told in many places, being an international business person, we need to be aware of different cultures, but eventually, nobody can understand and deal with all different cultures. Taking a small example, holiday, nobody really masters all holidays celebrating cross the world, even cross own country. Some holidays are commonly celebrated cross many countries, and there are much more distinctive holidays in every country. If you look at India, according to different regions and religions, they have hundreds of holidays, here, we can only list some of them. We list some major holidays in several countries (see Table 19.1), this gives you a small window to the world's culture.

Table 19.1 Some Major Holidays in Several Countries

Country	Holiday	Date
US	New Year's Day	January 1st
	Martin Luther King Day	January 18th
	President's Day	February 15th
	St. Patrick's Day	March 17th
	Good Friday	April 2nd
	Easter	April
	Memorial Day	May 31st
	Independent Day	July 4th
	Labor Day	September 6th
	Columbus Day	October 11th
	Halloween	November 1st
	Veteran Day	November 11th
	Thanks Giving	November
	Christmas	December 25th
Canada	New Year's Day	January 1st
	Easter Sunday and Monday	April
	Labor Day	May 1st
	Victoria Day	Third Monday in May
	Canada Day	July 1st
	Thanksgiving Day	Second Monday in October
	All Saints' Day	November 1st
	Remembrance Day	November 11th

Continued

Country	Holiday	Date
Canada	Christmas	December 25th
	Boxing Day	December 26th
	Carnival de Quebec	February
	St. Jean Baptiste Day	June 24th
UK	New Year's Day	January 1st
	St. Patrick's Day	March 17th
	Good Friday	April 2nd
	Easter Sunday and Monday	April
	May day	May 1st
	Commonwealth Day	May 24th
	Spring Bank Holiday	Last Monday in May
	Queen's Official Birthday	June 10th
	The Summer Holiday	Last Monday in August
	Columbus Day	October 12th
	Guy Fawkes' Day	November 5th
	Veterans Day	November 11th
	Christmas	December 25th
France	New Year's Day	January 1st
	Mardi Gras	February—March
	Easter Sunday and Monday	April
	Labor Day	May 1st
	Liberation Day	May 8th
	Ascension Day	May
	Whit Monday	May
	Bastille Day	July 14th
	Pentecost	May — July
	Assumption of the Virgin Mary	August 15th
	All Saints' Day	November 1st
	World War I Armistice Day	November 11th
	Christmas	December 25th
Germany	New Year's Day	January 1st
	Good Friday	March—April
	Easter Sunday and Monday	April
	Labor Day	May 1st
	Ascension Day	May
	Whit Monday	May
	Day of German Unity	October 3rd
	All Saints' Day	November 1st
	Day of Prayer and Repentance	November

Unit 19 Business Travel Etiquette

Continued

Country	Holiday	Date
Germany	Christmas	December 25th
Japan	New Year's Day	January 1st
	Coming of Age Day	January 15th
	National Foundation Day	February 11th
	Vernal Equinox	March 21st
	Greenery Day	April 29th
	Constitution Day	May 3rd
	Children's Day	May 5th
	Bon Festival	August 15th
	Respect for the Aged Day	September 15th
	Autumnal Equinox	September 23rd
	Sports day	October 10th
	Culture Day	November 3rd
	Labor Thanksgiving Day	November 23rd
	Emperor Akihito's birthday	December 23rd
South Korea	New Year's Day	January 1st
	The Lunar New Year	January or February
	Independence Day	March 1st
	Buddha's Birthday	April or May
	Memorial Day	June 6th
	Constitution Day	July 17th
	Liberation Day	August 15th
	Ch'usok, Harvest Moon Festival	September or October
	National Foundation Day	October 3rd
	Christmas Day	December 25th
Mexico	New Year's Day	January 1st
	St. Anthony's Day	January 17th
	Constitution Day	February 5th
	Carnival Week	February—March
	Birthday of Benito Juarez	March 21st
	Easter	April
	Labor Day	May 1st
	Cinco de Mayo	May 5th
	Corpus Christi	June
	Assumption of the Virgin Mary	August 15th
	President's Annual Message	September 1st
	Independence Day	September 16th
	Columbus Day	October 12th
	All Saints' Day	November 1st

Continued

Country	Holiday	Date
Mexico	All Souls' Day	November 2nd
	Revolution Day	November 20th
	Day of the Virgin Guadalupe	December 12th
	Christmas	December 25th
India	New Year's Day	January 1st
	Guru Gobind Singh Jayanti	January 9th
	Lohri	January 13th
	Pongal	January 14th
	Makar Sankranti	January 14th
	Republic Day	January 26th
	Vasant Panchami	February 5th
	Hazarat Ali's Birthday	February 15th
	Guru Ravidas Jayanti	February 16th
	Shivaji Jayanti	February 19th
	Maharishi Dayanand Saraswati Jayanti	February 26th
	Maha Shivaratri	March 1st
	Holika Dahana	March 17th
	Holi	March 18th
	Dolyatra	March 18th
	Chaitra Sukhlad	April 2nd
	Rama Navami	April 10th
	Ambedkar Jayanti	April 14th
	Eid-ul-Fitar	May 3rd
	Birthday of Ravindranath	May 9th
	Buddha Purnima	May 16th
	Rath Yatra	July 1st
	Eid Al-Adha	July 10th
	Muharram	August 8th
	Raksha Bandhan	August 11th
	Independence Day	August 15th
	Janmashtami	August 19th
	Ganesh Chaturthi/Vinayaka Chaturthi	August 31st
	Mahatma Gandhi Jayanti	October 2nd
	Maha Navami	October 4th
	Dussehra	October 5th
	Milad Un Nabi	October 9th
	Diwali	October 24th
	Guru Nanak Jayanti	November 8th
	Christmas Day	December 25th

Continued

Country	Holiday	Date
Russia	New Year's Day	January 1st
	Christmas Day	January 7th
	Old New Year	January 14th
	Defender of the Fatherland Day	February 23rd
	International Women's Day	March 8th
	Easter Sunday	April—May
	Spring and Labor Day	May 1st
	Victory Day	May 9th
	Russia Day	June 12th
	Day of Knowledge	September 1st
	Unity Day	November 4th

19.5 Typical Greeting Behaviors

When you travel internationally, one important business etiquette is greeting your host or guest with proper greeting manners which is regarding to local custom. Currently, there are different kinds of greetings available worldwide (see Table 19.2). With globalization in business world, some of greeting become more popular, like handshakes, but there are still some different greetings we need to understand. Even a simple handshake may hide some information that needs to be interpreted, e.g. how many times you shake hands, or how long you hold the other's hand.

Table 19.2 Different Kinds of Greetings Available Worldwide

Greeting	Origin	Usage Scenario	Remarks
Handshake	Europe	General applied	Not widely used in Middle Eastern countries Let a female offer her hand to the other part first
Kiss	Various	General applied	Air kiss Cheek to cheek
Hug	Various	General applied	
Bowing	Asia	Variousness, may be different due to gender, age, social status	Recognize differences among different countries

19.6 Basic Etiquette of Conference, Seminar or Training Program

If you are applied, invited, or assigned to any of Conference, Seminar, or training program, it could be a special kind of business travel. Besides the etiquettes we have mentioned above, you need to pay attention to some extra items.

(1) To bring and read the schedule and agenda.

(2) To prepare some relevant information about the event and participants.

(3) To prepare your speech or lecture as well as visual document in prior if you are invited to give one.

(4) To be on time.

(5) To be friendly with other participants.

(6) To be an active participant, i.e., providing your insight or participate in discussion.

19.7　Basic Etiquette of Trade Fair

There is one more kind of business travel you may experience, a trade fair. The company will participate in various trade fairs to promote its products. Arranging booth and attending the fair both have some etiquettes you should be aware the followings.

(1) To prepare stuffs you are going to carry with your colleagues if you do not travel alone.

(2) To plan the display before you leave to make sure everything you need are with you.

(3) To work as a team and respect your team members.

(4) To dress properly if uniform is not required.

(5) To show deserved attention to your visitors.

(6) To treaty your visitor equally.

(7) To direct your visitor to a free colleague if you are busy with others.

(8) To collect visitor's information, i.e., company, name, affiliation, phone number, interests, etc.

19.8　Case Study

Case One

Your company will send you to participate in the product exhibition held in country G next month. Please plan an international trip on this basis, and pay attention to business etiquette related matters that should be considered during the trip.

Meanwhile, the organizer of the exhibition will provide a booth for your company, and you will participate in the exhibition alone. Therefore, please consider the items required for the layout and the design of the booth. In this process, what business etiquettes do you need to pay attention to as well?

Case Two

You are invited to attend an international export conference and to give a speech in the conference too. Please prepare your international travel and list what you should bring with you.

19.9　Business Ethics

　　张岱在《游山小启》中写道："幸生胜地，鞋鞡下饶有山川；喜作闲人，酒席间只谈风月。野航恰受，不逾两三；便榼随行，各携一二。僧上凫下，觞止茗生。谈笑杂以诙谐，陶写赖此丝竹。兴来即出，可趁樵风；日暮辄归，不因剡雪。愿邀同志，用续前游。凡游以一人司会，备小船、坐毡、茶点、盏箸、香炉、薪米之属。每人携一簋、一壶、二小菜。游无定所，出无常期，客无限数。过六人则分坐二舟，有大量则自携多酿。约 x 日游 x 舟次。右启某老先生有道。司会某具。

　　白石苍崖，拟筑草亭招素鹤；浓山淡水，闲锄明月种梅花。有志竟成，无约不践。将与罗浮争艳，还期庾岭分香。实为林处士之功臣，亦是苏东坡之胜友。"

　　沈括在《梦溪忘怀录》中说的："游山客不可多，多则应接人事劳顿，有妨观赏，兼仆众所至扰人。今为三人，具诸应用物，共为两肩，二人荷之，操几杖持盖杂使三人便足矣。兼与者未预客有所携则照裁损，无浪重复，惟轻简为便。器皿皆木漆，轻而远道，惟酒杯或可用银钱一、二千，使人腰之，操几杖者可兼也。

　　行具两肩：甲肩：左衣箧一：衣，被，枕，盥漱具，手巾，足巾，药，汤，梳。右食匣一，竹为之。二鬲，并底盖为四，食盘子三，每盘果子楪十，矮酒榼一，可容数升，以备沽酒，匏一，杯三，漆筒合子贮脯修干果嘉蔬各数品，饼饵少许，以备饮食不时应猝。惟三食盘相重，为一鬲，其余分任之。署月果修合皆不须携。乙肩：竹鬲二，下为匣，上为虚鬲：左鬲上层书箱一：纸，笔，墨，砚，剪刀，韵略，杂书册。匣中食碗碟各六，匕箸各四，生果数物，削果刀子。右鬲上层琴一，竹匣贮之。折叠棋局一，匣中棋子，茶二、三品，腊茶即碾熟者，盏托各三，盂瓢七等。

　　附带杂物：小斧子，斫刀，劚药锄子，蜡烛二，柱杖，泥靴，雨衣，伞笠，食铫，虎子，急须子，油筒。"

19.10　Exercises

Exercise One

Departure:

When you arrive at the airport, the check-in of the flight you are about to take will be closed soon. Meantime, you find that your luggage is overweight. Please handle this situation delicately.

Exercise Two

Arriving:

When you landed at a foreign airport, you were randomly checked by the airport staff. They suspected that you were carrying contraband. How would you deal with this situation?

Exercise Three

In hotel:

You finally arrived at hotel. Your local partner called you and said that he would arrive at your hotel in an hour to discuss tomorrow's negotiation with you. How would you receive your guest?

Exercise Four

In trade fair:

A delegation composed of your five colleagues and you participated in a product show. Your products are very popular, and your company's booth was surrounded by lots of visitors and potential buyers.

You are receiving a potential customer, and there is another one is coming to you too. How will you deal with these two potential customers? What should you do when receiving potential customers?

Unit 20

Business Negotiation Etiquette

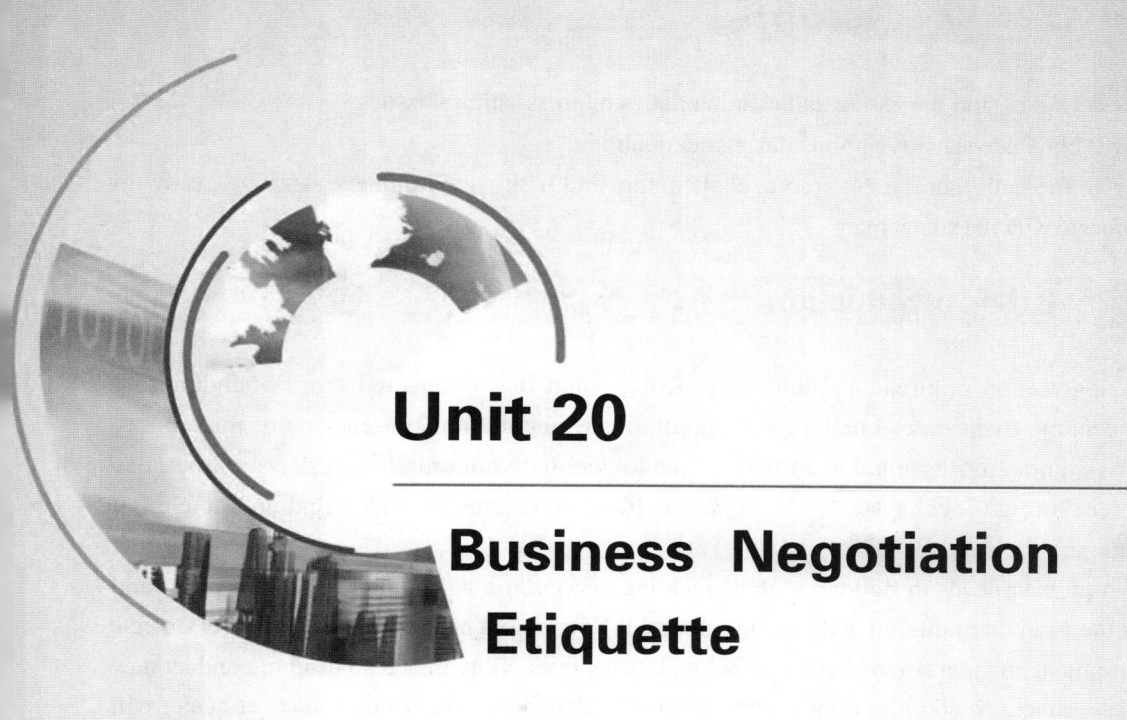

◆ **Case-Lead-in**

Suppose you were the general manager of a hamburger restaurant 30 years ago. Now your company has formulated a new business strategy and plans to enter an Asian market. Before entering the market, you conducted market research and found that consumers in this country take rice as their staple food. In the process of negotiation with your local partners, they proposed to localize your cuisines and develop new products with rice as the main raw material. But you insist on selling only traditional hamburgers. The negotiation was at an impasse for a time. If you were given a chance to review the decision at that time, what would you do?

20.1　Learning Objectives

(1) Understand the nature and characteristics of cross-cultural issues.
(2) Navigate sensitive points during negotiation.
(3) Prepare them for a more challenging and risky environment, and be ready to reciprocate with the counterpart.

20.2　Brief Introduction

Negotiation is already a delicate process, when it is conducted cross boundaries, it will become even more challenging. International negotiation presents more uncertainty and risk, and a professional negotiator needs to deal with not only business issues, but also different foreign legal system, natural and cultural environment, and verbal and nonverbal language.

A pioneer needs to figure out how much the new culture will influence their business and what they can do to minimize its negative impact. Negotiators need to prepare them for diverse environment and alert to important verbal and visual cues. They may also need to conduct new self-assessment to adopt to their international counterparts. A better negotiation etiquette will help them conquer these difficulties.

20.3　Negotiators as Hosts

Being a host negotiator, you're living in the culture you grow up with, which is as natural as breathing. If you receive visiting negotiators, you need to be aware that other countries, culture are different with yours. They may have a totally different religion, working relationship, management system, and company discipline.

In business negotiation, even if people gather together for business purpose, they are still strongly influenced by their cultural in behavior and belief, and their decision and desire still follow the patterns. To be a qualified negotiator, you should be aware difference between you and your counterpart, sensitive to their customs and behavior, recognize their core value and open to diversified preferences.

To do so, you need to understand basic concept related to culture. In this book, one theory among multiple of them will be introduced: Geert Hofstede's Cultural Dimensions. Prof. Hofstede defined his work in his website as follows.

"National cultures can be described according to the analysis of Geert Hofstede. These ideas were first based on a large research project into national culture differences across subsidiaries of a multinational corporation (IBM) in 64 countries. Subsequent studies by others covered students in 23 countries, elites in 19 countries, commercial airline pilots in 23 countries, up-market consumers in 15 countries, and civil service managers in 14 countries. Together these studies identified and validated four independent dimensions of national culture differences, with a fifth dimension added later.[1]"

These five dimensions are:

(1) Power Distance[2];

(2) Individualism[3];

(3) Masculinity[4];

(4) Uncertainty Avoidance[5];

(5) Long-Term Orientation[6].

Their explanations are provided in his website as well, and its analytical result is demonstrated in data. Figure 20.1 list some key countries' result to show their analysis and these numbers provide a visual result for different cultures. Through these data and graphics, you will have a more intuitive feeling of the cultural differences of various countries.

These theories analyze the differences of national cultures from different perspectives, but no matter which theory only analyzes a part of national cultures, and the culture they analyze cannot represent the national culture that everyone in this country understands and embodies. After all, everyone's growth environment, education and thinking will be different, especially in the business environment. With the development of internationalization and globalization,

---

1 Geert Hofstede's Cultural Dimensions

2 Hofstede's Power Distance Index measures the extent to which the less powerful members of organizations and institutions (like the family) accept and expect that power is distributed unequally. This represents inequality (more versus less), but defined from below, not from above. It suggests that a society's level of inequality is endorsed by the followers as much as by the leaders.

3 Individualism is the one side versus its opposite, collectivism, that is the degree to which individuals are integrated into groups. On the individualist side we find societies in which the ties between individuals are loose: everyone is expected to look after him/herself and his/her immediate family. On the collectivist side, we find societies in which people from birth onwards are integrated into strong, cohesive in-groups, often extended families (with uncles, aunts and grandparents) which continue protecting them in exchange for unquestioning loyalty.

4 Masculinity versus its opposite, femininity refers to the distribution of roles between the genders which is another fundamental issue for any society to which a range of solutions are found. The IBM studies revealed that (a) women's values differ less among societies than men's values; (b) men's values from one country to another contain a dimension from very assertive and competitive and maximally different from women's values on the one side, to modest and caring and similar to women's values on the other. The assertive pole has been called "masculine" and the modest, caring pole "feminine".

5 Uncertainty avoidance deals with a society's tolerance for uncertainty and ambiguity; it ultimately refers to man's search for Truth. It indicates to what extent a culture programs its members to feel either uncomfortable or comfortable in unstructured situations. Unstructured situations are novel, unknown, surprising, and different from usual. Uncertainty avoiding cultures try to minimize the possibility of such situations by strict laws and rules, safety and security measures, and on the philosophical and religious level by a belief in absolute Truth; "there can only be one Truth and we have it".

6 Long-Term Orientation is the fifth dimension of Hofstede which was added after the original four to try to distinguish the difference in thinking between the East and West. From the original IBM studies, this difference was something that could not be deduced. Therefore, Hofstede created a Chinese value survey which was distributed across 23 countries. From these results, and with an understanding of the influence of the teaching of Confucius on the East, long term vs. short term orientation became the fifth cultural dimension.

everyone's national culture reflected in the business environment is also different from that reflected in life.

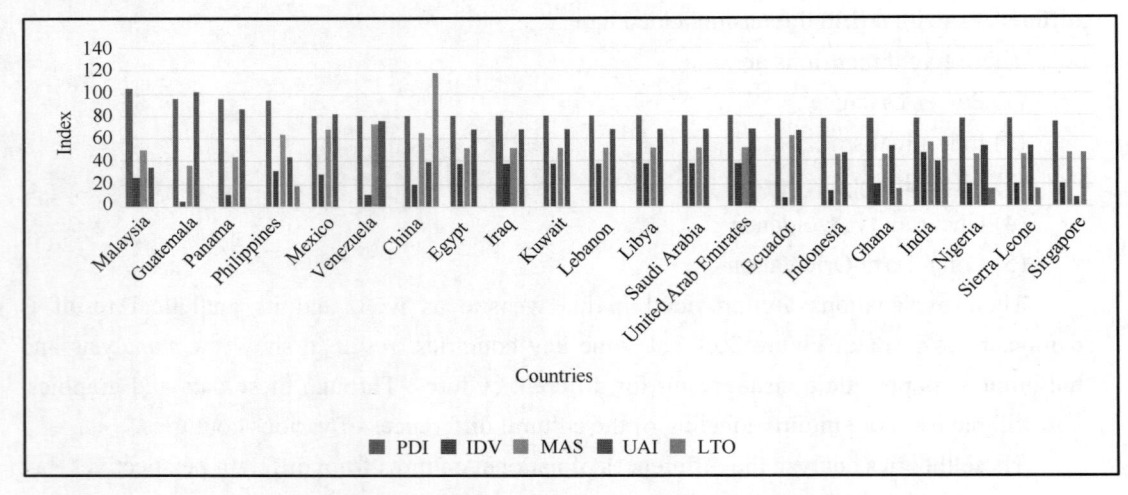

Figure 20.1 Analytical result of Geert Hofstede's Cultural Dimensions

20.4 Negotiators as Guests

Firstly, you need to evaluate how much cultural differences there may have, or saying, which part of their or yours will have significant influence, then to identify the influence is going to be positive or negative. This stage could be a part of preparation of your negotiation including to find out whether your counterparts and you have any experience in dealing with foreign culture or not. If some of you have relevant experience, it will give the group some advantages during the negotiation.

Secondly, you need to prepare yourself with knowledge of local legal system. Experiences remind us that refuse to understand the local legal environment, investment environment and social and cultural environment may lead to unpredictable consequences.

Thirdly, a qualified interpreter is a key successful element too. Say you are going to sign a purchasing contract with a local company L, a reliable interpreter will help you with legal terms, local custom and practice, and clarifying contract details.

Fourthly, you need to select appropriate team members. Your team members should be physically and psychologically suitable for international business negotiation. It must be admitted that some employees perform well in China, but they are not suitable for cross-cultural communication.

20.5 Verbal and Nonverbal Communication

In international business negotiation, communication is always a problem even with an appropriate interpreter. Since when a group of people come from the same culture, they intend to encode and decode messages in the same way, no matter these messages are sent by verbal or nonverbal approaches. It will virtually reduce communication costs. But when people come from different culture, the process will become more complicated, sometimes, it will lead to misunderstanding or hostile behavior.

Therefore, conducting effective communication and building mutual trust are the most important issues. Some people are quite sensitive and flexible to other people's feelings or characters, but most of us are trained to communicate with others.

Useful skills

(1) To choose your language carefully, avoiding slang and idioms, or regional phrase;

(2) To control your voice and facial expressions;

(3) To improve cultural sensitivity;

(4) To improve skills of encoding and decoding messages;

(5) To be aware of gestures and body language;

(6) To be reflectiveness;

(7) To keep an open mind;

(8) To embrace a diversified world;

(9) To dress properly.

20.6 Taboos of Business Negotiation of Different Cultures

The culture of a country is coupled by many determinants, including geography, politics, military economy and historical inheritance. Besides, factors, like religion, race, gender, population, are all contribute to recent evolving.

It is unrealistic for a person to understand or be familiar with all cultures in the world, but when we come into contact with a new culture, we can observe some gaps between this culture and our own culture from the following perspectives (see Table 20.1), so as to quickly understand the characteristics of this culture, most importantly, to avoid red flag in that culture, will help us in international business negotiations.

Table 20.1　Some Gaps between This Culture and Our Own Culture from the Following Perspectives

Factors	Yours	Counterpart
Value		
Belief		
Practice		
Social class		
Religion		
Age		
Physical ability		

Continued

Factors	Yours	Counterpart
Oral language		
Body language		
Gestures		
Touch		
Space		
Time		
Colors		

20.7　Case Study

Company A is a large enterprise located in country B in Asia, and its internal management system is rigorous. Company L is an enterprise located in country M in Latin America. This enterprise has been merged by company A last year. Company A dispatched some managers and staff to company L.

The products of company L have strong seasonality, and August is the hot season of the company's products every year. Therefore, the employees of the company began to increase production and formulate new marketing plans from May every year. This year is the first year after the merger, all employees stationed in company L from country B have worked overtime since May, including not only employees in the production department and sales department, but also employees in human resources, finance, logistics, warehousing and logistics departments. All employees from country B work overtime without overtime pay. But after a while, the employees from country B found a problem. All local employees didn't work overtime. When it was time to get off work, all them left the company.

Mr. F, the manager of the production department, is an employee from country B. Since he arrived in country M, he has been working in the production workshop without any weekends or holidays. Before this day's shift, he found that a machine had something wrong, so he asked the local engineer, Mr. W, to repair the machine as soon as possible, so as to ensure the smooth production of the next day.

Mr. F: Mr. W, our machine has broken down. Please repair it as soon as possible to ensure that tomorrow's production can be carried out on time.

Mr. W: I'm sorry, Mr. F, I'm about to leave work now. I just looked at that machine and found that the problem with that machine is relatively serious. I think the remaining time is not enough for me to complete the maintenance work, so I want to start the maintenance tomorrow morning.

Mr. F: I know the time is late, but you can understand that our production task is so heavy now. If this machine can't run on time tomorrow, our production progress may be delayed. I hope you can work an extra shift today to repair this machine.

Mr. W: I'm sorry, but I can't work overtime today, because I have promised my daughter that I will go to school to watch her football match this afternoon. I can't break my promise to her. I hope you understand that.

Mr. F: I understand your feelings as a father who wants to watch your daughter's important competition. But as you can see, now is the key time. If this machine can't work, tomorrow's production will be greatly affected. I hope you can sacrifice some personal time. After all, you can see that all employees from country B are working overtime, and none of us has been paid.

Mr. W: Mr. manager, your willingness to work overtime is your subjective behavior, which has nothing to do with me. The regulation does not expressly stipulate that I have the obligation to work overtime. In addition, as a person with independent personality, I need to remind you that during working hours, you are my direct boss and can give me orders related to my work. But you have no right to order me to do things during my off-duty hours. Sorry, I can't waste any more time here. My daughter's game will begin soon.

After that, Mr. W left the company.

Based on the above information, please combine with related theory to compare cultural differences between country B and L. This dialogue reflects the different views of the two countries' employees on overtime, as well as their different values on work and life. Suppose you are Mr. F, please combine the communication skills in cross-cultural negotiation, to persuade Mr. W to work overtime.

20.8 Situational Etiquette

To be aware following situations in certain countries.

Xiao Ming is a new employee in marketing department of an international company, today, he is going to attend a negotiation organized by his department. Before visiting group arrive, he asked a senior member in his team.

Xiao Ming: this is my first time in an international negotiation, I heard their team members come from various source, is there anything I need to pay attention to?

Ms. Yang, a senior member in the department: different cultures have different features and precautions, it is difficult to cover them in a short conversation. Here I have a few questions, let's see if you can answer them correctly.

(1) Can you shake hand with your guest with your left hand if your right hand is not available now?

(2) In casual chat, is family or spouse always an appropriate topic?

(3) If you visit a foreign negotiator's home, should you take off your shoes after entry

into their home?

(4) Should you always keep eye contact with your counterpart?

(5) Does nodding always indicate agreement?

(6) How do you interpret silence in different culture?

20.9　Business Ethics

Mencius said, "That whereby the superior man is distinguished from other men is what he preserves in his heart—namely, benevolence and propriety. The benevolent man loves others. The man of propriety shows respect to others. He who loves others is constantly loved by them. He who respects others is constantly respected by them. Here is a man, who treats me in a perverse and unreasonable manner. The superior man in such a case will turn round upon himself, I must have been wanting in benevolence; I must have been wanting in propriety — how should this have happened to me? He examines himself and is specially benevolent. He turns round upon himself, and is specially observant of propriety. The perversity and unreasonableness of the other, however, are still the same. The superior man will again turn round on himself. I must have been failing to do my utmost. He turns round upon himself, and proceeds to do his utmost, but still the perversity and unreasonableness of the other are repeated. On this the superior man says, 'This is a man utterly lost indeed! Since he conducts himself so, what is there to choose between him and a brute? Why should I go to contend with a brute?' Thus it is that the superior man has a life-long anxiety and not one morning's calamity. As to what is matter of anxiety to him, that indeed he has. He says, Shun was a man, and I also am a man. But Shun became an example to all the kingdom, and his conduct was worthy to be handed down to after ages, while I am nothing better than a villager. This indeed is the proper matter of anxiety to him. And in what way is he anxious about it? Just that he maybe like Shun: then only will he stop. As to what the superior man would feel to be a calamity, there is no such thing. He does nothing which is not according to propriety. If there should befall him one morning's calamity, the superior man does not account it a calamity."

孟子曰："君子所以异于人者，以其存心也。君子以仁存心，以礼存心。仁者爱人，有礼者敬人。爱人者人恒爱之，敬人者人恒敬之。有人于此，其待我以横逆，则君子必自反也：我必不仁也，必无礼也，此物奚宜至哉？其自反而仁矣，自反而有礼矣，其横逆由是也，君子必自反也：我必不忠。自反而忠矣，其横逆由是也，君子曰：'此亦妄人也已矣。如此则与禽兽奚择哉？于禽兽又何难焉？'是故，君子有终身之忧，无一朝之患也。乃若所忧则有之：舜人也，我亦人也。舜为法于天下，可传于后世，我由未免为乡人也，是则可忧也。忧之如何？如舜而已矣。若夫君子所患则亡矣。非仁无为也，非礼无行也。如有一朝之患，则君子不患矣。"

20.10　Exercises

1. Case Practice

Company H is a medium-sized auto parts production company located in country J. Its founders are three college students. With decades of development, company H has become a well-known auto parts manufacturer in this country. In this process, a management team composed of family members of the three founders, their friends, and senior employees who have served the company for a long time has been formed. Due to the deep influence of Asian culture, the management of enterprises has a strong "family management" feature, as well as a strong "family" feature in the composition of human resources.

In recent years, the development of company H has been limited, so the three founders decided to hire a professional manager Mr. Bobby from country in Europe to work in the company. Mr. Bobby is an engineer with rich experience, and has served as the deputy general manager of an internationally renowned large company for a long time.

After a month of research after Mr. Bobby arrived, he found that there were two problems in company H. First, the management mode is backward, the organization is overstaffed, there are too many members, the proportion of logistics administrators is large, and the non-production cost is high. Second, there is a lack of innovation. So when discussing with Mr. T, one of the three founders, Mr. Bobby puts forward the idea of merging some departments and integrating some overlapping jobs. Mr. T suggested that he should not put forward this idea at the board meeting for the time being.

Mr. Bobby didn't follow Mr. T's suggestion and put forward his idea at the board meeting on the second day, which was opposed by everyone on the spot, and someone proposed to dismiss Mr. Bobby.

If you are Mr. T, after the meeting, you invite Mr. Bobby for coffee, how will you point out his mistakes with great tact and technique?

2. Case Practice

Company R is a company located in country V in northern Europe, and plans to explore the market of country C in Asia. Therefore, Mr. D, a native of the marketing department, and Mr. O, a native of country C, were sent to the target customer company of country C to discuss the details of the sales contract. After the meeting, the two sides did not directly discuss issues related to the contract, but talked about many other topics. Mr. K, the representative of the other party, also mentioned his family situation. Mr. D felt that the opposite, customer didn't seem to have the willingness to cooperate with them. Instead of getting to the point, he was talking about irrelevant trivia. Looking at the fact that the client has not yet made any progress in the contract negotiation process, Mr. D believes that these conversations are a waste of time and tries to turn the topic to the sales contract. Mr. O knew that Mr. K tried to pull in this way. Close the relationship between the two sides and establish mutual trust. It is unwise to interrupt the other party at this time. Before arriving at country C, Mr. D had a little understanding of the country's culture, but he still couldn't adapt to this way of conversation.

When Mr. K finally talked about the terms of the contract, Mr. D directly raised the question of price. Mr. K didn't answer his question, but fell into silence. This makes Mr. D very uneasy, because silence is impolite in their culture. He didn't understand why Mr. K did this and how he should react. Mr. O knows that Mr. K is not refusing, but thinking.

If you are Mr. O, how will you explain to Mr. D the differences between the two cultures and what negotiation skills should be used?

3. Theory Practice

Please choose any three countries and compare their scores in the five factors with the cultural characteristics of these three countries in your mind (see Table 20.2). If different, please analyze the reasons for the difference.

Table 20.2 Countries and Compare Their Scores in the Five Factors with the Cultural Characteristics

Country	PDI	IDV	MAS	UAI	LTO
Malaysia	104	26	50	36	
Guatemala	95	6	37	101	
Panama	95	11	44	86	
Philippines	94	32	64	44	19
Mexico	81	30	69	82	
Venezuela	81	12	73	76	
China	80	20	66	40	118
Egypt	80	38	52	68	
Iraq	80	38	52	68	
Kuwait	80	38	52	68	
Lebanon	80	38	52	68	
Libya	80	38	52	68	
Saudi Arabia	80	38	52	68	
United Arab Emirates	80	38	52	68	
Ecuador	78	8	63	67	
Indonesia	78	14	46	48	
Ghana	77	20	46	54	16
India	77	48	56	40	61
Nigeria	77	20	46	54	16
Sierra Leone	77	20	46	54	16
Singapore	74	20	48	8	48

Continued

Country	PDI	IDV	MAS	UAI	LTO
Brazil	69	38	49	76	65
France	68	71	43	86	
Hong Kong	68	25	57	29	96
Poland	68	60	64	93	
Colombia	67	13	64	80	
El Salvador	66	19	40	94	
Turkey	66	37	45	85	
Belgium	65	75	54	94	
Ethiopia	64	27	41	52	25
Kenya	64	27	41	52	25
Peru	64	16	42	87	
Tanzania	64	27	41	52	25
Thailand	64	20	34	64	56
Zambia	64	27	41	52	25
Chile	63	23	28	86	
Portugal	63	27	31	104	
Uruguay	61	36	38	100	
Greece	60	35	57	112	
South Korea	60	18	39	85	75
Iran	58	41	43	59	
Taiwan	58	17	45	69	87
Czech Republic	57	58	57	74	
Spain	57	51	42	86	
Pakistan	55	14	50	70	
Japan	54	46	95	92	80
Italy	50	76	70	75	
Argentina	49	46	56	86	
South Africa	49	65	63	49	
Hungary	46	55	88	82	
Jamaica	45	39	68	13	
United States	40	91	62	46	29
Netherlands	38	80	14	53	44
Australia	36	90	61	51	31
Costa Rica	35	15	21	86	
Germany	35	67	66	65	31
United Kingdom	35	89	66	35	25
Switzerland	34	68	70	58	
Finland	33	63	26	59	
Norway	31	69	8	50	20

Continued

Country	PDI	IDV	MAS	UAI	LTO
Sweden	31	71	5	29	33
Ireland	28	70	68	35	
New Zealand	22	79	58	49	30
Denmark	18	74	16	23	
Israel	13	54	47	81	
Austria	11	55	79	70	

Unit 21

Business Dinner Etiquette

✧ **Case-Lead-in**

In business dining, even a normal social dining, you don't want to find yourself asking:
- "Where should we hold our banquet?"
- "Is this your soup or mine?"
- "Which fork is for my salad?"
- "Who is going to seat in the co-host position?"
- "What is the difference between vegan and vegetarian?"

That is why we all need to remember that business etiquette is important.

21.1　Learning Objectives

(1) Acquire basic etiquette for business entertaining.
(2) Master how to attend a business dinner when you are host/guest.
(3) Study some fundamental table manners when you go to a business meal.
(4) Learn how to toast in several foreign languages.
(5) Remember some key tips for business etiquette.

21.2　The Significance of Dining Etiquette

Business people always eat out, they need to settle down issues or build relationships during the meal. This idea is widely shared by most of cultures in the world, although they don't share table manners. If you eat in some Asian countries, like China or Japan, they use chopsticks. And lots of countries use fork and knife. In each culture, entertaining, seating, and toasting etiquettes are influenced by their long-time traditions and present their beliefs. Learning and respecting these manners are important for every business person.

21.3　Forms of Business Entertaining

After doing business, receiving your guest, or attending an offsite with your colleagues, these all include sightseeing, traveling, or visiting a resort. Some of these might require your personal time, but the purpose is still to build up social relationships with counterparts. In the process, delegate foods, drinks, entertainments or golf might be necessary. But how much is enough? Please keep this in your mind, no matter what you are doing, you do it for your company's, even with your own time. So, remember, keep it professional.

When you attend these entertaining, prepare yourself to present the best of yourself and your company.

- ◆ To dress properly.
- ◆ To have your invitation with you.
- ◆ To be on time.
- ◆ To control yourself.
- ◆ To greet and thank the host properly.
- ◆ To prepare your partner or spouse if you are allowed to bring one.
- ◆ To choose topics carefully.

21.4　Preparations for Business Meals

When you plan a business meal, you have three choices: breakfast, lunch, or dinner.

The decision should be made based on which meal is the better opportunity to reach your goal if you have plenty of time. Otherwise, you need to choose the most comfortable one for both sides.

(1) Breakfast

Can be held in various places with multiple kinds of food. People are in their early hour, might have a good mood and a clear mind. It also can be short and less costly.

(2) Lunch

Is a traditional working meal. When your group needs to return to your business, a lunch meal is highly suitable. It can be handled in a reasonable time and be a good opportunity to fix up the relationship.

(3) Dinner

Is the most important event in business dining and it always arranged on the purpose of improving relationships. Due to this feature, dining needs to be prepared more carefully.

When you are host.

It is your duty to arrange a well-prepared dining and it could be breath taking event. To do so, some basic etiquettes must be followed.

To consider your guest's taste. It is necessary to find out whether your guests have any special religion or habits. Is there anything they dislike or even cannot have at all?

To choose the right place. It can be fantastic, attractive, or amazing, but since this is a business dining, style, transportation, and environment are all need to be taken into consideration. So don't try anything strange and advance.

To make your reservation.

To send completed information to your guest, including direction, time, host (if you are not the host, but an organizer only), and transportation.

To arrive at the restaurant early than your guests, and make sure they are received.

To dress properly.

To arrange the table properly and decide seats. To make sure the honorable guest seats the best seat (facing out into the room).

To make sure all guests arrived, if someone is late, call them to make sure what happened.

To be aware of alcohol drinks, not too much, not too many round toasts.

To order the food with reasonable price, you don't want to order the most expensive dish of the group, especially you are the junior.

To order the food you know. If you really don't know anything about the food, do ask. You won't want to have any challenges this time.

To look after all guests and make sure they are not excluded.

To wait till your guest mentions the work.

To treat wait staff with respect.

To pay the bill.

When you are guest.

To confirm your attendance.

To attend on time.

To dress properly.

To follow the arrangement of host for seating.

To be aware of alcohol drinks.

To order the food with reasonable price, you don't want to order the most expensive dish of the group, especially you are the junior.

To order the food you know. If you really don't know anything about the food, do ask. You won't want to have any challenges this time.

To do what your host does if you don't know their table manners.

To treat wait staff with respect.

To tell your host your special dietary need.

21.5 Etiquette for Business Dinner

Since every country contains different culture in their table manners, including the choice of fork or chopsticks. You should research the dinner custom in other countries before you go. Here, we will introduce some western styles since we are basically familiar with our own.

1. Time

1) In US

7:00—9:00, breakfast

10:00—14:00, brunch

11:30—13:30, lunch

18:00—20:00, dinner

2) Latin America

7:00—9:00, breakfast

noon—15:00, lunch

17:00—18:00, afternoon refreshment break (coffee, tea, and some light snacks, in some countries, alcoholic beverages are served too. The drink is varied from country to country.)

3) European countries

7:00—8:00, breakfast

Around 13:00, lunch

20:00—21:00, dinner

In some European countries, they are used to have a light lunch, and on the other side, lunch is main meal. So, with or without alcoholic drinks, it totally depends on cultural issues.

4) UK
7:00—8:00, breakfast
Around 13:00, lunch
Around 17:00, tea time
19:00—20:00, dinner

5) Russia
7:00—8:00, breakfast
13:00—14:00, lunch
19:00—20:00, dinner

6) Asian countries
6:00—7:00, breakfast
noon—13:30, lunch
18:00—20:00, dinner

7) Special time schedule in India
16:00—17:00, snacks and tea
20:30—22:00, dinner

2. Table setting
Plates
A service plate: the large one
A bread plate: above the forks
A salad plate: next to the forks

Glassware
The water glass
The red wine glass: larger
The white wine glass: smaller

Utensils
Please remember, the traditional rule for setting is to use them following "outside in": to use your utensils from the outside every time you start to have a new dish. Here we will list most of utensils you might find in the traditional way.
1) Left to the service plate
Fish fork
Salad fork

Dinner fork

Oyster fork

2) Right to the service plate

Soup spoon

Fish knife/salad knife

Dinner knife

Steak knife

3) Extra setting

Butter knife

Dessertspoon and dessert fork

Tea or coffee spoon

Demitasse spoon

These formal place settings are not always available in business dinner. You usually have an informal table includes the followings.
- Two forks: one salad and one dinner;
- One knife: the dinner knife;
- Spoon;
- Glasses: water glass, wine glasses;
- Napkin.

Sometimes you are invited for a party or a meal in your host's home. If you accept the invitation, please bring some gifts, like a bottle of wine, it will be more polite. But giving gift is also a delegate issue. Do remember to wrap the gift carefully and beautifully, and do consider whether to open the gift.

Similar rules apply when you go to their home, do remember to respect their customs, like some countries eat with their hands, and the other seat on the floor.

21.6　Toasts

Toasting is a useful way to cheer the whole group up. If the culture do not drink alcoholic drinks, you can use nonalcoholic drink to propose a toast as well. The host should start with a short toast. And very country toasts different ways (see Table 21.1), it is polite to toast with your host in their language.

Table 21.1　Country Toasts in Different Ways

Country	Toasts
Denmark	Skol
French	A votre sante

Continued

Country	Toasts
German	Prosit
Greek	Prosit
Italian	Salute
Japan	Kampai
Korean	Gan bei
Malaysian	Slimat minim
Russian	Na zdorovie
Spain	Salud
Thailand	Choc-tee
United States	Cheers
	Bottoms up
	To your health

21.7　Useful Tips

There are if not thousands, but hundreds of dinner etiquette we need to remember. But it is impossible to do so, here we provide some tips for your meal.

To shake hand with your right hand.

To place your napkin in your lap right after everyone is seated.

To handle your tableware gently.

To handle your knife and fork in the right position.

To hold your white wine glass by the stem.

To hold your red wine glass by the bowl.

To leave your napkin in the chair if you want to leave temporary.

To place the knife below the fork in a X shape across the plate, if you want to leave temporary.

To fold the napkin loosely and place it to the left of your setting when you leave at the end.

Not to use the napkin as a tissue.

To hold your fork or spoon like a pen.

To hold the knife in your dominant hand and fork in the other hand.

To use fork and knife to cut your salad.

To use your normal knife if you don't have a butter knife.

To pass to the right, but it is fine to pass to the one left to you.

21.8 Case Study

Case One

Say your department received five guests from foreign partners, including an American, two Europeans, a Malaysian and a Middle Eastern. Now your department has assigned you to organize today's meal.

Please work with your part and list what business dinner etiquette you should pay attention to? During the process, please consider the following items.

(1) Which meal are you going to choose, breakfast, lunch, or dinner? And why?

(2) What kind of restaurant are you going to choose? And why you choose the restaurant? How did you know the restaurant? And how well you know it? Can you name four most famous dishes there?

(3) Is there any dietary need you should pay attention to?

(4) How can you make sure your guests are well informed and what information you should tell them? Please edit a note for these.

Case Two

Saving a disaster dining.

Please consider yourself dealing with following situations, what you shall do?

Scenes

(1) If your guest refused to attend your dining?

(2) If your guest was half hour late?

(3) If you arrived at the restaurant later than your guest, and you haven't order in prior. The restaurant is the best in town, but it is also famous in severing very slow.

(4) If you ordered the most expensive meal and your honor guest ordered the cheapest one?

(5) If you found your guest is vegan after ordering.

(6) If you took the last bread but your guest hasn't gotten one?

(7) If your guest asked you a question and your mouth was full?

(8) If you eat faster/slowly than everybody around the table?

(9) If you spill soup or drink onto the table?

(10) If you find your guest has something in his teeth?

(11) If you are invited to eat in the culture which eat food with their fingers, and the food is really hot?

(12) If you are invited by your boss to have a lunch with him/her along, who should pay the bill?

21.9　Business Ethics

《礼记·曲礼》里记载了古人宴饮的礼仪。

"凡进食之礼，左殽右胾，食居人之左，羹居人之右。脍炙处外，醯酱处内，葱渫处末，酒浆处右。以脯修置者，左朐右末。客若降等执食兴辞，主人兴辞于客，然后客坐。主人延客祭：祭食，祭所先进。殽之序，遍祭之。三饭，主人延客食胾，然后辩殽。主人未辩，客不虚口。

侍食于长者，主人亲馈，则拜而食；主人不亲馈，则不拜而食。

共食不饱，共饭不泽手。毋抟饭，毋放饭，毋流歠，毋咤食，毋啮骨，毋反鱼肉，毋投与狗骨。毋固获，毋扬饭。饭黍毋以箸。毋嚺羹，毋絮羹，毋刺齿，毋歠醢。客絮羹，主人辞不能亨。客歠醢，主人辞以窭。濡肉齿决，干肉不齿决。毋嘬炙。

卒食，客自前跪，彻饭齐以授相者，主人兴辞于客，然后客坐。侍饮于长者，酒进则起，拜受于尊所。长者辞，少者反席而饮。长者举未釂，少者不敢饮。长者赐，少者、贱者不敢辞。赐果于君前，其有核者怀其核。御食于君，君赐余，器之溉者不写，其余皆写。"

This is not the only document which records business etiquette in our history, many books, essays, poems, and historical classics provided numbers of records about dining etiquettes. China is a country of etiquette, which is reflected in all aspects, of which dinner etiquette is a very important part. We need to remember and respect ours while we are learning others.

21.10　Exercises

Exercise One

You and your intern were invited to have a business banquet in Upton Abbey, they served a full Utensil set. This is his first time attending a formal banquet like this, please complete following conversations.

Preparing for the banquet in your hotel.

Your intern: Ms. Wang, this is my first time to a banquet, I have never been any place like this. Please tell me what I should wear and bring?

You: _____

Your intern: I see, I will check my luggage to see what I have, and I don't have an invitation for myself, is that okay?

You: _____

Your intern: great, I got it. I have one more question, when we go to the banquet, what else should we bring? Do we need to bring a gift for them? Or follower maybe?

You: _____

Arriving at the banquet.

Your intern: wow, there are so many people attending, Ms. Wang, what should we do? Who we need to talk with?

You: _____

Your intern: can I have a drink?

You: _____

When you were guided to dining table.

Your intern: there are so many different forks and knifes, what I suppose to do with them?

You: _____

Your intern: what are differences between these two glasses?

You: _____

Your intern: why Mr. Ken is seating there?

You: _____

Your intern: I'm going to sit next to a senior manager from country N, what should I talk with him?

You: _____

Exercise Two

You are working in human resource department in an international company. You were asked to give a presentation about dinner etiquette. Please prepare a PPT for this lecture and present to your classmates.

Exercise Three

To answer following questions to check whether you have acquired some dinner etiquettes.

1) In North American (including US & Canada)

(1) Should you keep your hand/s above table while eating?

(2) Do they all have afternoon tea?

(3) What do they toast?

2) In UK

(1) Do they drink more coffee or tea?

(2) Do they have a light or normal lunch?

(3) Should you clean your plate before you leave the table at the end?

(4) What do they toast?

3) In Asian Countries (including China, Japan & Korea, etc.)

(1) Can you use fork and knife if chopsticks are too difficult for you?

(2) Should you clean your plate before you leave the table at the end?

(3) Is seating etiquette important?

(4) In which country/countries, you should remove your shoes when you entry into a restaurant or host's home?

(5) What do they toast?

4) In India

(1) How many meals they have a day?

(2) When do they arrange their dinner if there is one?

(3) Do they eat with their hand? If so, which one?

参 考 文 献

[1] MCCARTHY A, HAY S. Advanced negotiation techniques[M]. California: Apress Media, 2015.

[2] PACHTER B. The essentials of business etiquette[M]. New York: McGraw-Hill Education, 2013.

[3] SHWOM B L, SNYDER L G. Business communication: polishing your professional presence[M]. Londan: Prenrile, 2012.

[4] LANGFORD B. The etiquette edge: modern manners for business success[M]. New York: American Management Association, 2016.

[5] Bracknell Enterprise & Innovation Hub. Business communication: study text[M]. Berkshire: Emile Woolf International, 2015.

[6] CRAVER C. The intelligent negotiator: what to say, what to do, and how to get what you want every time[M]. New York: Three Rivers Press, 2002.

[7] HAMILTON C, L KROLL T L. Communicating for results: a guide for business and the professions[M]. 11th ed. Boston: Cengage Learning, Inc., 2018.

[8] HENDON D W, ROY M H, AHMED Z U. Negotiation concession patterns: a multi-country, multiperiod study[J]. American Business Review, 2003, (21): 75–83.

[9] HYNES G E. Managerial communication: strategies and applications[M]. 5th ed. New York: McGraw-Hill Corporations, Inc., 2015.

[10] LAURSEN G H N, THORLUND J. Business analytics for managers: taking business intelligence beyond reporting[M]. New Jersey: John Wiley & Sons, Inc., 2017.

[11] MARTIN J S, CHANEY L H. Global business etiquette: a guide to international communication and customs[M]. London: Praeger Publishers, 2006.

[12] THOMPSON L L. The mind and heart of the negotiator[M]. 5th ed. New Jersey: PearsonEducation, Inc., 2012.

[13] FLANNERY K. 50 essential etiquette lessons: how to eat lunch with your boss, handle happy hour like a pro, and write a thank you note in the age of texting and tweeting paperback[M]. Texas: Althea Press, 2019.

[14] LOCKER K O, KACZMAREK S K. Business communication: building critical skills[M]. 6th ed. New York: The McGraw-Hill Companies, 2014.

[15] GUFFEY M E, LOEWY D. Essentials of business communication[M]. 11th ed. Boston: Cengage Learning, Inc., 2019.

[16] MEIER M. Business etiquette made easy: the essential guide to professional success hardcover[M]. New York Berkshire: Skyhorse, 2020.

[17] CANAVOR N. Business writing for dummies [M]. 2nd ed. New Jersey: Pearson Education, Inc., 2017.

[18] POST P. The etiquette advantage in business[M]. 3rd ed. Sydney: HarperCollins Publishers (Australia) Pty. Ltd., 2014.

[19] SANDER P. Negotiation 101[M]. New York: Simon & Schuster, Inc., 2017.

[20] MOTSCHNIG R, RYBACK D. Transforming communication in leadership and teamwork[M]. Cham: Springer Nature Switzerland AG, 2016.

[21] DINNAR S, SUSSKIND L. Entrepreneurial negotiation: understanding and managing the relationships that determine your entrepreneurial success[M]. Cham: Springer Nature Switzerland AG, 2019.

[22] GATES S. The negotiation book: your definitive guide to successful negotiation[M]. 2nd ed. West Sussex: John Wiley and Sons Ltd, 2016.

[23] OBER S, NEWMAN A. 商务沟通[M]. 8 版. 北京：清华大学出版社，2013.

[24] 姚凤云，龙凌云，张海南. 商务谈判与管理沟通[M]. 2 版. 北京：清华大学出版社，2016.

[25] 张宏，蒋三庚. 商务谈判[M]. 北京：高等教育出版社，2016.

[26] 邓瑞平. 国际商事仲裁法学[M]. 北京：法律出版社，2010.

[27] 胡庚申. 国际商务合同起草与翻译[M]. 北京：外文出版社，2001.

[28] 黄霜林. 外贸合同与信用证[M]. 武汉：武汉理工大学出版社，2008.

[29] 黄水乞. 外贸英文信函范例与常用精句[M]. 广州：广东经济出版社，2011.

[30] 金双玉，钦寅. 外贸英语——函电与单证[M]. 上海：同济大学出版社，2006.

[31] 金泽虎，王桂平. 国际商务函电[M]. 北京：北京大学出版社，2013.

[32] 龙朝晖，马健美. 商务英语函电[M]. 北京：人民邮电出版社，2013.

[33] 罗恩·霍尔特，尼克·桑普森. 国际商业书信[M]. 北京：北京大学出版社，1999.

[34] 商乐，甘利. 商务外贸函电实训教程[M]. 北京：北京师范大学出版，2011.

[35] 滕美荣，许楠. 外贸英语函电[M]. 北京：首都经济贸易大学出版社，2014.

[36] 田运银. 国际贸易单证精讲[M]. 北京：中国海关出版社，2008.

[37] 王婧. 国际结算操作[M]. 北京：高等教育出版社，2008.

[38] 徐良霞. 实用英语教你写合同[M]. 北京：北京航空航天大学出版社，2004.

[39] 雪莉·泰勒. 商务英语写作实例精解[M]. 卢艳春，译. 北京：外语教学与研究出版社，2014.

[40] 杨华中，穆子砺，何贵才. 国际商事调解文集[M]. 北京：现代教育出版社，2007.

[41] 杨文惠. 现代商务英语写作集萃[M]. 广州：中山大学出版社，2005.

[42] 毅冰. 外贸高手客户成交技巧[M]. 北京：中国海关出版社，2012.

[43] 赵欣，吴士宝. 包装实用英语[M]. 北京：文化发展出版社，2012.

[44] 赵银德. 外贸函电[M]. 北京：机械工业出版社，2010.

[45] 张斌　外贸代理合同纠纷审理思路与疑难案例评析[M]. 北京：法律出版社，2014.

[46] 张东昌. 实用商务英语教程[M]. 北京：高等教育出版社，2015.

[47] 曾勇民. 国际商务函电[M]. 北京：北京理工大学出版社，2011.

[48] 周峰，魏莉霞. 商务英语函电[M]. 北京：北京大学出版社，2013.

[49] 仲鑫. 外贸函电[M]. 北京：机械工业出版社，2010.

[50] 诸葛林. 外贸英文书信[M]. 北京：对外经济贸易大学出版社，2000.